ASIAN AMERICA THROUGH THE LENS

CRITICAL PERSPECTIVES ON ASIAN PACIFIC AMERICANS SERIES

Volumes in *Critical Perspectives on Asian Pacific Americans* take on a spectrum of current issues facing Asian American communities by critically examining key social, economic, psychological, cultural, and political experiences. They are theoretically engaging, comparative, and multidisciplinary, reflecting the complexity of contemporary concerns that are of importance to the understanding and empowerment of Asian Pacific Americans.

BOOKS IN THE SERIES

Volume 1: Diana Ting Liu Wu, *Asian Pacific Americans in the Workplace* (1997)

Volume 2: Juanita Tamayo Lott, *Asian Americans: From Racial Category to Multiple Identities* (1998)

Volume 3: Jun Xing, *Asian America Through the Lens: History, Representations, and Identity* (1998)

SUBMISSION GUIDELINES

Prospective authors of single or co-authored books and editors of anthologies should submit a letter of introduction, the manuscript of a four- to ten-page proposal, a book outline, and a curriculum vitae. Please address proposals or questions to:

Critical Perspectives on Asian Pacific Americans Series
AltaMira Press
1630 North Main Street, Suite 367
Walnut Creek, CA 94596
(925) 938-7243

Asian America Through the Lens

HISTORY, REPRESENTATIONS, AND IDENTITY

Jun Xing

PRESS

A Division of
ROWMAN & LITTLEFIELD PUBLISHERS, INC.
Lanham • New York • Toronto • Plymouth, UK

ALTAMIRA PRESS
A division of Rowman & Littlefield Publishers, Inc.
A wholly owned subsidary of The Rowman & Littlefield Publishing Group, Inc.
4501 Forbes Boulevard, Suite 200
Lanham, MD 20706
www.altamirapress.com

PO Box 317, Oxford. OX2 9RU, UK

Cover photo: Visual Communications crew members (L to R): Eddie Wong, Robert
   Nakamura, and Alan Kondo. Courtesy of Visual Communications.
Still from the documentary film *Forbidden City, U.S.A.* provided courtesy of DeepFocus
   Productions.
Still from *Who Killed Vincent Chin?* courtesy of Filmakers Library, Inc.
Stills from *Maya Lin: A Strong Clear Vision* by Freida Lee Mock, courtesy of American
   Film Foundation.
Photo: Sokly "Don Bonus" Ny in *a.k.a. Dan Bonus* (1995) by Spencer Nakasako and
   Sokly "Don Bonus" Ny. Photo by Leland Wong. Courtesy of National Asian American
   Telecommunications Association.

British Library Cataloguing in Publication Information Available

Library of Congress Cataloguing-in-Publication Data
Hsing, Chun.
   Asian America through the lens : history, representations, and identity / Jun Xing.
      p. cm.—(Critical perspectives on Asian Pacific Americans series; v. 3)
   Includes bibliographical references and index.
   ISBN-13: 978-0-7619-9175-5 (cloth : alk. paper)
   ISBN-10: 0-7619-9175-1 (cloth : alk. paper)
   ISBN-13: 978-0-7619-9176-2 (pbk. : alk. paper)
   ISBN-10: 0-7619-9176-X (pbk. : alk. paper)
   1. Asian Americans in the motion picture industry. 2. Asian Americans in motion pictures.
I. Title. II. Series.
   PN1995.9.A77 H75   1998
   384'. 8'089935073—ddc21   98-19694

Printed in the United States of America

The paper used in this publication meets the minimum requirements of American National Standard for
Information Sciences—Permanence of Paper for Printed Library Materials, ANSI/NISO Z39.48–1992.

Interior design and production by Rachel Fudge
Editorial management by Jennifer R. Collier
Cover design by Jennifer R. Collier

Table of Contents

List of Illustrations

Acknowledgments

WRITING A BOOK IS VERY MUCH LIKE GIVING BIRTH to a baby. It is a very emotional process, from the initial excitement, the jitters along the way, to the final fulfillment. The idea of the project was conceived in an immigration history seminar I took with Dr. Rudolph Vecoli at the University of Minnesota back in 1992. My thanks should first go to Dr. Vecoli for his encouragement and guidance throughout. Many people have read various versions of this manuscript at different stages of its development. Among them are Dr. Gayle Graham Yates, my mentor at the University of Minnesota; Dr. Hisa Kuriyama, my former colleague at Emory University; Dr. Monica Chiu at University of Wisconsin, Eau Claire; Dr. Lane Hirabayashi at University of Colorado, Boulder; Dr. Jeanne Kilde at University of Notre Dame; Dr. Darrell Hamamoto at University of California, Davis; and my colleagues Dr. Paul Wong, Dr. Ruth Alexander, and Dr. Kai-Ho Mah at Colorado State University. I have often gratefully agreed with their suggestions but sometimes not. Mention of their names is not to say that they have certified the contents of the book.

Working on films, especially independent films, is a very expensive undertaking. Over the years several research grants and awards have kept the project going. The seed money came in the form of an Andrew Mellon fellowship award from Emory University in 1992. A research grant from the Virginia Foundation for the Humanities and Public Policy in 1993 enabled me to conduct initial interviews with East Coast–based Asian American filmmakers. Since 1994 a number of internal grants from Colorado State University have helped bring the project to a timely completion, including a Faculty Research Grant from the Graduate School in 1994, a Career Enhancement Award from the Provost Office in 1995, a Professional Development Grant from the College of Liberal Arts in 1996, and a generous Summer Research Award from the Tri-Ethnic Center in 1997.

In the past few years, several interested and talented students at Colorado State University have assisted me with the project in different ways. Katherine Leslie, Tam Nguyen, and Eric Ishiwata interviewed over two dozen Asian American filmmakers who are significant contributors to the Asian American film movement, and who found time for us in their busy schedules. Some of the interviews were conducted at Asian American film festivals, and some were based on media panel discussions at conferences. The majority were phone interviews recorded (with prior permission) and transcribed between February 1995 and April 1996. These interviews were woven into the fabric of the book. Claudia Manz should be lauded for her graciousness and patience in the tedious, and sometimes frustrating, process of acquiring all copyright permissions. Chris Peters and Karen Wong helped with library research, and Robert Koehler courageously accepted the daunting task of indexing the book.

I would like to thank all my colleagues in the Department of History and CASAE (Center for Applied Studies in American Ethnicity) at Colorado State University for their strong support and camaraderie. It has been a privilege to work in such a supportive environment. I want to thank Ms. Jennifer Collier at AltaMira Press for her great enthusiasm with the project and her extraordinary editorial skills. I have very much appreciated her support in putting this book into print in a timely manner.

I am deeply grateful to my wife, Shari, who has spent countless nights screening several hundred films with me, to my daughters Jane and Diana, to my parents, and to my sister Delia, whose love and friendship sustain the life out of which I write.

Finally, I want to dedicate this book to my newborn son Wilson for the new excitement and happiness he has brought into my mid-life.

Preface

ASIAN AMERICA THROUGH THE LENS IS A MILESTONE WORK in which Jun Xing presents the first sustained examination of Asian American independent films. Those who pursue this book because of their interest in cinema, or in pertinent theoretical debates, will not be disappointed. They will, in fact, find more here than they expected.

First, historian and ethnic studies scholar Xing fully succeeds in introducing a wide range of Asian American independent films in an intriguing way, including award-winning productions such as Wayne Wang's *Chan Is Missing* and Steven Okazaki's *Days of Waiting*. His discussions include information on the artists, as well as the collaborations and organizations behind the films. From the beginning, readers are also invited to grapple with the key question of what constitutes an Asian American film. Is it a matter of the filmmaker's ethnic or political identity? Is it contingent on the film's subject matter? Or is it fundamentally a matter of sensibility, point of view, style, or aesthetics? Because Xing frames his own response with careful attention to the literature on African American and Chicano/a cinema, the reader is able to understand the linkage between debates about Asian American independent film, and the wider field of critical discourse in ethnic, cultural, and American studies.

Second, through a judicious combination of original interviews and secondary sources, Xing richly documents the roles and contributions of Asian Americans to American film history, as he puts it, "in front of and behind the camera, creating alternatives to Hollywood's master narratives." To highlight even further the achievements of independent Asian American filmmakers, Xing skillfully reveals how corporate money, the insidious politics of imagery and representation, along with institutional practices, all combine to generate the misshapen media caricatures of Asians overseas and in the U.S.A.

In this context, Xing's careful documentation of Asian American cinema allows us to appreciate much more fully the work of the women and men who have created literally hundreds of social-issue documentaries, family dramas, experimental, and avant-garde films and videos. These productions capture the mundane and the extraordinary, the historical and the contemporary, the ostensibly traditional and the hybrid, and the local and the transnational dimensions of Asian America *from the points of view of those who have actually lived the experiences*. Because people of Asian descent have had fewer chances to empower themselves in the media by speaking in their own voices, and presenting themselves candidly on their own terms, these films stand as significant contributions to film art and to society at large.

The film artists whom Xing treats have striven to constitute themselves and other Asians in America as subjects. These artists exemplify how art can be subversive, how it can both resist and transcend established norms of representation. As Gilles Deleuze comments, in a brief discussion about minorities in *Negotiations*, "what counts . . . is the extent to which, as [minority subjectivities] take shape, they elude both established forms of knowledge and dominant forms of power" (1995, 176). Thus, as Xing convincingly argues, we should draw from independent films to generate new perspectives on what it means to be of Asian descent in America.

Xing identifies three contested narratives undergirding the production of Asian American films: the nationalist, the activist, and the aesthetic. In his meticulous discussion of these three narratives, Xing draws a parallel between them and the formulation of Asian American identities since the 1960s. For example, he points out that "personal diary" films often revolve around a protagonist from a specific national background. He also demonstrates that many social-issue documentaries promote a pan-Asian perspective and response, and that still other productions focus on the breakdown of borders that are now homologous with global capital. (Both borders and capital have become insistently fluid.) Precisely because assumptions and implications—in terms of the filmmaker's constitution of individual/family; home/society; past/present; local/global—are tangibly revealed in a cinematic product, each formulation of identity becomes clearer and more open to critical examination.

Moreover, if "[a] minority . . . has no model, it's a becoming; a process" (Deleuze 1995, 173), we should expect to be able to glean further insights from analyses of independent films. Some scholars, for example, contrast essentialist, instrumentalist, and diasporic formulations of identity as if they were somehow mutually exclusive. However, if we look at independent cinematic representations of, say, Asian Indians, we find a range of portrayals, all of which seem credible. For instance, an ethnic-specific depiction of South Asian Americans is presented in *The New Puritans*. This is a documentary that revolves around the attempts of Sikh farming families to maintain their cultural traditions in the rural setting of Yuba City, California, where there has been a large Sikh community for more than half a century. In the documentary *The Patels: The Owners of the Tenderloin*, the South Asian Americans who own hotels and motels in the San Francisco Bay Area are shown to be a diverse and rapidly acculturating population, even though they are predominantly new (post-1960s era) Asian immigrants who strive to retain their deeply held religious traditions. The Patel hotel owners' political battles, which stem from their position as the main providers of housing for low-income individuals in the city of San Francisco, involve formulations of identity that go well beyond those that are primarily energized by nationalistic and/or religious commitments. These owner-families are shown to be well aware of the service they provide to the larger society. They also clearly understand, as political activists, how to put pressure on San Francisco's City Hall if they become subject to negative (not to mention biased) publicity as Tenderloin "slum lords." What is more, recent productions such as *The Bhangra Wrap* or the feature-length movie *Mississippi Masala* allude to the diasporic context undergirding the contemporary construction of South Asian identities in overseas settings. What is fascinating is that these representations are quite attuned to the interface between South Asians and "others," and to the resulting disjunctures, but also very much to potential sites of multicultural understanding, even solidarity.

From this angle, there seems to be no point in arguing whether theories of Asian American identity are correct or incorrect for highlighting nationalist (essentialist), Asian American (including pan-Asian), or diasporic formulations. Identities may indeed be constructs, but—*contra* Deleuze—they are not merely fabulations on the part of either people or producers. I would like to suggest that this becomes clear when we attend to practices, as in the cases cited above, having to do with 1) the challenges of reproducing cultural beliefs and traditions; 2) the need to counter anti-Asian stereotypes and the potential for violence; and 3) the difficulties of constructing personal relationships in the interstices of migratory movements and pluralistic social formations. In other words, specific formulations of Asian American identity are created in response to different challenges that necessarily reflect the issues, resources, and strategies at hand. Instead of simply asserting the priority of one or the other, we can and should stipulate with much more care which formulation of Asian American identity is being deployed, for what reasons, and at what costs, in any given situation, cinematic or otherwise. Also, we should be aware of when, where, and under what conditions a given formulation, or combination of formulations, is likely to appear.

Xing makes an outstanding contribution by rightfully positioning independent film at the center of such debates. In addition to everything else he accomplishes in this book, Xing invites us to consider a range of topics, including the nature and formulations of Asian American identity, anew—through the lens.

Lane Ryo Hirabayashi
Department of Ethnic Studies
University of Colorado, Boulder

Introduction

IN 1992 IN THE TWIN CITIES of Minneapolis and St. Paul—the backwaters of Asian American history—an Asian American Renaissance Conference was held for the first time in Minnesota.[1] From April 29 to May 3, a group of vibrant and inspiring Asian American/Canadian films and videos were showcased, including Helen Lee's experimental short film *Sally's Beauty Spot* (1990), Trinh T. Minh-ha's feature-length documentary *Shoot for the Contents* (1991), Michael Cho's documentary video *Animal Appetites* (1991), and two experimental short videos: Cheng-Sim Lim's *My American Friends* (1989) and Sharon Jue's *My Mother Thought She Was Audrey Hepburn* (1989).

The Conference turned out to be an eye-opener for me, a homebound and snowbound graduate student in American Studies at the University of Minnesota. Since my arrival at UM as an international student ten years ago, I have maintained a special interest in American films. They were at first a window on American culture, and later became an invaluable resource, as I continued my research on Asian American experiences. The films offered a special way of explaining a culture—a way that, in some respects, was more powerful than printed words alone. Throughout my graduate years at the university, films on Asians in one form or another would not escape my attention. The wide-ranging talents of the Asian American independents, however, took me totally by surprise. I was deeply touched by the artistry and political consciousness of these films and videos.

Intrigued, I decided to learn more about Asian American productions. I checked the online catalogue at the Wilson Library and searched the Internet. I found it unbelievable that I could not find anything significant on the subject. While substantial literature had been published beginning in the 1970s on independent filmmaking by women, Blacks, and Chicano/as, films by Asian Americans were still absent or nearly absent in American public discourse.[2] *Moving the Image: Independent Asian Pacific American Media Arts* (1991), a collection of essays and interviews by fifty Asian American media artists, and the only book-length work available now, was still in press back then.[3] Future works by such scholars as Gina Marchetti (*Romance and the "Yellow Peril:" Race, Sex, and Discursive Strategies in Hollywood Fiction* [1993]), Sumiko Higashi (*Cecil B. DeMille and American Culture: The Silent Era* [1994]), and Darrell Hamamoto (*Monitored Peril: Asian Americans and the*

Politics of TV Representation [1994]) would touch on the independent scene, but their research primarily focused on the Orientalist discourse in the Hollywood and TV industries. When I considered the celebrated publicity of Asian American writers (from Maxine Hong Kingston and Amy Tan, to David Mura and David Henry Hwang), as well as the increasing popularity of Asian films (by Japanese as well as by fifth-generation Chinese directors), I wondered why there had been such little recognition for Asian American films.

I began to search for clues. "The literary is very different from the visual," one friend speculated. "Traditionally, Asians have been disembodied in American culture. Asians could be intelligent, but not physical." To buttress his point, he pointed out that lately we had seen many Asian doctors and engineers in stories appearing in both print and broadcast media, but we rarely saw Asian sports stars or fashion models. "Asians had gotten the brain power," my friend asserted, "but not the raw physical ability, according to the popular mind." Although my friend sounded a bit cynical, his contention seemed to be corroborated on the other side of the coin by John Hoberman, in his analysis of America's popular obsession with chiseled Black bodies. In his book *Darwin's Athletes: How Sport Has Damaged Black America and Preserved the Myth of Race,* Hoberman argues that mainstream American culture has always been fixated on the Black body, and "[O]ne of the ironic consequences of integrated sports is that it is a racial theater."[4] Steven Okazaki, an award-winning Japanese American filmmaker, offers a different interpretation. He believes that independent films need a core audience to support them. But, unlike African Americans (who make up almost 32 percent of the American movie-going population), Asian Americans simply do not have that numerical weight. Historically, race movies, for example, were made specifically for the Black audience, never intended to be viewed by white Americans. Black filmmakers have always had a core audience behind them, while Asian Americans have not.[5]

But how could I explain the difference in popular reception between Asian American fiction and films? I began conducting interviews. In the process of gathering comments, several filmmakers and writers pointed out to me that the difference was largely due to their contrasting content areas. They cited *Woman Warrior* and *The Joy Luck Club* as examples. Both books, they argued, were heavily imbued with traditional Chinese themes and appealed to the mainstream readers partly because of the Chinese mythologies, from the legend of Fa Mulan to the myth of the Moon Lady. In contrast, Asian American films (especially the documentaries) focused on identity issues, history, family, and immigrants' everyday lives in the United States. Such films often represented alternative Asian images, bringing to the foreground issues central to the Asian communities and, while doing so, criticizing racism and sexism in American society. Of course, they did not carry the selling points of either exotica or erotica.

I found those opinions interesting and thought-provoking, but there were still many important questions left unanswered. For example, what was the genesis of the Asian American film movement? How do their film narratives take shape, and under what social conditions? Where do the filmmakers get their funding for their projects? How do Asian American works get onto the silver screen, and which works are excluded, and why? Who is the primary audience in the filmmakers' minds? What are their expectations? How, in short, are Asian American films different from Hollywood movies? To truly understand the lack of (or limited) recognition of Asian American films, I felt we needed to look behind the camera and into both the history and the process of Asian American filmmaking. That belief served as the starting point for this study.

GOALS OF THE STUDY

In view of the ongoing nature of the Asian American film movement, this book is not in any sense a "definitive study." Rather, it is intended "to throw out the stone to solicit the jade," to use an old Chinese saying. Specifically, I have three aims:

First, I want to introduce to a wider public, or broaden the exposure of, the growing ranks of Asian American films.[6] Bill J. Gee, director of Asian Cine-Vision, the largest Asian American media center, which is based in New York, used the following words to highlight the achievements of Asian American cinema:

> Asian American filmmaking, once a barely noticeable trickle along the sidestream of minority cinema, has now grown into a forceful expression of Asian American life. The emergence of filmmakers, who, by the artistic force of their creations, have called attention to their individual talents and to the Asian American community as the cultural heart that both gives inspiration to and supports their work, has brought about an enlargement of cultural sympathies, a broadened appreciation from the movie-going public of what it truly means to be of Asian heritage in America.[7]

Indeed, in the past three decades, Asian American cinema experienced an explosion of creativity and productivity. Asian Americans have independently produced hundreds of social-issue documentaries, as well as experimental films, videos, and dramas dealing with various aspects of the Asian American experience in the United States.[8] In this short period of thirty years, they have won numerous national and international film awards, including twelve Oscar nominations from the Academy of Motion Picture Arts and Sciences and five Academy awards.[9] In 1989 alone, three Asian American–directed films were nominated for Oscars: Renee Tajima and Christine Choy's *Who Killed Vincent Chin?*, Lise Yasui's *Family Gathering*, and Mira Nair's *Salaam Bombay!*[10] The latter film was also a winner of the Cannes Camera D'Or. Steven Okazaki's *Days of Waiting* garnered an Oscar in 1991. In 1993 *The Wedding Banquet* by Ang Lee was nominated for an Academy Award for best foreign language film and won the prestigious Golden Bear Grand prize at the Berlin Film Festival. Hawaiian-born and New York–based Japanese American director Kayo Hatta's *Picture Bride* (1994) was the winner of the Audience Award at the 1995 Sundance Film Festival. Ang Lee won another nomination in 1995 for *Eat Drink Man Woman.* Asian American women, Freida Lee Mock and Jessica Yu, won two Oscars, for their documentaries *Maya Lin: A Strong Clear Vision* in 1995 and *Breathing Lessons: The Life and Work of Mark O'Brien* in 1996. These are clear indications that Asian American films have come of age. "It's not quite the golden age yet, but there's no question that Asian-American film and video are enjoying an unprecedented burst of creativity," says James Yee, former executive director of the San Francisco–based National Asian American Telecommunications Association (NAATA).[11]

Although Asian American filmmakers have lately begun to receive a degree of recognition (largely because of distribution by independent filmmakers, activist groups, and small, alternative companies), Asian American cinema's current boom is still fairly unknown to the American public. Intended for both the academic community and educated nonspecialists, this book introduces Asian American films as possible tools for teaching the Asian American experience, as well as potential resources for public education. Because Asians are the fastest growing minority group in the United States, the demographics of Asian immigration will have a tremendous impact on American life. The emerging Asian American film culture is playing, and will continue to play, a potent role within and beyond these communities. Together with other forms of Asian American art, these films have become a source of empowerment for the communities. Historians have already recognized the important work that such filmmakers are doing. Sucheng Chan, for example, provided a list of documentary films (alongside the usual bibliography) suitable for classroom use in the textbook she wrote about Asian American history (*Asian Americans: An Interpretive History*). Harry Kitano and Roger Daniels have likewise listed films in the second edition of their textbook on Asian Americans (*Asian Americans: Emerging Minorities*).

A second aim of this study is to attempt to offer an alternative approach to the "positive image" dilemma confronting Asian Americans as viewed by and considered in the media. In my research I have found that although most Asian

American films *do* create more authentic and affirmative images, they should not be taken as simple reactive responses to Hollywood stereotyping.[12] As Kayo Hatta put it,

> I try to present genuine, interesting, complex people the way I know them. If this counters a stereotype by virtue of them being complex, then that's great. But I'm not trying to consciously defy those stereotypes. What I'm trying to do is to be more proactive in my work in presenting really interesting images rather than being reactive.[13]

Hatta's sentiment is broadly shared among the majority of filmmakers my research assistants and I interviewed.

This study refutes the notion of "positive image" as a useful critical concept for looking at minority representation in the media.[14] Much of the work on cinematic representation has stressed the issue of the "positive" imagery as opposed to stereotypes. But, as African American scholar bell hooks states, "Often what is thought to be good is merely a reaction against representations created by white people that were blatantly stereotypical."[15] To move the discussion beyond a single-minded "image analysis," several film scholars posed significant questions as to whether positive image, as a theoretical framework, was too simplistic and misleading. To quote Robert Stam and Louise Spence:

> Much of the work on racism in the cinema, like early work on the representation of women, has stressed the issue of the "positive image." This reductionism, though not wrong, is inadequate and fraught with methodological dangers. The exact nature of "positive," first of all, is somewhat relative; black incarnations of patience and gradualism, for example, have always been more pleasing to whites than to blacks.[16]

What is more, this "imprecise nature of the positive/negative distinction," as Black film scholar Valerie Smith has noted, "has the potential to essentialize racial identity and deny its dynamic relation to constructions of class, gender, sexuality, religion, and so on."[17] Even worse, "positive-image" productions often run the risk of reifying rather than ameliorating the same stereotypes that they had initially intended to challenge. An often-cited case in point was the debate over Black male–produced films such as Spike Lee's *Do the Right Thing* (1989) and *Jungle Fever* (1991), and John Singleton's *Boyz N the Hood* (1991). Some critics charged that "those emotionally powerful yet cognitively empty movies" played Black positive male images against Black women. As Kalumu ya Salaam put it bluntly, "Just as the bravado gesture of flashily fondling our male genitalia is actually an indicator of identity insecurity, the not-so-subtle subtexts of most contemporary Hollywood films directed by African American males revel in celluloid crotch-grabbing, subliminal sexual imagery and emotional textures drenched in macho/male chauvinism."[18] This critical controversy is a perfect example of the so-called viewer-image identification problem. There is no essentialized notion of blackness. What is considered "positive" or "negative" depends on the point of view of the audience as well as the viewer's positioning.

Not only is the positive image notion logically indefensible, but also it is misleading as a political strategy. Richard Fung, an Asian American/Canadian filmmaker, has shrewdly observed:

> To the extent to which positive images are a response to negative stereotypes, it is a limited strategy in that it takes its cue from what the white man or what the straight man thinks. Reaching out with alternative images for a mainstream is valuable but we can become so obsessed with how others might interpret what we have to say that we can cast our own Asian or gay audiences into passivity.[19]

By a similar reasoning, Valerie Smith argued that the positive/negative concept "focuses critical scrutiny on the ways in which African Americans have been represented in Hollywood cinema, often at the expense of analytical, theoretical or historical work on the history of Black-directed cinema."[20]

Conscious efforts to correct this phenomenon entail a sustained inquiry into the roles of Asians in American film history, which is the third purpose of this study. Being a historian, I believe the most logical way to analyze Asian American cultural productions is to measure them closely against the historical and cultural contexts under which those productions were made. Asians have a substantial history of work, contributions, and resistance to oppression in this country. Despite their long (more than 150 years) and often dramatic history in the United States, the Asian American story remains virtually unknown to the average American. In the context of studying Asian American arts, John Kuo Wei Tchen once called for critical attention to "a long, largely unacknowledged American tradition of anti-Orientalism."[21] This study is an attempt to reclaim the history of Asian Americans as a force both in front of and behind the camera, creating alternatives to the Hollywood "master narratives."

This Asian American film history of resistance against the mainstream dates back to the early twentieth century. Early instances of this anti-Orientalist discourse were found in both studio groups and individuals. For example, to combat Hollywood's images of the Chinese, James B. Leong Productions was set up in the 1920s in Los Angeles, financed by Chinese businessmen. Although social and political conditions made it a short-lived experiment, it left some important legacies for later Asian American filmmakers.[22] More successful was Haworth Pictures, founded by actor Sessue Hayakawa in 1928; altogether, twenty-five movies were produced by this independent company. Recently, some of its finest productions, such as *The Dragon Painter* (1919), were restored.[23] Resistance has also shown through the work of various individual actors in the first decades of the twentieth century. Two of the earliest (and arguably the best-known) Asian American performers in the film industry were Anna May Wong and Sessue Hayakawa. Each experienced similar frustrations with racism at the peak of their career and left the country temporarily. Anna May Wong was among the earliest to protest Hollywood's portrayals of the Chinese, asking, "How should we be, with a civilization that's so many times older than that of the West? We have our own virtues. We have our rigid code of behavior, of honor. Why do they never show these on the screen? Why should we always scheme, rob, kill? I get so weary of it all—the scenarist's concept of Chinese characters."[24]

Understandably, Asian American actors and actresses were battling tremendous odds. When she felt she was losing her fight against racism, Wong suddenly dropped out of the picture business in America. She went to Europe in 1928, at the peak of her fame, to protest against the negative roles she had been offered. Described as "one of the screen's greatest dramatic characters," Sessue Hayakawa, a Japanese actor, faced a similar situation. When interviewed in 1929 by *Motion Picture Magazine* about his sudden departure for Europe, Hayakawa revealed an incident. A film company executive insulted him because of a debt situation. "No man can help where he is born," he bitterly complained, "—what is his blood. Only an ignorant coward throw up to a man that he does not like his race. I come of a proud people—a man of my quality could not endure an insult. Still I did not speak. I stare at this face, but I say nothing. He say then, 'People in this country have no use for Chinks.' I am not Chink. I am Japanese gentleman, and the word *Chink* is not fit to be spoke."[25] Tom Gubbins, an Englishman born in China, was reported to have helped organize strikes and protests in Hollywood against "the lurid screen portrayals of the Chinese."[26] "They do not like to appear in roles which in any way seem degrading," Gubbins recalled. "Honor and honesty are characteristics of their race." He asserted, "Do you think the Chinese would appear in those scenes? Not on your life! They chattered among themselves, shook their heads, backed off. It looked like mutiny."[27] Gubbins recalled a particular incident:

> The situation got so bad that when a company arrived to film sequences for *Pied Piper Malone* (1924) in New York's Chinatown, they were met with a near riot. Young Chinese tore the Mandarin clothes from the extras (also Chinese), and the company was bombarded with milk bottles, bricks, and old vegetables. The film people took cover until the police arrived. The main complaint was against the movies showing the denizens of Chinatown smoking opium.[28]

The new Asian American cinema should be placed in this historical context of its evolution.[29] Lately, the hidden history of Asian American resistance has begun to be told. Yoshio Kishi, for example, laboriously sorted through credit records, press books, and reviews, to create a name list of Asian American pioneers and groundbreakers in the film industry.[30] Drawing on the extensive literature on Black filmmaking, from the early "race movies," through the "Blaxploitation genre" in the 1970s and 1980s, to the recent Asian diaspora films, my book explores Asian American filmmaking as a historical process, in terms of its social contexts (origins and changing missions), its support mechanisms (invention, funding, and distribution), its call-and-response dialectic between the filmmakers and audience (film criticism), as well as its narrative strategies (an Asian American aesthetic).

IDENTITY POLITICS AND FILM REPRESENTATION

Since the 1960s, identity politics has played a key role in ethnic revival and community empowerment. Identity politics was central both to challenging the cultural homogeneity of 1950s-era America and to enabling many formerly silenced and displaced groups to assert their suppressed voices and experiences. However, over recent years identity politics has reached a theoretical dead end, so to speak, dominated by a notion of difference structured in polarizing dichotomies and an uncritical appeal to a discourse of authenticity. As Chinese American writer Gish Jen recently asserted in *The New Republic,* "In any case, many minority writers like me, once marooned by prejudice, now find ourselves marooned again by identity politics. For the first allegiance of artists in general is to the very inner life that identity politics denies."[31]

For Asian Americans, issues of identity politics have taken center stage in academic and popular debates over the past three decades. Asian American historians and scholars alike have methodically studied the formations of Asian American communities, and a great deal of work has been done on the definition of Asian American identity.[32] Analysts of the Asian experience in the United States have seen the construct of "Asian American" in primarily racial and political terms. For historical reasons, our understanding of identity formation and group membership often begins with the primordial tradition, or "ethnicity of descent," as some scholars call it. This view defines Asian American identity as a self-contained and naturally given category that derives from one's cultural heritage. In other words, Asian American groups are bound mostly by a common culture and tradition traced to their primordial past. In this process, the dynamics of racial assignment by the dominant society also has played and continues to play a critical role in the designation of Asian American cultural identities. When a person is automatically labeled as "Oriental" or "Asian," strictly on the basis of his or her physical features without regard to birth or nationality, that person is uncaringly lumped together with *any* immigrant to America from the Asian continent. This externally imposed racial "assignment," however incorrect it may be, has entered into both public perceptions and self-conceptions of individuals of Asian descent living in America.

This primordial definition of Asian American identity, however, increasingly encounters challenges. Again, as Gish Jen wrote, "In identity politics, to define oneself from without is to acknowledge the 'truth'; to define oneself otherwise is to deny the 'truth.' This sort of thinking represents a failure of self-knowledge. . . . A person is more than the sum of her social facts."[33] British cultural studies scholar Stuart Hall outlines "two different ways of thinking about 'cultural identity.' " The first, he explains, "defines cultural identity in terms of the idea of one, shared culture, a sort of collective 'one true self,' hiding inside the many other, more superficial or artificially imposed 'selves' which people with a shared culture and ancestry hold in common."[34] The second mode qualifies, if it does not replace, the first primordial definition:

> [Cultural identity] is not something which already exists, transcending place, time, history and culture. . . . Far from being externally fixed in some essentialized past, [cultural identities] are subject to the continual play of history, culture and power . . . identities are the names we give to the different ways we are positioned by, and position ourselves within, the narratives of the past.[35]

Indeed, primordial ties *do* break and ancestry does *not* guarantee a common identification. Culture can be inherited, but it could also be created and re-created. By focusing solely on ancestry or cultural heritage, the primordial approach often overlooks structural conditions, together with economic and political circumstances that are so tightly bound up with ethnic identification. Lisa Lowe views the essentialist position of Asian American as a manipulable tool:

> . . . a strategic use of a positive essentialism . . . suggests that it is possible to utilize specific signifiers of ethnic identity, such as Asian American, for the purpose of contesting and disrupting the discourses that exclude Asian Americans, while simultaneously revealing the internal contradictions and slippages of Asian American so as to insure that such essentialisms will not be reproduced and proliferated by the very apparatuses we seek to disempower.[36]

Here Lowe argues forcefully against an essentialized Asian American identity, and "emphasize[s] the dynamic fluctuation and heterogeneity of Asian American culture."[37] Indeed, there are some inherent theoretical and practical pitfalls to beware if one pursues a biologically determined understanding of what it means to be Asian American. First, the imprecise nature of Asian American identity itself creates conceptual problems. Who, after all, is an Asian American? Is there a pan-Asian identity or representation? These seemingly straightforward questions involve fundamental issues in ethnic and cultural identity formation (its flexible and relational nature) and in the importance of socialization. As veteran Chinese American filmmaker Loni Ding perceptively points out, "Asian American is not a matter of birth. It is a perspective you assume, you adopt. You have an opportunity by being born into a language, culture, or some kind of background. . . . But that is no substitute for the active adoption of the perspective itself."[38] For Ding, identity politics is more concerned with questions of subjectivity, culture, and self-reflexivity than birth. Clearly, Asian American identities are neither fixed nor naturally given, but instead are historically contingent and politically negotiated. In identity politics, Asian immigrants in America often face two kinds of binarism: the Asian American cultural divide, which is evocative of the famous "double-consciousness" described by W. E. B. Du Bois, and the dichotomous scheme of the black/white racial divide. Within dominant regimes of representation, particularly in Hollywood, Asians are "Orientals" grounded in a set of categories that are fixed, transhistorical, and racial.

Some observers contend that the relatively recent construct of "Asian American," with its genesis in the Civil Rights Movement of the 1960s, is an invention based on political goals rather than a sense of cultural commonality (whether shared lineage or common ancestor). Brought together by their common racial status and experience in American society, Asians have formed strategic political coalitions, to protect and advance their own interests. As Lane Hirabayashi writes about the strategic character of a pan-Asian ethnicity, "The 'Asian American' concept was largely a vehicle for forming coalitions between the Chinese, Japanese, Filipinos, and Koreans for political reasons. . . . it is a strategic, political, and rhetorical resource for struggle and ultimately for empowerment—especially when 'ethnic specific' resources can't do the trick."[39] A pan-Asian formation has been driven in important ways by the strategic advantages that are associated with forming large and unified groups. Under this historical context, the invention of the term *Asian American* is not a natural cultural formulation (that is, people sharing affectionate or cultural ties), but rather becomes a political choice (interest groups mediating power). The pan-Asian term or consciousness is meant to convey a set of common historical experiences that stemmed from the dynamics of racial politics (for example, anti-Asian immigration laws and hate-crimes against Asians).

However, this political understanding of Asian American (ethnicity of consent) contains its own contradictions, and has serious limitations as well. For many Asian immigrants themselves, for example, the term *Asian American* serves only as a symbolic label, even meaningless trappings. The term provides no sense of solidarity, nor does it clear up serious dis- or mis-identification among the various groups.

Perhaps this watering-down of Asian American consciousness and activism should be viewed in the context of changes in American society and international politics. With the end of the Cold War, the worldwide decline of communism has disillusioned the idealistic and activist groups. Cuba, whose "guerrilla filmmaking" inspired the first group of Asian American filmmakers in the 1960s, became a political outcast and remains so. The Tienanmen Square massacre in Beijing in 1989 had fundamentally shaken the image of China (which in the early years instilled in Asian American youth a utopian image of Mao's Cultural Revolution). The ideological mass appeal driven by Third World revolutions in the 1960s and 1970s was very much lost to the younger generations by the late 1980s. What is more, since the change of the immigration law in 1965, particularly since the end of the Vietnam War, the demographics of Asian American communities have undergone drastic changes. New immigrants and professionals from Taiwan, South Korea, and India, as well as Southeast Asian refugees, have transformed the communities. These new communities have a vastly different political and social agenda from the better-established ones. For example, because of their experience, the Southeast Asian refugees were very anticommunist and more easily bought into the "melting pot" ideology. Take Trinh T. Minh-ha's *Surname Viet Given Name Nam,* for example. When the film was screened by an audience from her own community, the majority missed the message of decolonization, and interpreted it as an anticommunist documentary.

It is also important to note that the mass media, both print and broadcast, have co-opted Asian Americans in the course of their struggle with racial and ethnic conflicts in the society. Politicians carefully orchestrated the "model minority" image, and the mass media proceeded dutifully to pit Asian Americans against other minorities. The popularity of Asian American works in literature and theater, from such luminaries as Maxine Hong Kingston, Amy Tan, and David Henry Hwang, by default has lent credibility to a false sense of euphoria that some Asian Americans feel. With this political realignment, the artificial category of "Asian Americans" has imposed limited and prescriptive boundaries on the communities, and in doing so has fallen far short of accounting for the hybrid quality and extremely divergent nature of the expanding Asian American communities. Furthermore, new questions have been raised, and continue to be raised, about identity politics. For example, do we all need to identify ourselves as belonging to a given culture or ethnic group, and to whom should we do that? Is the politically charged label addressed to Asian American themselves, or to their communities? Or is it merely meant as a multicultural spectacle for the "general" population, which often turns out to be white males?

Within the imperatives of the newly emerging transnational market economies and migrations, the identity of being Asian is no longer static or secure. Collective Asian identity or pan-Asianness and their rigid boundaries seem hopelessly outdated as the cultural landscape of the communities is being redrawn within the new and shifting borders of identity, race, and ethnicity. New political vocabulary and concepts need to be developed for rethinking an Asian American identity predicated on broader formulations of decolonization across national boundaries. It is increasingly acknowledged among Asian American scholars that we cannot interpret the Asian American experience in the United States alone without a thorough comprehension of the global relations of power, the capitalist world-system, and European colonization. Migration of Asians as cheap labor, the displacement of refugees, and the forced exile of large groups have developed the different Asian diasporas around the world. New cultural spaces, borderlands, or crossings began to emerge and to challenge any essentialized notion of identity and subjectivity. Asianness is increasingly viewed as a historical and cultural formation shaped in complex, related, and multiple ways through its interaction with numerous and diverse communities.

The most provocative thinking about ethnic and cultural identity, emerging out of the current debate, is produced in the context of Black and Asian diasporic cultures and communities. Scholars such as Paul Gilroy, among others, first introduced diaspora as a theoretical framework in understanding the Black experience. In a thoughtful study of racism and nationalism in Great Britain, Gilroy challenges the parochial and ethnocentric nature of cultural studies, which deals with culture along strict national boundaries. He argues that the new racism in Britain gives "direct attention to national boundaries, focusing attention on the entry and exit of blacks. It specifies who may legitimately belong to the national community and simultaneously advances reasons for the segregation or banishment of those whose 'origin, sentiment or citizenship' assigns them elsewhere."[40] Interestingly, Gilroy cites Asians as a comparable example, "Asians on the other hand . . . are understood to be bound by cultural and biological ties which merit the status of a fully formed, alternative national identity. They pose a threat to the British way of life by virtue of their strength and cohesion."[41] This new racism described by Gilroy, where "the limits of 'race' have come to coincide so precisely with national frontiers," is a forceful voice in the debates over multiculturalism in this country as well.[42] Education specialist Diana Ravitch, for example, has invented the dichotomy of a pluralistic and a particularistic multiculturalism. Advocating a "pluralistic" approach to multicultural education, which celebrates "American culture," she accuses those "particularists" of "encouraging children to seek their primary identity in the cultures and homelands of their ancestors."[43]

This celebration of Americanness systematically excludes Asians and other racial minorities alike. Actually, this debate on American identity has been going on for years among Asian American scholars. Elaine Kim, among others, has highlighted this crucial question:

> So much writing by Asian Americans is focused on the theme of claiming an American, as opposed to Asian, identity that we may begin to wonder if this constitutes accommodation, a collective colonized spirit—the fervent wish to "hide our ancestry," which is impossible for us anyway, to relinquish our marginality, and to lose ourselves in an intense identification with the hegemonic culture. Or is it in fact a celebration of our marginality and a profound expression of protest against being defined by domination?[44]

To find a viable alternative framework, Paul Gilroy put forth the idea of an African diaspora, which refers to Black individuals and societies linked by both a common heritage and a history of struggle against similar (and in many cases the same) forces of oppression and domination. One of the key features of the diasporic culture is that social groupings or collective identities are not based on rigid racial, national, geographical, religious, or linguistic denominators. Instead, what is developed is a new and ambiguous formulation of identities at a point where race, gender, and class intersect. The so-called nomadic principle is another defining characteristic proposed by Paul Gilroy and elaborated by film scholar Teshome H. Gabriel.[45] In a seminal essay entitled "Thoughts on Nomadic Aesthetics and the Black Independent Cinema: Traces of a Journey," Gabriel argues that migration and displacement are common themes in Black culture that call on Black filmmakers to travel like nomads, in a free open space, outside the rigid confines of national boundaries.

This groundbreaking concept of diasporic cultures and sensibilities holds equally true for the loosely defined Asian immigrant communities dispersed throughout the world (for example, the Indians in Africa, the Chinese in Southeast Asia, and the Japanese in South America). Actually, the idea of a diasporic culture is not entirely new to Asian Americans. Trinh T. Minh-ha's widely-quoted statements "There is a Third World in every First World and vice versa," and " 'other' is inside each of us," articulate precisely the defining features of diasporic identities characterized by migration and displacement. The New York–based Third World Newsreel, with a strong Asian American component, has used "the Asian diaspora" concept in distributing films made by Asians and Asian Americans—films that truly address widely disparate concerns. Scholarly attention has also begun to focus on films from the Black and Asian diasporas that explore a multifaceted nomadic subjectivity or identities.[46]

This opening discussion of Asian American cultural identities provides the overall theme for this book. Over recent years, cultural critics, who investigate the interplay of identity and ideology, have argued convincingly that identities are cultural constructs formed largely through representation. Stuart Hall, for example, in a much-quoted essay, "Cultural Identity and Cinematic Representation," emphasizes that ethnic or cultural identity is "always constituted within, not outside, representation."[47] Film, Hall adds, is a "form of representation which is able to constitute us as new kinds of subjects and thereby enable us to discover who we are."[48] Along the same line of reasoning, Edward Said calls on cultural critics not only to question "the politics of identity as given, but to show how all representations are constructed, for what purpose, by whom, and with what components."[49] Hall's and Said's comments here suggest that identity cannot solely be grounded in essentialism of any sort (whether biological or cultural), but must be constructed simultaneously through various sites of representation, including the medium of film. As its title indicates, *Asian America Through the Lens: History, Representations, and Identity*, this book employs these insightful, pertinent strategies for critically reexamining the tensions about Asian American identities through a cinematic lens across different film genres. "Asian American" as a trope for the filmmakers themselves, as Lane Hirabayashi points out, "has at least three manifestations: ethnic specific [the primordial focus on 'communities of culture'], the pan Asian [the instrumental emphasis on 'community interests'], and diasporic [beyond national or geographical boundaries]."[50] By taking the critical concept of a representational pedagogy, this book locates these varying positions over questions of subjectivity, power, and identity politics in the Asian American cinema movement.

The first chapter, *A Cinema in the Making*, defines Asian American cinema as an important subject for scholarly inquiry. Asian American films have been made for more than thirty years now, but there is yet little agreement as to what constitutes an Asian American film. Does the term *Asian American* refer to the ethnicity of the filmmaker or to the thematic content of the film? Are formal and technical properties equally important defining characteristics, if not more so? In other words, is there even such a *thing* as an Asian American film aesthetic (as Thomas Cripps describes Black films)? If there is, what are its thematic and structural conventions? How has this Asian American film tradition, as in the case of the slave narrative in literature, come to define the structure of subsequent works on the subject? The initial chapter explores a working definition through the three contested understandings of Asian American cinema: the essentialist paradigm; the activist and political criteria; and the aesthetic approach, which calls for critical attention to "Asian American aesthetic sensitivities." My argument is that the best way to define Asian American cinema should be through a careful analysis of each individual film, looking at their production process, their points of view, and their formal styles.

To contextualize Asian American cinema, Chapter 2, *Cinematic Asian Representation*, offers an overview of the history of Asian and Asian American images on the silver screen. Borrowing a methodology from Chicano film historian Carlos E. Cortés, the chapter critically looks at three distinctive but interrelated dimensions of Asian representation in Hollywood: the "Oriental" image embodied in the "yellow peril" formula, the "Madame Butterfly" narratives, and the "Charlie Chan" genre; "politics of representation," the ideological functions of stereotypes as powerful means of social control; and the institutional aspect of representation in the industry, the "yellow-facing" tradition where Asian roles were played by "adhesive tape actors" in Hollywood.

The next three chapters offer a close reading of a selected group of "representative" Asian American films drawn from three different genres: social history documentaries (Chapter 3), family dramas (Chapter 4), and avant-garde films by Asian American women (Chapter 5). My discussion of these films focuses on how their thematic and cinematic elements—that is, their discursive innovations—differ from Hollywood conventions. I will explore how they document the various aspects of the Asian American experience. Critical attention will also be paid to their narrative strategies, mise-en-scène, montage, and sound.

Chapter 6, *Marginal Cinema and White Criticism*, takes a close look at the critical review of Asian American films by both mainstream and community sources. The chapter is divided into three sections, each dealing with one of the three coexisting but mutually conflicting patterns in this growing literature, namely, marginalization, appropriation, and cultural misreadings. The first section explores the underlying causes for the marginalization of Asian American productions by the literary establishment, in comparison, for example, with Asian American literature and with Japanese and Chinese films. The second section examines cultural debate over strategies for the culturally resistant film practices arising from the recent commercial success and popular acceptance of a few Asian American films like *The Joy Luck Club*. Specifically dealt with are whether the mainstream establishment has taken over the judgment of Asian American productions without giving due attention to community concerns, and whether going commercial constitutes an automatic "sell-out" to Hollywood on the part of independent filmmakers. Finally, two problematic practices in Asian American film criticism are identified: first, that Asian American films are universally considered foreign films, and, second, that they are often defined in racial or ethnic terms alone, with their artistic merits being discounted or totally ignored.

The concluding chapter assesses the present status and speculates on the future of Asian American filmmaking. Two current trends are analyzed: "crossover" films and diasporic films. The first trend is represented simultaneously by the growing ranks of non-Asian-themed and nonactivist productions by Ang Lee and Wayne Wang, among others, as well as by Asian filmmakers and actors such as John Woo and Jackie Chan, who are literally marching or hurtling into Hollywood. For the second, we witness an increasing number of films distributed in the United States (by NAATA and Women Make Movies, for example), which are produced by Asian immigrants elsewhere in the English-speaking world in such countries as Canada, Australia, and Great Britain. These films from the Asian diaspora display a bold heterogeneity in both content and form. Accordingly, they refuse to claim (or to have imposed on them) any essentialist or totalized group or individual identity. It remains to be seen whether these growing trends represent future directions for the booming Asian American cinema.

NOTES

1   The conference was part of a ten-month National Tour of Asian CineVision's 14th Asian American International Festival.

2   For studies on Black cinema, *The Negro in Films* (1948) by Peter Noble is a pioneering work that traces the ignominious career of the Black stereotype in film through both the silent and sound eras. Edward Mapp's *Blacks in American Films: Today and Yesterday* (1972) serves as a useful supplement to Noble's book. Other earlier publications include: Thomas Cripps's *Black Film As Genre*, an analysis of Black films as a coherent genre through examination of six key films, Murray James's *To Find An Image: Black Films From Uncle Tom to Super Fly*, and Mbye Cham, *Blackframes: Critical Perspectives on Black Independent Cinema*. For more information on Chicano/a cinema, see *Chicano Cinema: Research, Reviews, and Resources*, edited by Gary D. Keller, and *Chicanos and Film: Essays on Chicano Representation and Resistance*, edited by Chon A. Noriega.

3   *Moving the Image: Independent Asian Pacific American Media Arts* edited by Russell Leong (jointly sponsored by UCLA Asian American Studies Center and Visual Communications in Los Angeles in 1991) is a good resource book. A single-author comprehensive monograph on the subject is called for in the field.

4   See Christopher Shea, "In 'Darwin's Athletes,' a Professor Explores Americans' Reverence for Black Sports Stars," *Chronicle of Higher Education* (March 7, 1997), A-15.

5   Phone interview with Katherine Leslie, April 1996.

6   By definition, Asian American films in this study mean "films by, for, and about Asian Americans." Renee Tajima defines Asian American cinema in broader terms as a "socially committed cinema; created by a people bound by 1) race; 2) interlocking cultural and historical relations; and 3)

a common experience of western domination characterized by diversity shaped through 1) national origin; and 2) the constant flux of new immigration flowing from a westernizing East into an easterning West." See Renee Tajima, "Moving the Image: Asian American Independent Filmmaking 1970–1990," *Moving the Image*, 10.

7   Asian CineVision, "Tributes, Retrospectives, and New Films to Celebrate AAIFF's First Decade," *CineVue* 2:3 (May 1987), 1.

8   *Asian American Media Reference Guide*, 2d ed., ed. Bill J. Gee (New York: Asian CineVision, 1990).

9   James Wong Howe, the renowned Chinese American cinematographer, received Oscars in 1956 for *The Rose Tattoo* and in 1963 for *Hud*.

10   For more details, see Daryl Chin, "Asian American Filmmakers Harvest Oscar Nominations," *CineVue* 4:1 (March 1989).

11   As quoted in Frank Viviano, "From Charlie Chan to Hyphenated Cinema," *Far Eastern Economic Review* (July 30, 1987), 34.

12   Since 1991, *CineVue* has given five Asian American filmmakers/video artists "a carte jaune" (a "yellow card") to remake any film they choose from an Asian American point of view, including Arthur Dong, Deborah Gee, Jon Moritsugu, Norman Yonemoto, and Renee Tajima. See Marsha Tajima, "Carte Jaune Fantasies," *CineVue* 6:3 (Sept. 1991), 1–3.

13   Phone interview with Katherine Leslie, April 1996.

14   For further information, see Diane Waldman, "There's More to a Positive Image Than Meets the Eye," *Jump Cut: Hollywood, Politics and Counter Cinema*, ed. Peter Steven (New York: Praeger, 1985), 202–208.

15   bell hooks, *Black Looks: Race and Representation* (Boston: South End Press, 1992), 4.

16   Robert Stam and Louise Spence, "Colonialism, Racism, and Representation: An Introduction," in *Movies and Methods: An Anthology*, ed. Bill Nichols (Berkeley: University of California Press, 1976), 639.

17   Valerie Smith, *Representing Blackness, Issues in Film and Video* (New Brunswick: Rutgers University Press, 1997), 4.

18   Kalamu ya Salaam, "Black Macho and The Myth of the Positive Message," *Black Film Review* 7:1 (1991), 6.

19   Richard Fung, "Centering the Margins," *Moving the Image*, 67.

20   Smith, 3.

21   John Kuo Wei Tchen, "Believing Is Seeing: Transforming Orientalism and the Occidental Gaze," *Asia/America: Identities in Contemporary Asian American Art*, ed. Margo Machida (New York: New Press, 1994), 23.

22   Kevin Brownlow, *Behind the Mask of Innocence* (New York: Alfred A. Knopf, 1990), 330.

23   Available for rental from George Eastman House in New York.

24   Brownlow, 333.

25   Ibid., 352.

26   Ibid., 332.

27   Ibid., 333.

28   Ibid., 334.

29   For a four-stage development history, see Yoshio Kishi, "Final Mix; Unscheduled," *Moving the Image*, 157–65.

30   Yoshio Kishi, "Pioneers and Groundbreakers," *Moving the Image*, 167–70.

31   Jen's essay was originally published in the April 21, 1997, issue of *The New Republic*. The quote is taken from Gish Jen, "A person is more than the sum of her social facts," *Chronicle of Higher Education* (May 23, 1997), B-11.

32   For a good summary of the theories on ethnicity, see Yen Le Espiritu, *Asian American Panethnicity: Bridging Institutions and Identities* (Philadelphia: Temple University Press, 1992), especially Chapter 1.

33   Jen, B-11.

34   Stuart Hall, "Cultural Identity and Cinematic Representation," *Framework* 36 (1989), 69.

35   Ibid., 70.

36   Lisa Lowe, "Heterogeneity, Hybridity, Multiplicity: Marking Asian American Differences," *Diaspora* 1:1 (Spring 1991), 39.

37   Ibid.

38   Phone interview with Katherine Leslie, April 1996.

39   Quoted from Hirabayashi's comments on my book.

40   Paul Gilroy, *"There Ain't No Black in the Union Jack": The Cultural Politics of Race and Nation* (Chicago: University of Chicago Press, 1991), 45.

41   Ibid., 45–46.

42   Ibid., 46.

43   Diana Ravitch, "Diversity and Democracy: Multicultural Education in America," *American Educator* (Spring 1990), 18.

44   Elaine Kim, "Defining Asian American Realities Through Literature," *Cultural Critique* 6 (Spring 1987), 88.

45   Teshome H. Gabriel, "Thoughts on Nomadic Aesthetics and the Black Independent Cinema: Traces of a Journey," *Blackframes: Critical Perspectives on Black Independent Cinema*, ed. Mbye Cham (Cambridge: MIT Press, 1988).

46   For example, see Gwendolyn Audrey Foster, *Women Filmmakers of the African and Asian Diaspora: Decolonizing the Gaze, Locating Subjectivity* (Carbondale and Edwardsville: Southern Illinois University Press, 1997). Foster studies six women directors of African and Asian descent: Zeinabu Irene Davis, Ngozi Onwurah, Julie Dash, Pratibha Parmar, Trinh T. Minh-ha, and Mira Nair.

47   Hall, 69.

48   Ibid., 80.

49   Edward Said, *Culture and Imperialism* (New York: Knopf, 1993), 314.

50   Quoted from Hirabayashi's comments on my manuscript; the explanatory notes within the brackets are mine.

A Cinema in the Making

IN MARCH 1994, NEW YORK UNIVERSITY organized a panel discussion on the topic "Whose Black Cinema Is It, Anyway?" as part of a week-long program on Black film.[1] The seven panelists, including filmmaker Spike Lee, writer Ishmael Reed, and film critic Joel Siegel, debated the following questions: Should only Blacks make movies about Blacks? Should Black filmmakers be limited to Black themes? Are Black-controlled films guaranteed to portray the Black experience with sensitivity? Should Blacks see films directed by non-Blacks, and should the race of the audience affect which movies they see? Deceptively simplistic, those questions touch on some of the fundamental issues in ethnic representation: authenticity, creative control, and community empowerment.

This debate is not unique to Black filmmaking, but is also a highly contested topic among Asian Americans. Over the past three decades, Asian American film and video artists have produced hundreds of films and videos in the narrative, documentary, and experimental modes, yet much confusion remains about what constitutes an Asian American film. Does the term *Asian American* refer to the ethnicity of the filmmaker or the topic of the film, regardless of who makes it?[2] Would a film made by an Asian American in Asia or elsewhere—such as Ang Lee's *Eat Drink Man Woman* (1994), made in Taiwan, or Tran Anh Hung's *The Scent of Green Papaya* (1993), filmed in France—be considered Asian or Asian American? How do we categorize an Asian American–directed "nonethnic" movie, such as Wayne Wang's *Smoke* (1995) and *Blue in the Face* (1995), or Ang Lee's *Sense and Sensibility* (1995) and *The Ice Storm* (1997)? Where do we draw the boundaries? Do films with a clear Asian American theme, but shot by a multiracial crew—such as Oliver Stone's *Heaven and Earth* (1993) and David Cronenberg's *M. Butterfly* (1993)—qualify as Asian American? Furthermore, do we even *need* this naming, labeling, or categorizing of Asian American films?

Informed by similar themes in Black independent cinema, this chapter attempts to define Asian American films as a distinctive cinema.[3] Asian American film has not been satisfactorily defined or named. Many Asian American filmmakers regard the label of Asian American film or filmmaker as externally imposed and limiting. Peter Wang, director of the critically acclaimed cross-cultural comedy *A Great Wall* (1986), for example, considers himself a filmmaker first and foremost. When asked if he had ever considered himself an Asian American filmmaker, he responded in a resigned manner, "Not by choice. It is not my choice. I think I am just a filmmaker, period."[4] Filmmakers and media activists who have tried to categorize Asian American films have often done so from either an essentialist or a political perspective. Neither approach provides a working definition, and, therefore, the classification remains open-ended. In this context, the first two sections of this chapter address cultural essentialism and media advocacy, two main points of view on the subject. An alternative aesthetics approach will be proposed in the third section. Also in that final section, a critical reading of Wayne Wang's *Chan Is Missing* (1982), arguably America's first feature film utilizing an all–Asian American cast and technical crew, will be showcased as an Asian American film.

Defining the subject is an important critical task for this book, for both descriptive and analytical purposes. By identifying Asian American films as a distinctive cinema, I hope to establish some formal parameters for lining up a representative corpus of film texts and isolating them from other types of films. Asian American cinema can, therefore, be judged as a tradition in its own right, both for its unique cultural and discursive practices, and for its complex dialectical relationship with Hollywood narrative and other forms of Asian American art. Furthermore, this critical process itself would help develop a historically specific and culturally innovative framework for interpreting the political and artistic meanings of these works, thus controlling the process of self-comprehension and criticism. As Asian Canadian videomaker Midi Onodera puts it precisely, "Criticism by well-informed, well-intentioned white critics tell us mainstream beliefs, but it does not tell us what we mean. We must begin this process of comprehension ourselves."[5]

CULTURAL ESSENTIALISM AND ASIAN AMERICAN FILMS

In 1926, W. E. B. Du Bois laid down the following four terms for an authentic Black theater:

> The plays of a real Negro theater must be: 1. *About us.* That is they must have plots which reveal Negro life as it is. 2. *By us.* That is they must be

written by Negro authors who understand from birth and continual association just what it means to be a Negro today. 3. *For us.* That is, the theater
must cater primarily to Negro audiences and be supported and sustained
by their entertainment and approval. 4. *Near us.* The theater must be in a
Negro neighborhood near the mass of ordinary Negro people.[6]

Three-quarters of a century later, this ethnicity-defined essentialism has
also been accepted and adapted by Chicano/a filmmakers. In his introduction to
Chicanos and Film, Chon A. Noriega wrote,

> Although what constitutes a "Chicano" film continues to be the subject of
> debate, we can start with the definition offered by the filmmakers: a film
> (or video) by and about Chicanos. The word "by" is taken to mean that
> the writer, producer, or director is Chicano. The filmmakers tend to apply
> a third criterion when the producer alone is Chicano: that he or she had
> significant involvement in the creative process. . . .[7]

Among veteran Asian American filmmakers and critics, this "by, for,
about" standard also strikes a strong chord. Writing on the history of Asian American media centers, Stephen Gong, a longtime Asian American media activist,
emphasized that Asian American independent filmmaking was largely based on
the assumption of a pan-Asian ethnicity (the belief that "being Asian American
transcended the experience of being solely Chinese, Korean, or Japanese American").[8] Adopting the same reasoning, John Esaki, an Asian American media artist,
wrote in 1990 that "only by believing in the compelling nature of our lives as Asian
Pacific Americans and by trusting in our own creative ways of seeing those lives
and framing them on film can we forge a true Asian Pacific American cinema."[9]
Daryl Chin, a Chinese American playwright and cofounder of the Asian American
International Film Festival (AAIFF) in New York City, was instrumental in helping lay down the parameters for Asian American film. In defining standards for
admission (as well as categories for awards, at the film festival) the identity of the
filmmaker was taken as the primary criterion. On various occasions, Chin insisted
on the primacy of filmmakers' ethnicity over film topics: "[I]f an Asian American
made the movie, but the movie did not have specific Asian American content, was
it still an Asian American movie? My answer is always, yes."[10] Based on this understanding, for two decades since its beginning in 1978, AAIFF, the country's primary showcase for Asian American films, has welcomed submissions of any works
in which one of the principals (meaning director or producer) is Asian by birth or
heritage. Its guidelines place no limits on length, genre, or subject matter, which can
be specifically Asian or otherwise. By its second year, the festival had expanded to
include foreign feature films from Asia.

It is an agreeable idea that ethnic filmmakers, with their cultural knowledge, enjoy some edge over outsiders in portraying their culture in a more sensitive way. As Spike Lee stated in the film panel at NYU, "Just as Francis Ford Coppola and Mr. [Martin] Scorsese brought rich experience to their films about Italian-Americans, so [I], as a black American[,] naturally gravitated to black subject matter and brought to it a special kind of knowledge."[11] Many Asian American filmmakers agree with Lee. Duane Kubo, one of the cofounders of Visual Communications in Los Angeles, told his interviewer, "I don't think that Asian Americans are necessarily better filmmakers. I think Asian American filmmakers can, yes, make better Asian American films because of their background, heritage, and community. Any number of things might give them that advantage."[12] Peter Wang, for another example, saw little authenticity (or perhaps a lack of sincerity) behind non-Asians making films about Asians. He contended:

> If you want me to make a film about people in East Europe, I wouldn't recommend you go see it. It would be horrible. The camera is such a magic tool. It doesn't hide. It shows definitely the director's intention, his background, his preference, even to a degree you can tell whether this director likes the actor or actress or not. If you try to fake an orgasm, it doesn't work that way. It doesn't work.[13]

Wang's point on authenticity is enthusiastically embraced by the "cultural guardians" in the Asian American community. Just look at the controversy over Margaret Cho's 1994 television sitcom *All-American Girl,* which aired on the ABC network. Bill Wong, an *AsianWeek* columnist, accused the show of being "stupid, inane, and ethnically inauthentic."[14] Because only two of the show's eleven writers were Chinese American and none of them Korean American, the comedy was dubbed "a cast of Asian American entertainers delivering lines written by Hollywood writers who have little understanding of how Asian Americans interact with each other in real life."[15] "Very rarely has a commercial sitcom come in for so much nit-picking and unseemly angst," wrote Carlos Mendez in *AsianWeek.* " 'Even the rice they eat,' exclaimed a high-school intern for the Korea Times; 'we eat sticky rice.' "[16] Margaret Cho was shocked by the harshness of the criticism from the Korean-language press and within her own Korean American community. In a very emotional and blunt speech delivered at an awards banquet in honor of her as "Asian Pacific American of the Year," Cho admitted the personal attack "is painful to me." She compared her position among Koreans to that of rapper Ice Cube after the release of his 1992 single "Black Korea," an angry racist rap tune, which viciously maligned Korean store merchants and advocated their murder following the Latasha Harlins court case.[17] Gary Jacobs, the executive producer of *All-American Girl,* was equally "surprised by the intensity of the negative reactions from Asian

Pacific Americans." Addressing its detractors, he said that unrealistic demands and expectations were placed on a show that "never presumed to represent the definitive Asian Pacific American experience."[18]

Playwright and filmmaker Philip Kan Gotanda looks at ethnicity in terms of historical experience. "So in some senses," said Gotanda, "a film that an Asian American directs, whether it be about an Asian subject matter or not, is still going to carry, in some degree, the nuances, the historical psychology inside that person's makeup."[19] Chinese American writer Amy Tan expressed a similar view (in a post-screening interview about *The Joy Luck Club*): "I met with dozens of people who wanted to make the book into a movie. Five actually made offers, but I never took them. I wasn't entirely convinced that it *should* be a movie." But after meeting Wayne Wang, "I . . . ended up having such a wonderful conversation about our own histories that I knew I wanted him on the project."[20]

It is important to bear in mind that this type of discourse about authenticity results directly from a long period of frustration and anger among Asian Americans over the degradation of their images on the silver screen.[21] Even the most perfunctory review of Hollywood films reveals a constant recycling of grotesque representations of Asians, from the inscrutable Charlie Chan to the diabolical Fu Manchu, down to the exotic Suzie Wong and the happy-go-lucky Jackie Chan. The 1985 release of *Year of the Dragon* was so offensive that it was met with the largest protest ever generated by the Asian American community. But the picket lines and mass protests had little impact on the movie (except for the addition of an empty disclaimer at the film's beginning).

The relationship between power and representation has become the underlying argument for the essentialist position. To create alternatives to Hollywood portrayals and control the screen images that define so much of their lives, Asian Americans feel they have to take control over what goes on both in front of and behind the camera. Japanse American director Kayo Hatta reflects, in a private interview, "I feel it is really important that Asian Americans get more into the producing, controlling the means by which films are made and distributed. That's where the artistic control comes in. If you don't have the means to make the film, you can't control the content. On the financial and the distribution end, filmmaking is going to be white, with Asian Americans being more in the background."[22]

Even more important, in American media it is the essentialist ideology of "whiteness" that has been used by the "white" population against "nonwhites" as a conceptual form of social control. Hollywood's institutional racism, carefully documented by Eugene Wong, among others, lends credibility to this essentialist argument.[23] The longtime practice of "role segregation" places Asians as sidekicks or as extras, and allows Caucasians to play major Asian roles through what Wong calls racist cosmetology. The list of "yellow-facing" (putting on crudely stereotypical Asian makeup) in Hollywood is a long one. Actors Warner Oland, Boris Karloff, and Peter Sellers played Fu Manchu for four successive decades, until as recently as the 1980s. The role of Charlie Chan, the most famous Chinese detective in movies, was played by a number of white actors, from Warner Oland, Sidney Toler, and Roland Winters, all the way down to Peter Ustinov. The much-publicized controversy over the casting of the Broadway musical *Miss Saigon* in 1990 was probably the most recent example of this yellow-facing tradition.[24] The practice of yellow-facing was so common in American popular culture that it had once become a matter of de facto reversed cultural authenticity. A case in point, about the casting of Cho-Cho-San in a New York production of the opera *Madame Butterfly*, was documented by Nick Browne. The engagement of a certain Japanese Mme. Tamaki Miura of Tokyo for the lead role gave rise to the question "as to whether a woman from the West can better portray the Butterfly of Puccini's opera than a woman of her own nation."[25] One critic was reported to demand that "Mme. Miura had to divest herself of most of the artistic traditions of her own land before she could impersonate the character imagined by an American novelist and set to music in Italy."[26]

The history of racism and discrimination against Asian Americans in the film industry validates Gayatri Spivak's concept of "a strategic use of positivist essentialism."[27] For Spivak, essentialism (read "ethnic identity") could be used "in a scrupulously visible political interest."[28] Like Nietzsche's concept of "genealogy in place of historiography," Foucault's "construction of a 'counter-memory,'" and Derrida's "affirmative deconstruction," according to Spivak, the strategy of positive essentialism "becomes most useful when 'consciousness' is being used in the narrow sense, as self-consciousness."[29] For Asian American filmmakers, the strategy of ethnic collective/community consciousness could become means for their own empowerment. Kayo Hatta was very positive on the strategy. She stated:

> I think using a so-called label to identify yourself was more for the purpose of saying, "This is not business as usual. This is from a different perspective." For me, I am always interested when I hear "Latina filmmaker" or "Black filmmaker," because I know that this is going to be a work that is a little bit different. . . . So until [filmmaking] becomes more multiethnic, the labels just help people of color.[30]

For director Wayne Wang, the debate is not so much a matter of essentialsism as a matter of equity:

> I don't agree with people who say that you can only make films about blacks if you're black, you can only make films about Chinese if you're Chinese . . . as long as Chinese-Americans are able, and have the resources to make films about Chinese-Americans, then I think it's fine for a white

American director to make a film about the Chinese-American community, because it's another perspective from the outside looking in.[31]

Cultural critics have long argued that identities are formed through representations rather than ethnic heritage. If we accept this understanding of identity, defining Asian American films based solely on filmmakers' ethnicity would
become at best a dubious concept. How does the ethnic heritage of filmmakers
affect their artistry? In other words, does the mere ethnic background of filmmakers ensure that they make truer representations of Asian Americans? Obviously,
this assumption would lead us helplessly into the value-laden judgments of authenticity and into elusive concepts of realism. Recent controversies over some commercial films by ethnic filmmakers have demonstrated that a person's genetic
makeup might not automatically guarantee authenticity. The debate among
Blacks surrounding Spike Lee's film *Malcolm X* (1992) is an illuminating test case.
Manning Marable, for example, accuses Lee of making the Black activist into a
myth or cultural icon—something the Black community does not need, because
"it desperately requires practical solutions to its pressing problems."[32] As controversial as *Malcolm X* was Wayne Wang's *The Joy Luck Club* (1993). Despite the rave
reviews the latter movie received for breaking down stereotypes of Asian women,
the critical reaction from the various Asian communities was mixed. As one angry
reader of *AsianWeek* wrote, "There are only two typecasts of Chinese men [in the
movie], assholes and sissies." Even mainstream critics were wary of the disturbing
and offensive stereotypes of Chinese men. Brian Johnson of *MacLean's* commented,
"All the women are beautiful, successful and affluent, a fact that is simply taken for
granted. And all their men are stupid, evil or, at the very least, unfaithful."[33] Stuart Hall's comment about Black filmmakers might be relevant for Asian Americans as well. He says, "Films are not necessarily good because black people make
them. They are not necessarily 'right-on' by virtue of the fact that they deal with
the black experience."[34]

The fundamental question would be: Who possesses the authority to
write about or depict an ethnic or racial group? Does the making of Asian American films require "insider" cultural knowledge, similar historical experience, and
even membership in the given group?[35] Can we seriously take the position (which
Werner Sollors labels "biological insiderism" in *Beyond Ethnicity*) that outsiders can
never produce films about an ethnic group because they view it only through their
inherently dissimilar, different-from-the-group value system?[36] These authenticity
standards are often used to make judgment in film criticism. "Legitimacy tests" of
one kind or another must be passed. For example, in adapting Alice Walker's novel
The Color Purple (1985) to the screen, Steven Spielberg's credentials were challenged
from an essentialist position. "He is not a Southerner," Rita Dandridge wrote in the

Black Film Review. "He has no background in the black experience, and he seems to know little about feminism."[37]

Furthermore, the essentialist orientation could turn out to be a double-edged sword. Could the essentialist turf argument be used against Asian Americans? And is there going to be a backlash against Asian Americans making non-Asian movies? A ready example would be Ang Lee's bold adventure in *Sense and Sensibility,* the Jane Austen classic. Lee from the beginning was regarded as a novelty in the production of the movie. The fact that Lee, an unknown (in Hollywood terms) Chinese director, landed the directorial job on a medium-budget studio movie (with a major star, Emma Thompson, as both scriptwriter and lead actress) has been commented on frequently. Most people thought he was an exceedingly odd choice. In an interview, the film's producer, Sidney Pollack, recalled, "Lee had somehow got hold of the script and made a phone call through his agent about it. First we thought this was insane, having a Chinese director make an American-produced English period piece." But Pollack took a gamble and was vindicated. "Sometimes, but not always," Pollack stated after the movie won seven Oscar nominations, "it happens that someone from another culture is more objective about your own than you can be yourself. We were amazed in the 1960's when [British director] John Schlesinger did *Midnight Cowboy* and caught a piece of America that most Americans hadn't seen. It could be we have been just as lucky."[38] Because of Pollack's open-mindedness, Lee was lucky enough to be given the opportunity to prove himself. For another example, Trinh T. Minh-ha, a Vietnamese American filmmaker who made her first two films (*Reassemblage* and *Naked Spaces: Living Is Round*) about West Africa, was often questioned by African Americans about her positioning. As the Black writer bell hooks noticed, "There was often a resentment behind those questions about what her place was in this place."[39] For hooks, the resentment reflects "a failure to understand subjectivity and what freedom is."[40] For the late Black film historian James Snead, it is an ideological problem. "The fixation upon racial or even ethnic pedigree," he said, "has tended to separate American blacks from British blacks, American blacks from West Indian blacks, American blacks from Chinese- and Japanese-Americans, American blacks from Hispanic and Latino-Americans, not to mention American blacks from British Indians and Asians."[41]

In a sense, this essentialism tends to work against nonwhite filmmakers more forcefully than against their white counterparts. Trinh T. Minh-ha describes the confining boundaries of this essentialism against minority artists:

> We have been herded as people of color to mind only our own cultures.
> Hence, Asians will continue to make films on Asia, Africans on Africa,
> and Euro-Americans on . . . the world. Every time you hear similar reac-

tions to your films, you are bound to realize how small the limits and
the territory remain in which you are allowed to work.[42]

From an essentialist imperative, an additional question, regarding Asian
American filmmaking, can be raised. "No filmmaker is independent," wrote Snead,
"in the way, say, a poet is. Filmmaking, both capital- and labor-intensive, is the
most dependent art form."[43] Indeed, film production is a collaborative process, and
sometimes it can hardly be controlled by one single ethnic group. Cross-over productions between Asian Americans and non-Asians are bound to occur. Two 1993
movies, *M. Butterfly* and *Golden Gate*, were based on Tony Award winner David
Henry Hwang's original screenplays, but were directed by two whites, David Cronenberg and John Madden. The making of *Heaven and Earth,* well-documented by
Michael Singer in *Oliver Stone's Heaven and Earth: The Making of an Epic Motion Picture,* is another successful cross-racial production.[44] The movie is based on Le Ly
Hayslip's life story, with Oliver Stone's screenplay and Kitaro's music score. In
making *The Joy Luck Club*, Wayne Wang devised a rule that no Caucasians would
play roles written for Asians. Regardless, the movie was made by a multiracial
crew. The screenplay, based on Amy Tan's 1989 best-seller, was a joint effort
between Tan and Ronald Bass (a Caucasian Academy Award–winning screenwriter). Tan seemed very happy working with Bass. "Our collaboration was so
thorough," Tan recalls, "that by the time we saw the movie during screenings, we
often could not remember who wrote what. In fact, there's a particular line the
audience seems to love, where the daughter character Rose says to her mother, 'I
like being tragic, Ma—I learned it from you.' Ron and I argue over who wrote that
line. He says I did. I say he did."[45] Believe it or not, this kind of cross-over production will certainly increase as more Asian Americans get into the studio system.

In view of these inherent contradictions, it is obvious that the biologically
determined definition of Asian American films does not help inform the discussions
of Asian American films. The essentialist criteria were important historically in the
cultural politics that inspired a whole generation of Asian American media activists.
They have addressed, and continue to counter, Hollywood's institutional racism
against Asian Americans. However, biology (race) itself is a problematic category
and cannot, and should not, overdetermine Asian American film practices and criticism. New formulations have to be explored, which leads to another popular con-
ception: the politically grounded definitions of Asian American films.

"BETWEEN A WEAPON AND A FORMULA"[46]

Faced with all the difficulties in defining "black film," Tommy Lott offers the notion of Third Cinema as his "no-theory" theory for contemporary Black cinema. "What makes Third Cinema third (i.e., a viable alternative to Western cinema)," he writes, "is not exclusively the racial makeup of a filmmaker, a film's aesthetic character, or a film's intended audience, but rather a film's political orientation."[47] In the context of Asian American literature, Garrett Hongo has identified "three dominant modes" in its critical practices:

> (1) an unconscious assumption that what was *essentially* Asian American was a given work's overt political stance and conformity to sociological models of the Asian American experience, (2) the related notion that a writer writes from a primary loyalty to coherent communities, and (3) vehement castigation or rude, categorical dismissal for literary qualities deemed "assimilationist" or "commercial."[48]

This political orientation is useful in describing Asian American film-making as a political movement, especially during its early development. In the relatively short history of Asian American cinema, two broadly defined stages have arisen, corresponding to the political and social contexts in the United States. From the 1970s to the early 1980s, Asian American cinema, as Stephen Gong observed, was "fundamentally a political (rather than a cultural or ethnic-based) movement."[49] Inspired by the Third Cinema movement in Latin America, Asian American filmmaking was a direct outgrowth of the Civil Rights Movement and political activism in the 1960s. In the wake of the Black civil rights, sexual minority rights, and ethnic pride movements, young people of diverse Asian ancestry joined together to form a new political coalition. United under an Asian American banner, they began to exert collective political clout, seeking reparations for past injustices and challenging racial stereotyping. From the beginning, the path-breakers tried to build a so-called "triangular cinema" of community, storyteller, and activist.[50] Visual Communications (VC) in Los Angeles, the first Asian American media group, for example, emerged out of the Ethno-Communications program (an affirmative action experiment that began in 1968 at UCLA). Social consciousness and political activism were obvious goals of the group. They made their first project filming the antiredevelopment demonstrations in the Little Tokyo area of Los Angeles. As committed filmmakers, they produced films "not only about people engaged in these struggles, but also with and by them as well."[51] The late Steve J. Tatsukawa, former VC administrative director, and later director of Asian CineVision in New York, recalled, "We were always out there to shoot. But sometimes, it was more important to drop our cameras and join the demonstration—well, uh, maybe not drop the cameras. But put them down carefully, and then be part of the struggle ourselves."[52]

The Asian American movement, studied by William Wei, had a very active cultural component, spawning visual arts collectives, literary groups, independent film cooperatives, and nonprofit theater companies. Discontent with a long history of stereotypical rendering of their culture and history, the young filmmakers made a passionate and conscious choice for community-based filmmaking. This notion of filmmaking as a method for social change, instead of as a showcase of the artist, has understandably produced a cinema that is more concerned with its message. Loni Ding, a twenty-year veteran Chinese American documentarist, explains her priorities: "It's a story [communal history] that needs to be told twice, three times, more before making art out [of] it. Film is such an expensive undertaking that you can't just say I'll do that and the other, too. You do one, or the other. You gotta make your choice."[53] Arthur Dong, the director of many social issue documentaries (from Asian American history to gay rights), dropped out of school to engage in making social change. "Film is a medium to talk about social issues, to make social change possible," he wrote. "It is something that gets shown to thousands and thousands of people if you're lucky, if it's good enough, if it's acceptable to the general public."[54] Thus, for young Asian Americans, the camera, the most powerful artistic invention of modern times, became both a logical tool in achieving community mobilization and an agent for social change. They regarded filmmaking as a unique way to initiate recognition of the community and also as a method of obtaining long-overdue civil rights.

Three thematic concerns dominated their works: identity politics, historical injustice, and contemporary racism. They started with the so-called "personal diary" films, dealing with identity issues, which will be discussed in detail in Chapter 3. No subject received more coverage than the internment experience for the Issei (first-generation Japanese immigrants to the United States) and Nisei (the second generation). Scores of documentaries were produced by both Japanese and other Asian American filmmakers. Steven Okazaki's *Days of Waiting*, the story of Estelle Ishigo, a gifted Caucasian artist who was interned with her Japanese American husband, won an Academy Award in 1991. Loni Ding's *The Color of Honor: The Japanese-American Soldier in World War II* was screened before Congress as part of the debates for reparations for Japanese Americans interned during World War II. Visual Communications's first major feature-length movie, *Hito Hata: Raise the Banner* (1980), directed by Duane Kubo and Robert Nakamura, was also devoted to the World War II experience of an Issei (played by Mako) in the Little Tokyo district of Los Angeles. Christine Choy and Renee Tajima's *Who Killed Vincent Chin?* (1989) is perhaps the best-known Asian American social issue documentary. In the context of Japan-bashing and anti-Asian violence, this compelling documentary became the rallying cry for Asian American activists in the 1980s. Christine Choy's newly released film *The Shot Heard 'Round the World* (1997) examines the tragic death of Yoshi Hattori, a teenage Japanese exchange student who was shot to death by Rodney Peairs on October 17, 1992, in Baton Rouge, Louisiana.

The politically charged terms of "oppositional," "resistant," and "subversive," however, are often freely employed by Asian American film critics without giving sufficient attention to the other dimensions of the films under discussion. In short, such critics sometimes fall into the trap of being too eager to read a political agenda into the productions. While most of the works produced in the 1970s or early 1980s dealt with the struggle to define Asian American identities, reclaim untold stories, and fight racism, the recent wave of Asian-directed films demonstrates a much wider range and variety of content, styles, and perspectives. A new generation of artists have emerged, and they produce films that are not necessarily culturally introspective or politically active. In recent years, more fictional and narrative films have been made, and with them has come some mainstream recognition. Indeed, there has been increasing resistance among Asian American filmmakers to the kind of cultural confinement expected in previous decades. Peter Wang, for example, bluntly rejected any political mission, saying, "I don't think that I am on a mission or a kind of crusade to correct the wrongs. I don't think I am capable of doing that or that there is even a necessity for it. All you have to do is tell a genuine and truthful story that you feel that is important. That is all you ask of any filmmaker."[55] Kayo Hatta agrees:

> I am not really trying to educate people, not in a conscious way. I try to present genuine, interesting, complex people the way I know them. If this counters a stereotype by virtue of them being complex, then that's great. But I'm not trying to consciously defy those stereotypes. What I'm trying to do is to be more proactive in my work in presenting really interesting images rather than being reactive. . . . I don't like my work to be reactive.[56]

Playwright and screenwriter David Henry Hwang describes himself "as an Asian American artist not particularly dedicated to telling the essential Asian American story." Hwang told his audience at the 1989 Show the Right Thing conference in New York City that "speaking sincerely and passionately about nonculturally specific issues was more effective than half-heartedly trying to speak universally on concerns of race and culture."[57] Valerie Soe, a Chinese American videomaker, argues against elevating cultural content above individual creativity. She wrote, "It's more important not to pigeonhole Asian Pacific artists into only dealing with culture specific topics and themes."[58] The crux of the matter, according to her, is that different strategies of representation would be foreclosed if too much political pressure were placed on these artists to speak for the community.

Los Angeles–based director Gregg Araki, who was sometimes attacked for not engaging Asian subjects in his films, told *The Independent* magazine that he would not be dictated to by any political agenda. "My feeling about both the gay issue and the Asian issue," he said, "is that I don't let Hollywood or *anybody* tell me how to make my films. I'm certainly not going to let some Asian American media group say I should make a film about the relocation camps." For Araki, staying away from the topic of internment camps was also an ethical decision. He continued, "My parents were interned just like everybody else's, but I feel that if they want to make a film about that, that's their experience. I personally think that's a little bit exploitive of the pain that your own parents went through."[59] Even Wayne Wang, after making several Asian American dramas, was reluctant to take on *The Joy Luck Club* because, as he told the *New York Times*, "I didn't want to do another Chinese movie."[60] And after the highly acclaimed movie was made, he broke out of his "ethnic mold" and directed *Smoke* and its sequel *Blue in the Face*, neither of which is related to Asians directly. In a similar way, Ang Lee, having won acclaim for his Asian American trilogy *Pushing Hands* (1992), *The Wedding Banquet* (1993), and *Eat Drink Man Woman*, directed the Oscar-winning *Sense and Sensibility* and went on to direct *The Ice Storm* (1997), a drama based on the novel by Rick Moody about two upper-class, suburban Connecticut families in 1973. Lee is reportedly planning to do a blockbuster Chinese martial-arts epic in the next few years.[61]

Philip Kan Gotanda saw this depoliticalization as a natural progression for almost any emergent group. "[T]he political growth of any movement . . . first starts with a kind of anger, looking back on history, a sense of self-empowerment," he said. "Once those things are established, then you can move on to explore other themes, which are perhaps less explicitly politicized. I think that's the stage we've reached in terms of Asian Pacific Americans in filmmaking."[62] As Jesse Algeron Rhines cogently writes on the three coexisting, nonexclusive, and intersecting areas in Black independent cinema: filmmaking is a business, filmmaking is an artistic endeavor, and filmmaking is a tool for socioeconomic development.[63] If Rhines's comment is equally true of Asian American cinema, a more inclusive framework is called for in reading Asian American films across a number of diverse styles, stories, and modes in its growing ranks.

ASIAN AMERICAN AESTHETICS

Two decades ago, in defining Black genre films, film historian Thomas Cripps emphasized that Black films should be seen as a genre "for what it says and how it's said, rather than who is saying it."[64] In the same vein, Wayne Wang once asserted in an interview with Diane Mei Lin Mark, "There's a part of me that's very American [coded 'white'], and I want to make movies that have no Asian [coded 'Asian American'] characters. But my aesthetic, which is very much Chinese, would still come through."[65] Although stated in different contexts, Cripps's and Wang's comments raise important questions for Asian American films. Is there a Chinese—and, by extension, Asian—American film aesthetic? Are formal and technical properties equally important in defining characteristics of Asian American cinema, or does one take primacy? Or, to put it differently, has an Asian American film tradition even emerged?[66]

Obviously, no easy answers can be given to these critical questions. Actually, one finds more skepticism and self-doubts than answers. First, *Asian American* is itself a very slippery label. Asian Americans in the United States do not share a common cultural or linguistic heritage. Among Asian Americans, Renee Tajima is one of the earliest to call for critical attention to "Asian American aesthetic sensitivities," as well as being one of the first to search for the Asian American soul. As she wrote, "The notion of plurality as the fabric of our own cultural identity contradicts our need for cohesion, our search for Asian American soul."[67] Second, there is so much debate about the normal hyphen (omitted in this book) in the label of *Asian Americans*. Do we really need a hyphen between *Asian* and *American*? In other words, what is the essence of Asian American aesthetics—Asian, American, or a combination of the two? Daryl Chin is quoted as saying, "Any definition of Asian-American aesthetics must be ipso facto partial, because the idea of Asian aesthetics must be pluralistic."[68] In comparison, Black cinema could claim "presence of cultural practices rooted in black vernacular experience (jazz, gospel, rootworking, religion and so on)."[69] Chicano/a cinema also carries more easily identifiable subcultural forms that provide the conventional, formulaic genres and narrative structures. Chon A. Noriega has clearly outlined the cultural narratives of *corridos, floricanto, teatro, telenovelas,* and *testimonion* that constitute some distinctive cinematic codes within bicultural and bilingual contexts.[70]

Despite these difficulties, in our interviews with many Asian American filmmakers, there seems to be a strong dialectical attitude toward categorizing Asian American films as a separate cinematic tradition. On the one hand, the filmmakers are absolutely opposed to "pigeonholing" of any kind, because, as Loni Ding puts it, "any classification of people tends to limit them to the extent that a category or a way you are framing who someone is or what their work is about and what their film is similar to. I am just against that." On the other hand, she acknowledges that a category is useful as "a way of understanding the significance of the work, in terms of what it relates to in the past, where it is now, and where it might be going next. That kind of categorization, a naming or framing, is normal, natural, and fine."[71] In our discussions, many of the filmmakers have expressed the idea of defining Asian American aesthetics as a "consciousness," or a "sensitivity," because filmmakers create films out of their consciousness, arising out of both who they are and how they position themselves in the society. Again, Loni Ding does not think the ethnic background of a filmmaker is as important as, to use her own words, "adopting the consciousness." She asserts, "Your consciousness is everything, your perspective, sensitivity, or talent, your willingness to work like a dog, to get inside of it, or to be faithful to that subject. I think that is more important than anything."[72] Philip Kan Gotanda describes this consciousness as "a state of mind." According to him, "It begins with the filmmaker, himself or herself, her own and his own state of mind and how he or she perceives herself or himself. That to me defines what is Asian American film."[73]

To translate this "sensitivity," "consciousness," or "state of mind" into a critical analysis of Asian American film texts, I borrowed Sau-ling Cynthia Wong's concept of reading Asian American films as "an emergent and evolving textual coalition," a two-pronged approach of contexts and intertexts.[74] According to Wong, the context "stresses the indispensability of historical knowledge to any responsible reading of the corpus." That is to say, reading Asian American films contextually is not just a literary or aesthetic, but also a sociological, historical, and cultural enterprise. In turn, the intertext, in Wong's very precise words, refers to "how mutual allusion, qualification, complication, and transmutation can be discovered between texts regarded as Asian American, and how a sense of an internally meaningful literary tradition may emerge from such an investigation."[75] In the place of seeking an Asian American aesthetic tradition, this literary reading strategy of textual coalition provides useful references for Asian American films. For analytical purposes, I have identified three critical elements of Asian American films: an authentic Asian American point of view, a sensitive portrayal of Asian American characters and communities, and a set of culturally specific artistic innovations.[76]

Further, this approach of textual coalition could be implemented through what Henry Louis Gates calls "text-specific" strategy (a careful analysis of each individual film, looking at production process, points of view, and formal styles).[77] Chon A. Noriega made a similar point that "production history should be central to the criticism or interpretation of Chicano film and video."[78] To me, this strategy may help to transform the process of defining Asian American cinema from passive identification (uncritical acceptance) into active criticism (which both appreciates and interrogates the productions). Wayne Wang's *Chan Is Missing* is chosen as an illustration of this "text-specific" approach.[79]

Released more than a decade ago, *Chan Is Missing* is now considered an Asian American independent classic. It stands out indisputably as the first Asian American independent theatrical feature ever made in the United States. Employing an all-Asian cast and crew, the movie was produced on a meager budget of $20,000. As Diane Mark observes, the film's low budget is evident "in its simplified, sometimes repetitive camera technique," static "thinking head" shots, and numerous close-ups of news clippings. However, despite its grainy texture and economical look, the film's rich cultural allusions and innovative film practices made it one of twenty-five films added to the National Film Registry in 1995, on a par with some of the most treasured American films ever produced, including *Top Hat* (1935), *Gone with the Wind* (1939), *Citizen Kane* (1941), *Casablanca* (1942), *Singin' in the Rain* (1952), and *2001: A Space Odyssey* (1968).[80]

Chan's story line is quite simple. It follows two San Francisco Chinatown cabbies in their search for Chan Hung, a missing partner who is in possession of $4,000 of their money. As the two cabbies, Jo and Steve, comb Chinatown for clues leading to their partner, they encounter a full range of characters in the community, each imbued with a unique personality, and each giving a different impression of the missing character.

The film's power and appeal lie in the way Wang offers an insider's perspective into the intricate conflicts and tangles of Chinatown life. "Wang's Chinatown is inside—inside the Chinese restaurant, inside the kitchen, inside the wok. It is inside family apartments, cafes, and even inside Jo's head."[81] Although Wang's movie is part of the mystery genre, he refuses to exploit Chinatown as the exotic, dark, mysterious locale it is portrayed as in Roman Polanski's *Chinatown* (1974). Wang's portrait of Chinatown is multidimensional and diverse, with the typical contradictions of ethnic communities. The crisis of assimilation and the characters' struggle with identity are revealed very vividly. The conflict between ABCs (American-born Chinese) and FOBs (fresh off the boat) becomes the movie's subplot. When Jo and Steve argue on the waterfront about the identity of Chan Hung, for example, Steve says that there are no limitations for Chinese Americans—they are all self-imposed. Jo responds, "You don't know what it's like to be an immigrant, or understand the problems." Since Jo is second generation, and Steve is third, Jo is closer to the immigration experience. He easily empathizes with Chan Hung. The flag-waving incident during a Chinese New Year parade illustrates the destructive political passions based on old-country ideological differences within the community. The heartbreaking gap between the older, foreign-born Chinese Americans and their American-born children is also ruthlessly exposed.

The movie presents an interesting character study of an entire, diverse ethnic community. Even characters' personalities are very different: the brassy Steve, a Sansei; the philosophical Jo; the quizzical Presco; the cynical Henry, a Chinese cook in a "Samurai Night Fever" T-shirt, singing "Fry me to the Moon"; the pompous Chinese scholar Fong; the shrewd language center administrator George; and the young streetwise Asian males wearing baseball caps—these are just a few. Helping to defuse stereotypes, director Wang does not paint every character in a positive light. For example, Mr. Lee, the insurance salesman, is racist and sexist. But his character is important for the plot; for, as Jenny, Chan Hung's daughter, says earlier in the film, "My mother didn't like my father because he's not like Mr. Lee." Lee is being held up as the image of a role model. The everyday characters in the movie are emotional, political, and fallible. They laugh, cry, swear, and fight. They don't always keep their cool, stay on top of the situation, or succeed as do-no-wrong heroes. They are ordinary human beings. This portrayal serves as an important corrective to the widely held stereotype of Asian Americans as the "model minority."

These myriad characters serve as a critique of the single essentialized Asian American identity. This challenge is dramatized in the following argument between Jo and Steve. Jo summarizes his struggle to define his identity: "It's hard enough for guys like me who've been here so long to find an identity. I can imagine Chan Hung's problem, somebody from China coming over here and trying to find himself." Steve protests, "That's a bunch of bullshit, man! That identity shit. That's old news. Man, that happened ten years ago." Jo retorts, "It's still going on." Steve argues, "Bullshit. That don't mean nothing. I ran into an old friend of mine downtown. . . . We used to run together in high school. He's all decked out in his fuckin' *GQ* look. . . . And he didn't want to talk to me, man. He knew who I was. . . . He's playing a game, man. Fuck the identity shit. He knew what he was doing. I knew what I'm doing. I could have kicked his fuckin' ass. The Chinese are all over this fuckin' city, man. Whaddaya mean about identity? They got their own identity. I got my identity!"

Equally important for this identity critique is the "negative" character of Chan Hung, whose presence is felt but not seen throughout the film. His physical absence but haunting presence on our minds has more to do with our subjectivity. What we learn about Chan Hung is contradictory and secondhand. The twelve people who know Chan provide as many different descriptions of him. Jo summarizes the ambivalent Chan Hung:

> Mr. Lee says Chan Hung and immigrants like him need to be taught everything as if they were children. Mr. Fong thinks anyone who can invent a word processing system in Chinese must be a genius. Steve thinks Chan Hung is slow-witted, but sly when it comes to money. Jenny thinks that her father is honest and trustworthy. Mrs. Chan

thinks her husband is a failure because he isn't rich. Amy thinks he's a hot-headed political activist. The old man thinks Chan Hung's just a paranoid person. Henry thinks Chan Hung is patriotic, and has gone back to the mainland to serve the people. Frankie thinks Chan Hung worries a lot about money and his inheritance. He thinks Chan Hung's back in Taiwan fighting with his brother over the partition of some property. George thinks Chan Hung's too Chinese, and unwilling to change. Presco thinks he's an eccentric who likes mariachi music.[82]

In sharp contrast to Hollywood's convention of glossy surface, continuity editing, and "invisible style," *Chan* is noted for its various discursive innovations. The montage in the film, for example, is highly experimental. A typical Hollywood movie is often characterized by a linear narrative scheme with a beginning, middle, and end. As Robert Rosenstone remarks, "[It] tends to focus on heroic individuals and, more importantly, to make sense of its material in terms of a story that moves from a beginning through a conflict to a dramatic resolution."[83] As a parody of Charlie Chan films, the narrative structure of *Chan* represents a distant departure from the Hollywood norm. Whereas the typical classical Hollywood detective drama is characterized by a relentless narrative acquisition of clues that eventually climaxes in the solution of the mystery, *Chan* offers no solution to Chan Hung's whereabouts. Each clue that develops in the film only raises more questions—"indeed, the clues are not real clues: they include a gun that may or may not have been fired, a newspaper with the important article torn out, a spot on the wall where a picture used to hang, a series of former addresses no longer occupied by Chan Hung, and a Polaroid in which Chan Hung's face is obscured by shadows."[84] So these clues add up to nothing. As Jo complains, "The murder article is missing. The photograph's not there. The other woman is not there. Nothing is what it seems to be." All such ambiguities testify to the unique features of this Asian American film.

The film's ending is particularly symbolic. Towards the end of the film, Jo announces in a voice-over that "if this were a TV movie, an important clue would now pop up and clarify everything." No clue leads anywhere and Chan is never found. Instead, Jo explains that even the search for such neat coherence is a Western trait. For those who can "think Chinese," what is not there becomes as meaningful as what is. Nothing means what it seems to mean. The open-ended plot seems to stand in direct contradiction to the Charlie Chan mode, where there is always a solution to the mystery. Wayne Wang asserts, "Asians tend to have a much higher tolerance for ambiguity, and have always historically been able to deal with ambiguity a lot more than so-called Caucasian minds, or Western minds."[85]

The narrative sensitivities are supported by a significant use of mise-en-scène (all the elements placed in front of the camera to be photographed), which suggests a syncretic mix of Chinese rituals, music, and languages. Cinematographer Michael Chin revealed that he used the documentary-type "shoot from the hip" format. His Chinatown mise-en-scène, often viewed through the front windshield or window of a taxicab, is filled with the visual and aural texture of Chinatown life: Kung-Fu Warrior posters, pagoda rooftops, smoked chickens hanging in restaurant windows, Chinese-character signs, a Christmas-decorated Buddha with tinsel and flashing lights, and Chinese rock and roll ("Rock Around the Clock"). If language is a medium of culture, then in this film we are brought to the heart of Chinese American cultural life. Our ears are flooded with Cantonese, Mandarin, and Chinese American English/Black dialect; professional dialect; Chinatown dialect; even cook dialect. It is Wang's deliberate decision to privilege the Asian audience by not using subtitles for the Chinese that is spoken. The music on the soundtrack is a mixture of Hong Kong pop, Pat Suzuki (Grant Avenue), and Kikuchi-Yngojo's own Asian American music, a significant symbol of Wang's Chinese Americanism:

> They call it Grant Avenue, San Francisco, California, U.S.A./ Look for Chinatown. You travel there in a trolley, up you climb, dong-dong, you're in Hong Kong, having yourself a time./ Sharkfin soup, beancake fish, the girl who serves you your food is a dish, you know you have a Grant Avenue way of living./ That's where it's at. San Francisco, California, U.S.A./ A Western street with Eastern manners, tall pagodas with golden banners, you can shop for precious jade, or silk brocade, or see a bold and brassy night club show on the most exciting thoroughfare./ I know they call it Grant Avenue, San Francisco, U.S.A.

In this chapter, I have proposed to read Asian American films as an evolving cinematic tradition. Further, given the tremendous heterogeneity in both their thematics and aesthetics, I suggest adopting the critical practice of reading each individual text closely (contexts and intertext). Intended as a showcase of the text-specific strategy, I argue that *Chan Is Missing* can be loosely defined as an Asian American film. Its box-office success and classic status have helped define the structure of subsequent works in Asian American cinema. In this sense, it might be plausible to suggest that a distinguished Asian American cinematic tradition, if it has not already emerged, is definitely in the making.

NOTES

1   William Grimes, "Should Only Blacks Make Movies About Blacks?" *New York Times* (March 28, 1994), B1 and B2.

2   Some 80 percent of the films are nationality-specific and only about 10 percent are pan-Asian. Japanese American– and Chinese American–produced and –themed films account for the majority of the films under discussion.

3   Similar questions are being debated in other areas of artistic production among Asian Americans. In Asian American theater, for example, it is difficult to come up with an agreeable definition. Velina Hasu Houston emphasizes the importance of subject in identification. "It is a play written by a American citizen of Asian ancestry. Because, however, the subject matter of Asian American playwrights is not limited to Asian American topics, subject matter also may become a consideration (from a theater's point of view) in labeling a play an 'Asian American' play." See *The Politics of Life: Four Plays by Asian America Women*, ed. Velina Hasu Houston (Philadelphia: Temple University Press, 1993), 11; see also James Moy, *Marginal Sights* (where Moy quotes Du Bois's definition of Negro Theater).

4   Phone interview with Katherine Leslie, April 1996.

5   Midi Onodera, "A Displaced View: What Are We Reconsidering about the Yellow Peril?," *Yellow Peril: Reconsidered,* ed. Paul Wong (Vancouver: On Edge, 1990).

6   W. E. B. Du Bois, "Krigwa Players Little Negro Theater," *The Crisis* 32 (July 1926), 134.

7   Chon A. Noriega, *Chicanos and Film: Essays on Chicano Representation and Resistance* (New York: Garland Publishing, Inc., 1992), xviii. For more information on the debate over the definition of Chicano/a films, see also Rosa Linda Fregoso, *The Bronze Screen: Chicana and Chicano Film Culture* (Minneapolis: University of Minnesota Press, 1993), xiii–xxiii.

8   Stephen Gong, "A History in Progress: Asian American Media Arts Centers 1970–1990," *Moving the Image: Independent Asian Pacific American Media Arts*, ed. Russell Leong (Los Angeles: UCLA Asian American Studies Center, 1991), 1–2.

9   John Esaki, "Back to Real Asian American Filmmaking," *Moving the Image*, 36–37.

10   Daryl Chin, "After Ten Years: Some Notes on the Asian American International Film Festival," *Program Notes* (New York: Asian CineVision, 1988), 16.

11   Grimes, "Should Only Blacks Make Movies About Blacks?" B1.

12   Phone interview with Katherine Leslie, April 1996.

13   Phone interview with Katherine Leslie, April 1996.

14   Darby Li Po Price, " 'All American Girl' and the American Dream," *Critical Mass: A Journal of Asian American Cultural Criticism* 2:1 (Winter 1994), 129.

15   Joann Faung Jean Lee, "Margaret the 'All-American' Bust of TV," *AsianWeek* (Dec. 1994), 6.

16   Carlos Mendez, "Melodramatic Margaret Minces the Media Mavens," *AsianWeek* (Dec. 23, 1994), 24.

17   Ibid.

18   Ibid.

19   Phone interview with Katherine Leslie, April 1996.

20   Preeti Chawla, "Wayne's World: 15 Minutes with Wayne Wang," *A. Magazine* 3:1 (1994), 32.

21   See Chapter 2 for a survey of Hollywood representations of Asians and Asian Americans.

22   Interview with Katherine Leslie, April 1996.

23   Eugene F. Wong, *On Visual Media Racism: Asians in the American Motion Pictures* (New York: Arno Press, 1978).

24   See Angela Pao, "The Eyes of the Storm: Gender, Genre and Cross-Casting in *Miss Saigon*," *Text and Performance Quarterly* 12 (1992), 21–39.

25   As quoted by Nick Browne, "The Undoing of the Other Woman: Madame Butterfly in the Discourse of American Orientalism," in Daniel Bernard ed., *The Birth of Whiteness: Race and the Emergence of U.S. Cinema* (New Brunswick: Rutgers University Press, 1996), 232.

26   Ibid.

27   Gayatri Spivak, *In Other Worlds: Essays in Cultural Politics* (New York: Methuen, 1987), 205.

28   Ibid.

29   Ibid.

30   Phone interview with Katherine Leslie, April 1996.

31   bell hooks, "The cultural mix: an interview with Wayne Wang" *Reel to Real: Race, Sex, and Class at the Movies* (New York: Routledge, 1996), 128.

32   Manning Marable, "Malcolm as Messiah: Cultural Myth vs. Historical Reality in Malcolm X," *Cineaste* 19:3–4 (March 1993), 8.

33   Brian Johnson, "The Joy Luck Club," *MacLean's* 27 (Sept. 1993), 70.

34   Stuart Hall, "New Ethnicities," *ICA Documents*, 28.

35   Scholars from the "ethnicity school" call this approach exclusive "biological insiderism," or "exceptionalism." See Sau-ling Cynthia Wong, *Reading Asian American Literature: From Necessity to Extravagance* (Princeton, N.J.: Princeton University Press, 1993), 4.

36   Werner Sollors, *Beyond Ethnicity: Consent and Descent in American Culture* (New York: Oxford University Press, 1986), 13.

37   Rita Dandridge, "The Little Book (and Film) that Started the Big War," *Black Film Review* 2:2 (1986), 28.

38   "The Roddick Interview: They would say 'Jane who?', then 'Emma who?' " [http://www.tvmovie.de/kino/filme/sense_and/ang_lee.html].

39   hooks, "The cultural mix," 128.

40   Ibid.

41   James Snead, *White Screens/Black Images: Hollywood from the Dark Side* (New York: Routledge, 1994), 124.

42   Trinh T. Minh-ha, "Why a Fish Pond," *Framer Framed* (New York: Routledge, 1992), 164.

43   James Snead, *White Screens/Black Images,* 125.

44   Michael Singer, *Oliver Stone's Heaven and Earth: The Making of an Epic Motion Picture* (Boston: Charles E. Tuttle Company, 1993).

45   Amy Tan, "Joy, Luck and Hollywood," *Los Angeles Times* (Sept. 5, 1993), 105: D7.

46   This subtitle is borrowed from an essay on Chicano cinema by Chon A. Noriega in *Chicanos and Film*, 159–88.

47   Tommy L. Lott, "A No-Theory Theory of Contemporary Black Cinema," *Representing Blackness*, 92.

48   Garrett Hongo, Introduction to *The Open Boat: Poems from Asian America* (New York: Anchor Books/Doubleday, 1993), xxxv.

49   Gong, "A History in Progress," 8.

50   Haile Gerima, "Triangular Cinema, Breaking Toys, and Dinknesh vs. Lucy," *Questions of Third Cinema*, eds. Jim Pines and Paul Willemen (London: British Film Institute, 1989), 65.

51   For the early VC history, see Robert Nakamura, "Visual Communications: The Early Years," *In Focus*, 6:1; Ron Hirano, "Media Guerrillas," in *Counterpoint: Perspectives on Asian America*, ed. Emma Gee (Los Angeles: UCLA Asian American Studies Center, 1979), 295–302; Renee Tajima, "Ethno-Communications: The Film School Program That Changed the Color of Independent Filmmaking," in *Anthology of Asian American Film and Video* (New York: Third World Newsreel, 1984). The documentary *Claiming a Voice: The Visual Communications Story* by Arthur Dong also provides valuable personal recollections about the media organization.

52   As quoted in *Anthology of Asian Pacific American Film and Video* on the inside front cover.

53   As quoted in Shirley Kwan, "Asian American Women Behind the Camera," *Anthology of Asian American Film and Video*, 35.

54   Lia Chang, "Filmmaker as Activist, Arthur Dong makes award-winning films that also seek to change the world," *AsianWeek* (May 10, 1996). The interview was done after Dong won the year's Peabody Award for *Coming Out Under Fire*, a critically acclaimed documentary based a book of the same name by Allan Berube. The film uses the oral histories of nine gay and lesbian World War II veterans to chronicle the origins of the U.S. military's anti-homosexual policy.

55   Phone interview with Katherine Leslie, April 1996.

56   Phone interview with Katherine Leslie, April 1996.

57   Valerie Soe, "Inspired Purpose and Exhibition Practices: A Review of the Show the Right Thing Conference," *The Independent* (March 1990), 12.

58   Valerie Soe, "On Experimental Video," *Moving the Image*, 238.

59   See Release Print, "Ultra Low-Budget Feature Filmmakers Explore Youth and Nihilism," *The Independent* (May 1991), 23.

60   Jessica Hagedorn, "No Joy, No Luck," *Ms.* (Jan./Feb. 1994), 76.

61   Sarah Kerr, "Sense and Sensitivity," *New York* (April 1, 1996), 47.

62   Phone interview with Katherine Leslie, April 1996.

63   Jesse Algeron Rhines, *Black Film/White Money* (New Brunswick, N.J.: Rutgers University Press, 1996).

64   Thomas Cripps, *Black Film as Genre* (Bloomington: Indiana University Press, 1978), 9.

65   Diane Mei Lin Mark, "Interview with Wayne Wang," *Chan Is Missing* (Honolulu: Bamboo Ridge Press, 1984), 112.

66   The term *genre*, a French word meaning *category*, *kind*, or *type*, is used in literary criticism "to designate the distinct types or categories into which literary works are grouped according to form or technique." The cinematic applications of genre equally emphasize the narrative conventions recognizable to both audiences and filmmakers. See William Flint Thrall, Addison Hibbard, and C. Hugh Holman, *A Handbook to Literature* (New York: Odyssey Press, 1962), 211; see also David Bordwell and Kristin Thompson, *Film Art: An Introduction*, 4th ed. (New York: McGraw-Hill, 1993).

67   Renee Tajima, "Moving the Image," *Moving the Image*, 11.

68   Daryl Chin, "Film Forums: The Asian American Case," *CineVue* 1:3 (1986), 9.

69   Valerie Smith, *Representing Blackness*, 2.

70   See Noriega, *Chicanos and Film: Essays on Chicano Representation and Resistance*, 172.

71   Phone interview with Katherine Leslie, April 1996.

72   Ibid.

73   Ibid.

74   Wong, 9–11.

75   Ibid.

76   I have modeled the critical elements of Asian American film partly on Cripps's five identifying characteristics of Black genre films: (1) an authentic Black in-group point of view; (2) a sensitive narrative treatment of Black aspiration; (3) an accurate anatomy of Black social mores; (4) the symbolic repertoire of Black symbols; and (5) an urgent sense of advocacy for the Black cause.

77   Henry Louis Gates, Jr., *Figures in Black: Words, Signs and the "Racial" Self* (New York: Oxford University Press, 1987), xix.

78   Noriega, 170.

79   I have chosen *Chan Is Missing* over the more recent *The Joy Luck Club* for a number of reasons. Except for the simple fact that both films are produced by the same director, I find the two very different. *Chan Is Missing* is a low-budget black-and-white feature shot on 16mm stock, while *The Joy Luck Club* is noted for its slick and color-saturated images. Whereas *Chan Is Missing* builds its narrative strength on an insider's perspective of Chinatown life, the power of *The Joy Luck Club* as a tearjerker comes from its universal themes. The story of *Chan Is Missing* draws on a matrix of cultural idioms and symbols, while *The Joy Luck Club*, in the process of adaptation, has emptied much of the cultural mythology from Amy Tan's original novel. The myth of the Moon Lady in Ying-Ying's life and the Red Candle–burning scene for Lindo's marriage are two ready examples. To go into details about the differences between the two movies, however, would lead us astray from the topic at hand.

80   In 1988, Congress established the National Film Registry within the Library of Congress to promote the preservation of motion pictures as they were originally created and to advance public awareness of American film as a cherished form of art. Beginning in 1989, each year twenty-five films are chosen and added to the National Film Registry. See Cassandra Burrell, "Library of Congress honors 25 old films," *Fort Collins Coloradoan* (December 28, 1995), A4.

81   Mark, Introduction to *Chan Is Missing* script, 6.

82   *Chan Is Missing* script, 74.

83   Robert A. Rosenstone, "History in Image/History in Words: Reflection on the Possibility of Really Putting History onto Film," *American Historical Review* 93:5 (Dec. 1988), 1179.

84   Peter Feng, "Chinese American Identity and Asian American Subjectivity: the Films of Wayne Wang," paper read at AAAS Conference, Ann Arbor, April 7, 1994. See also his published article "Being Chinese American, Becoming Asian American: *Chan Is Missing*," *Cinema Journal* 35:4 (Summer 1996), 101.

85   Mark, "Interview with Wayne Wang," 112.

Cinematic Asian Representation

ASIAN AMERICAN INDEPENDENT CINEMA has come into being largely as a result of the long history of abusive portrayals and stereotypical renderings of Asians, Asian Americans, and their cultures. For Asian American filmmakers, consciously or subconsciously, there always exists a host of Hollywood images and conventions (in both Hollywood-style and documentary films). In other words, although produced outside the traditional image-making system, Asian American films have engaged in an intertextual dialogue with Hollywood films.[1] Asians began to appear in film almost as soon as celluloid was invented in the late nineteenth century, and their imagery can be found in movies of every decade throughout the twentieth century.

With this in mind, this chapter aims to provide a critical overview of Asian representation in mass media, especially in Hollywood cinema. Starting in the late 1960s and early 1970s, there has been an explosion in literary and historical writing on Asian and Asian American film representation.[2] However, most works on Asian film representation, like literature on general ethnic representation, focus on image analysis, overlooking other dimensions of media. To help address this problem, Chicano film historian Carlos Cortés identifies three categories in the historiography of ethnic film analysis: content analysis (films as visual texts), control analysis (process of filmmaking), and impact analysis (influence of films over the audience and vice versa).[3] The studies of Asian representation in cinema can easily be grouped along these lines. Essentially, scholars have attempted either to construct a typology of images, focusing on stereotypes as ideological phenomena, or to examine the institutional aspects of racism.

Using Cortés's model as a theoretical framework, this chapter is divided into three sections. Each section critically engages one aspect of cinematic Asian representation: film as celluloid imagery, film as a political process, and film's institutional dimension. By reviewing this literature, I hope to demonstrate how Asian

American artists have had, by necessity, to operate within this historical, ideological, and institutional context. A critical survey of Asian and Asian American representation in Hollywood also helps to answer one of the organizing questions for the book: how do Asian American productions differ from Hollywood movies? Above all, I want to offer an intertextual and revisionist framework for understanding Asian American films in the following chapters.

REPRESENTATION AS IMAGE

Over the years, particularly since the 1960s, a large, if somewhat uneven, literature has been produced on Asian film images. Dorothy B. Jones's *Portrayal of China and India on the American Screen, 1896–1955* is often credited as the pioneering work.[4] Jones sampled over 300 feature and short-subject movies and traced the changing screen images of China and India from the turn of the century to the mid-1950s. A large number of scholarly essays followed this model of Asian "stock character" analysis.[5] These studies uniformly focus on identifying ethnic stereotypes. Jones, for example, has categorized specific character types for both groups. The evil mandarin, the pirate or bandit, the warlord, the detective, the peasant, the houseboy, the cook, and the laundryman were the major Chinese stock characters. For the Indians, there were the primitive tribesman, the rajah, the benighted native, and the Bengal soldier.[6] In a similar fashion, Christine Choy, a prominent Korean American documentarian, grouped Asian American images into four main stereotypes: the "stock" image, the "mysterious villain," the "china doll" or "geisha," and the "Banzai war crime" image.[7]

All images are created as a matter of specific setting and particular timing. Because Asian screen images are historical constructs, they do not remain static. Some scholars have traced the changes of those images and grouped them along certain historical lines. Harold Isaacs, in his seminal study of Asian images, *Scratches on Our Minds: American Images of China and India* (dealing not merely with film images), has classified American imagery of China into six historical periods. They are: (1) the Age of Respect (eighteenth century); (2) the Age of Contempt (1840–1905); (3) the Age of Benevolence (1905–1937); (4) the Age of Admiration (1937–1944); (5) the Age of Disenchantment (1944–1949); and (6) the Age of Hostility (1949–).[8] Focusing partly on genre conventions and partly on international politics, Dick Stromgren has conveniently placed the history of Asian screen images into four periods: (1) the Silent Era: Exotic Melodrama; (2) the Burma Road and Beyond; (3) the Red Menace; and (4) a New China and Fiendish Old Plots.[9]

In this section, instead of summarizing film character types or repeating the historical timelines, I will organize my survey of Asian images, based loosely on three formulaic traditions: the "yellow peril" formula, the "Madame Butterfly" narratives, and the Charlie Chan stories. These three Hollywood formulations represent the staples of America's popular imagination of the "Orientals." As narrative conventions, they are noted for their incredible staying power and their wealth of sexist and racist clichés.

The Yellow Peril Formula

In their perceptions of Asians, nothing is more ingrained in American popular consciousness than the "yellow peril" image. A term first used mainly for Japanese and Chinese in the United States, it soon collapsed all of Asia into one yellow horde and became a catchword signifying the "yellow menace" to Western Christian civilization. As Harold Isaacs noted, the yellow peril concept originally came to America from Europe, rooted in medieval fears of Genghis Khan and his Mongol hordes.[10] By the late nineteenth century, the growth of the Chinese presence in California gave birth to the anti-Chinese movement that was partly based on the threat of the yellow hordes of invaders. The germ theory, intermixed with racial, anti-immigrant, and xenophobic rhetoric, provided theoretical and political support for the yellow peril thesis. In the twentieth century, the Boxer Rebellion in China and Japan's 1905 victory over Russia appalled the Western world, giving further proof of the threat from the "bloodthirsty hordes" of Chinese fanatics and warning that the "rejuvenescent Japanese race [had] embarked on a course of conquest."[11] The call to protect the national body politic from the attack of the impending yellow peril proved especially potent during World War II, the Korean War, and the war in Vietnam.[12]

The yellow peril image has spawned two of Hollywood's favorite genres: the rape narratives, and the "Banzai" type war films. By the same token, Gina Marchetti, in her study of the various strategies deployed by Hollywood to influence the American public perception of Asia, has found the fantasy of miscegenation in three kinds of narratives: the rape stories, captivity tales, and seduction narratives.[13] Indeed, in Hollywood films, images of race and sexuality are always intimately intertwined, and sexual aggression against white women has become a metaphor for the racial threat posed to Western culture by the "other." Gary Hoppenstand described the significance of this strategy:

> The threat of rape, the rape of white society, dominated the action of the
> yellow formula. The British or American hero, during the course of his
> battle against the yellow peril, overcame numerous traps and obstacles

in order to save his civilization, and the primary symbol of that civilization: the white woman. . . . The yellow peril stereotype easily became
incorporated into Christian mythology, and the Oriental assumed the
role of the devil or demon. The Oriental rape of the white woman signified a spiritual damnation for the woman, and at the larger level,
white society.[14]

The rape narratives also found their way into Hollywood cinema during
the silent era. One of the first feature-length films to exploit the image of the sinister Oriental rapist was Cecil B. DeMille's highly acclaimed *The Cheat* (1915),
described by Kevin Brownlow as "one of the most sensational films of the early cinema."[15] The sadistic Burmese ivory king Arakau (originally a Japanese money
lender named Tori), played by Sessue Hayakawa, best exemplifies the classic Asian
male image. He is mysterious, exotic, and sinister. But ultimately, the libidinous
Arakau represents a sexual threat to the Christian social order through his desire
to possess the body of Edith Hardy, a white social butterfly. This symbolic miscegenation is intended to arouse a white-supremacist fear: Asian males pose a racial
threat to white womanhood. The emotional grip on the viewers climaxes in the
notorious branding scene, when Arakau tears the gown from Edith's shoulder and
brands her like an object in his collection. It was reported that audiences screamed
and some women even fainted in their seats.[16] The famous courtroom sequence at
the end illustrates the solution to the racial threat: mob lynching. Not as blatantly
racist was D. W. Griffith's classic *Broken Blossoms* (1919), a film commonly
described as "sensitive and humanitarian," in which the fantasy of rape and the
possibility of lynching form its subplot.[17] The film features Lillian Gish as Lucy, the
daughter of a murderously brutal prizefighter, and Cheng Huan, a "Yellow Man"
from China. Intended as a sympathetic treatment of the Asian character, the film
displays the Yellow Man as dreamy, frail, but lustful. After a vicious beating by her
father, Lucy collapses before the "Chink" storekeeper. The sequence of Lucy's first
night at the Chinese man's home raises the tantalizing suspense of rape. Robert
Lang describes the details of the following scene: "We see in the shots of an increasing intimacy between the Yellow Man and Lucy, an extreme close-up of the Yellow
Man's face . . . and Lucy drawing away from the Yellow Man in wonder tinged
with fear."[18]

As a pervasively displayed stereotype in popular culture, Asian men were
routinely portrayed as gangsters or rapists with perverted sexual appetites for white
women. Often, the white women victims would eventually be rescued by a white
male hero and the Asian rapist lynched by white male vigilante groups. As Tom Gubbins recalled, "You remember, back in the old days of serials, the spectacle of the
heroine being snatched by villainous Orientals and dragged into a den of vice. It was

quite common. The truth of the matter is that fewer white girls have been attacked by Chinese than by any other race of people."[19]

Since the beginning of this century, another mainstay of yellow peril discourse has been linked to war. "The majority of white Americans," John Dower wrote in his book *War without Mercy*, "have been intimately introduced to Asians in the context of war and violence on the motion picture and television screens."[20] Two of the earliest and most durable Asian villains were Ming the Merciless and Fu Manchu. Together, they represented the incarnations of the yellow peril in the Oriental crusade to conquer the world. The prototype of Emperor Ming, the Merciless, appeared in the *Flash Gordon* movie series in the 1930s. The character was delineated as a sharp contrast to the pure and honest Flash Gordon and Miss America, Dale Arden. Fu Manchu, the archvillain of the Sax Rohmer novels, was cruel, vicious, and a throwback to Genghis Khan. To paraphrase Richard Oehling, the diabolical Fu Manchu symbolized for the American audience three main strands of racial fears: Asian mastery of Western knowledge and technique (denoted by his degrees from three European universities in chemistry, medicine, and physics); his access to mysterious Oriental "occult" powers (his eyes can hypnotize victims); and his ability to mobilize the yellow hordes.[21] In the war narrative, sometimes an evil dragon lady (for example, Fu Manchu's various female companions) is paired with her male counterpart. Often sexy, sly, and terribly cruel, the dragon lady has a notorious penchant for white men. Other early yellow peril movies include *Limehouse Blues* (1934), *Chinatown Squad* (1935), *She* (1935), *China Seas* (1935), *Secret Agent* (1936), *The Soldier and the Lady* (1937), *Lost Horizon* (1937), *China Passage* (1937), and *Shadows of the Orient* (1937).

The three wars fought in Asia—World War II, the U.S. intervention in Korea, and the American fiasco in Vietnam—have left an important legacy for the war stereotype of Asians. "Pearl Harbor enabled Hollywood to revive all the old 'Yellow Peril' characteristics," wrote William Everson. "The Jap [was] a screaming, unshaven, wizened fanatic, crouched low over his machine guns, bombing Red Cross ships."[22] Hollywood practically developed a subgenre around World War II: *Destination Tokyo* (1943), *Guadalcanal Diary* (1943), *The Purple Heart* (1944), and, most important of all, *The Bridge on the River Kwai* (1957). Within the war narrative, a subgenre of tong wars or crime melodramas has utilized the same yellow peril theme. Chinatowns, known as isolated, sordid, violence-ridden urban ghettos, have long been the ideal stock settings for gangster movies, from *The Hatchet Man* and *The Mysterious Mr. Wong* in the 1930s to *Big Trouble in Little China*, *China Girl*, and *Year of the Dragon* in the 1980s.

The yellow peril formula may not be as blatant now as in the past, but stories of "white slavery" and war continue to haunt the silver screen. Recent movies like *Girls of the White Orchid* (1985), a made-for-television exposé of white slavery in contemporary Tokyo, *Year of the Dragon,* and the *Karate Kid* series all have the threat of rape as their subplots. Yellow peril representations of Japan have also taken a new twist over the last ten years or so. Economic competition with Japan is often analogized to World War II battles. Flippant suggestions of using the *Enola Gay* to drop another atomic bomb as the final solution to trade friction provides further evidence of this point. For example, in 1992 Senator Ernest Hollings of South Carolina suggested "jokingly" that a factory's employees "draw a mushroom cloud and put underneath it: Made in America by lazy and illiterate workers and tested in Japan."[23] Screen images of the yellow peril continue to feed this Japan-bashing movement. Productions like *Gung Ho* (1985) and *Rising Sun* (1993) are two better-known examples. The latter, a Michael Crichton novel-turned–blockbuster movie, is a clear reincarnation of the Fu Manchu who competes with whites in a fashion not unlike the incarnation of evil.[24] "Business is war," declared Eddie Saka-mura in the movie of *Rising Sun.* The recent controversy over the re-release of a World War II–era cartoon, *Bugs Nips Nips,* testifies how such a war mentality is alive and well today. One scene shows Bugs Bunny giving ice cream cones, with hidden bombs, to a crowd of Japanese as he remarks, "Here's you go bowlegs, here you go monkey face, here you go slant-eyes, everybody gets one."[25] Only after strong protest by Japanese American Citizens League (JACL) did MGM–UA Home Video reluctantly pull the tape from the shelves.

The Madame Butterfly Narratives

David Henry Hwang's 1988 Tony Award winning play *M. Butterfly* tells an incredible story. In his twenty-year-long affair with a Beijing Opera performer, including the birth of a child, the French diplomat Rene Gallimard had learned nothing at all about his lover—not even the truth of his sex. Gallimard had never seen his "girlfriend" naked, and is quoted as saying, "I thought she was very modest. I thought it was a Chinese custom." At Gallimard's trial it is revealed that his lover was not only a Chinese spy but also a man. This baffling true story of a Frenchman duped by a Chinese man masquerading as a woman serves as a perfect footnote on *Madame Butterfly*, the best-known cinematic inscription of Asian women. Disruptive of naturalized gender categories, Hwang's *M. Butterfly*, as Jessica Hagedorn observed, tells "more about the mythology of the prized Asian woman and the superficial trappings of gender than most movies that star real women."[26] As a direct reversal of the miscegenation threat presented in the yellow peril stereotype, Asia (in these yellow fever narratives) ceased to be a place of peril, becoming instead a place of tropical beaches, magical cultures, exotic landscapes, and sexual encounters, where "Asian women are objects of desire, who provide sex, color and texture in what is essentially a white man's world."[27]

It has long been Hollywood tradition for a white male lead to freely conduct liaisons with any nonwhite women. East-West romances in particular have sparked many literary and theatrical works in the West, perhaps the most enduring of which is *Madame Butterfly*, the archetype of Oriental femininity. First written as a magazine short story by John Luther Long in 1898, *Madame Butterfly* was adapted into a one-act play by David Belasco two years later. Giacomo Puccini's opera, at first a fiasco in its 1904 premiere at La Scala, Milan, quickly became one of the most widely performed and long-lasting in the repertory.[28] The story of Madame Butterfly is well known. Pinkerton, a bored U.S. naval officer stationed in Nagasaki, fakes a wedding to develop a liaison with Cho-Cho-San, a local Japanese prostitute. After he departs, she gives birth to his child and then anxiously awaits his return. Several years later, Pinkerton returns with his elegant American wife, but only to claim his child, not his abandoned lover. Heartbroken, Cho-Cho-San commits suicide. *Madame Butterfly*, as Endymion Wilkinson observes, became a master narrative in Orientalist discourse:

> In recent centuries the rich tradition of Oriental exoticism took a new form as colonial conquest and rule provided the opportunity in the form of readily available girls, and encouraged Europeans and Americans to think of the West as active and masculine and the East as passive and feminine.[29]

Various Hollywood versions of the Butterfly tale have been set in Japan (Mary Pickford's drama [1915], Sessue Hayakawa's "sequel" to *Madame Butterfly*, *His Birthright* [1918], *Sayonara* [1957], *The Crimson Kimono*, [1959]), China (Anna May Wong's *Toll of the Sea* [1922] and *Sand Pebbles* [1966]), Hong Kong (*Love Is a Many-Splendored Thing* [1955] and *The World of Suzie Wong* [1960]), Vietnam (*China Gate* [1957]), and several Chinatowns (*Daughter of the Dragon* [1931] and its contemporary sequel *The Year of the Dragon* [1985]). As Marchetti has observed, in the Western vision of Asia, the entire continent becomes an exotic, beckoning woman, who can always satisfy white males' forbidden desires.

In numerous Hollywood films, Asian women were routinely depicted in film as spoils of war and objects of pleasure for lonely soldiers. In *The World of Suzie Wong*, for example, the sexy and pretty Suzie (played by Nancy Kwan) works out of a bar frequented by white sailors. William Holden plays a white "nice guy" painter. Suzie falls madly in love with him. She and the other prostitutes in this movie are cute, giggling, dancing sex machines. In all these stories, the Asian-white love must be illicit, and, because it breaks taboos, it offers forbidden pleasures for the audience. In the 1990s, this Asian whore image was perpetuated in a

British musical megahit *Miss Saigon* (1991). A slight reworking of the Butterfly construction, its plot cannot be more familiar. Cho-Cho-San has become Kim, a Saigon prostitute, while Lieutenant Pinkerton now is an enlisted man named Chris. He goes away. She has his child. He returns with an American wife. She kills herself. The producers themselves have advertised *Miss Saigon* as an updated adaptation of *Madame Butterfly*. Replete with Orientalist touches, exotic costumes, and peculiar actions, the musical renews the stereotype of the destitute, helpless, and ultimately disposable Asian woman who is foolish enough to pin her hope on a white lover.

Not until 1954 were the long-standing U.S. laws banning interracial marriage between Asians and Caucasians struck down. As the propaganda arm of the American dream machine, Hollywood promoted the romantic fantasy between American GIs and local Asian women. The yellow fever syndrome witnessed a narrative development from the hooker with a heart of gold to the domesticated war bride. The image of Asian war brides came first in the 1950s during the American occupation of Japan. The liaisons between American GIs and Japanese women were vividly captured in James Michener's *Sayonara* (1954)—a best-seller that was subsequently made into a film. In his novel, Michener profusely extols both the strength and gentleness of the Japanese women through his descriptions of two characters: the beautiful Takarazuka actress Hana-ogi and the rather homely Katsumi. Hana-ogi is the radiant heroine with an iron will, who devotes herself to her art and profession, and Katsumi is the comforting, wifely woman who could "take a wounded man and make him whole." In many ways, *Sayonara* became the prototype of the war bride image. The characters' seduction may represent a symbolic conquering of Japan, and indeed of the Orient itself, by the West. Their sexual acquiescence to the GIs, in allowing them to take over their body like their homeland, is perhaps symbolic wish-fulfillment, expressing a desire for Japan's capitulation to Western hegemony.

In media of more recent decades, we continue to see shadows of the *Sayonara* heroines, such as Mariko in James Clavell's best-selling book *Shogun* (1975) and Kumilo in the movie *Karate Kid II* (1986), both of which depict their Japanese heroines as being devoted, selfless, and brave. However, the subtle suggestion is that the beautiful heroines are so suppressed and deprived by society that they must be saved from their own destinies by powerful, gallant Western lovers. George Cosmatos's *Rambo II*, Jerry London's film version of *Shogun*, and Eric Van Lustbader's *The Ninja* are all familiar examples to careful viewers. In a "love" scene from *Rambo*, for example, the white American hero avenges the slaughter of a beautiful half-Asian woman by a group of male Asian enemy soldiers by gunning them down en masse. Before her death, the victim begs Rambo to take her to America, the "promised land" every Asian woman is supposed to dream about.

Unlike Black women, who are consistently reduced to mammies by Hollywood, Asian women find their bodies are more often fetishized as objects of sexual conquest and seduction, as casualties of war, as mail-order items.[30] These Lotus Blossoms, as Renee Tajima calls them, are utterly feminine, delicate, and quiet, a rare antithesis of their often allegedly loud independent American counterparts.

The Charlie Chan Genre

Asian and Asian American screen representations are often classified into good guys and bad guys, with some slight variations. A new order of "good" Asian representation is created in the Charlie Chan stories. As early as the 1930s, a "Good boy, Charlie" character, the Asian manservant, began to appear in Hollywood movies. Based on a derogatory term for Japanese houseboys, like the fawning houseboy in *Auntie Mame* (1958), this domestic servant character was often known as Charlie.[31] With his typical traits, such as submissiveness, loyalty, and lack of sexuality, Charlie would soon become the prototype for another reigning Asian stereotype, the famous Oriental detective Charlie Chan.

Beginning in the 1930s the "inscrutable Oriental detective" stories were developed by 20th Century Fox and Paramount, including the films about Mr. Moto and Mr. Wong. However, Charlie Chan, based on Earl Derr Biggers's novels, was the best-known. "Chan was the epitome of the 'damned clever Chinese,' " as Harold Isaacs wrote, "blandly humble in the face of Occidental contempt and invariably confounding all concerned by his shrewd solution of the crime."[32] Created at almost the same time in Hollywood, the benevolent Charlie Chan balanced out the diabolical Fu Manchu. The two are inextricably intertwined in Hollywood fiction. John Stone (the producer of the original Chan films at Fox Studios) was quoted as saying that the Chan characterization "was deliberately decided upon as a refutation of the unfortunate Fu Manchu characterization of the Chinese, and partly as a demonstration of his own idea that any minority group could be sympathetically portrayed on the screen with the right story and the right approach."[33] Having appeared in forty-six films, the Charlie Chan character became institutionalized as the nonthreatening Asian (read: a physical wimp, a sexual deviant, and a political yes-man).

Evidently Charlie Chan films have developed the narrative tradition of depicting Asian males as stealthy and nonassertive, devoid of all the traditional masculine qualities associated with Anglo-American males. Frank Chin compared this Asian image to the "house nigger" stereotype for African Americans. "House niggers is what America has made of us," Chin wrote, "admiring us for being patient, submissive, aesthetic, passive, accommodating and essentially feminine in character . . . what whites call 'Confucianist,' dreaming us up [as] a goofy version of Chinese culture to preserve in becoming the white male's dream minority."[34] If we put this stock Asian male character in a comparative perspective with the portrayal of other ethnic groups, Frank Chin's observation seems quite true. Hispanic males, for example, are often presented as extremely macho individuals, who are subject to uncontrollable fits of temper, drinking, and violent outbursts.[35] The earliest "greaser" movies were typical examples of this character type. And Black male film images have been changing drastically over the years, in Donald Bogle's words, from "toms, coons and servants to bucks and heroes." The earlier submissive image of the "good Negro" Uncle Tom has largely been replaced since the 1960s by Black tough guys, in the so-called blaxploitation films. The full-grown tough, arrogant, and very decisive John Shaft in the early 1970s helped to create what Bogle called a period of Buckmania. In a sense, the emerging Black tough guy "seemed to be avenging all those earlier black males who had to bow and kowtow."[36] (Interestingly, *kowtow* is well-chosen, coming from a Chinese word for obsequious deference.)

In sharp contrast, Asian male characters have been and continue to be feminized. Chiung Hwang Chen, for example, has located a cinematic castration, so to speak, in the 1993 movie *The Ballad of Little Jo*. The plot of the movie, writes Chen, portrays Asian men as effeminate and "devoid of the typical American maleness."[37] Peter Feng, for another example, addresses Asian masculinity (or lack of it) through a comparative analysis of Steven Okazaki's *American Sons* (1995) and mainstream media.[38] It is also interesting to note that in the last couple of decades the Asian sissy male image in heterosexual relations has spread into homosexual relations. In the gay community, the derogatory term "rice queen" has often been used to refer to a gay Caucasian man primarily attracted to Asian men. In their relationships, the Asian virtually always plays the role of the "woman" and the so-called "rice queen" is the "man" both culturally and sexually. "This pattern of relationships had become so codified," David Henry Hwang noted, "that until recently, it was considered unnatural for gay Asians to date one another."[39] The symbolic meaning of this pattern is well-articulated by bell hooks in *Black Looks*:

> Within white supremacist, capitalist patriarchy the experience of men dressing as women, appearing in drag, has always been regarded by the dominant heterosexist cultural gaze as a sign that one is symbolically crossing over from a realm of power into a realm of powerlessness.[40]

In the 1960s, a new rendering of the "model minority" entered the long Hollywood Charlie Chan tradition. Intended to be read as a positive and sympathetic portrayal of Asians, the model minority image is a new variation of the old

Charlie Chan genre. *Flower Drum Song* (1961), the first and possibly only all-Asian-cast Broadway musical, portrayed the Chinese community as humble, quiet, and successful. As Renee Tajima commented, *Flower Drum Song* "gave birth to a whole new generation of stereotypes—gum chewing Little Leaguers, enterprising businessmen and all-American tomboys of the new model minority myth."[41] The model minority image represents "a new bent on racist representations of Asian Americans," as Marchetti points out, and it can also be traced to the Charlie Chan prototype.[42] This deliberate social positioning is grounded in a kind of white paternalism. Historian Roger Daniels has perceptively pointed to overt racist comparisons by neoconservatives between the Black underclass and more upwardly mobile Japanese and Chinese Americans.[43]

What is more, the female Asian newscaster image (modeled after Connie Chung) "has [also] come to embody a new bent on racist representations of Asian Americans as the 'model minority.' "[44] Representations of Asian broadcast anchorwomen have lately appeared even in some mainstream movies and TV series like *The American President* (1995), *Hard Copy* (1994), and *Quantum Leap* (1994). However, the best footnote to this new twist of Asian cinematic representation is Miramax Films's plan to resurrect the Charlie Chan movie.[45] In sharp contrast to the portly hero of the past, the new Chan, according to Gary Granat, senior executive vice president at Miramax, will be a "more well-rounded character" who is hip, slim, cerebral, sexy, and (naturally) a martial arts master. Best of all, this new Chan of the 1990s will be played by Russell Wong, a Chinese American, instead of a white man. "Clearly, by the casting of Russell Wong as the new Chan," Granat promises, "our efforts are to make him into a real role model for Asian and non-Asian audiences."[46]

As the twentieth century draws to a close, these Asian images are still alive and thriving in the media. To any careful observer it is no secret that with very little variation the same racist and sexist fantasies about Asians and Asian Americans continue to flourish and to command the popular consciousness. As Herbert Schiller describes in his book *The Mind Managers*, the recycled or reinscribed screen stereotypes of Asian Americans in television and film are constantly consumed by the general population.[47] Thanks to new conceptual studies (for example, in psychology and linguistics) on ethnicity in film, media's impact on spectators' attitudes toward others, particularly with regard to prejudice and stereotyping, is beginning to receive more critical attention. Scholars in social psychology, for example, have applied a social-cognitive approach to the film-viewer relationship. Film audience members as social cognizers "actively select, organize, transform, and interpret film information, at times in a biased or distorted way, guided by their needs, values and beliefs, especially those concerning 'self' and 'others.' "[48]

This alternative reading of the spectator's role is further developed in the field of linguistics. Film scholars have also borrowed the critical concept of "dialogism" from Russian scholar Mikhail Mikhailovich Bakhtin in the study of race and ethnic representation.[49] For Bakhtin, language, text, and media are essentially a matter of utterances or voices rather than sentences and images. "Each cultural voice," he claims, by nature "exists in dialogue with other voices."[50] Even though listeners, readers, and spectators do not speak from the film itself, they are already in the conversational process with it. Thus, the Bakhtinian formulation of dialogism posits an active role for the audience members, who are not passive recipients of the film message but rather are constantly in internal dialogue with the film they are viewing. This politics of representation is the subject of the second section of this chapter.

"POLITICS OF REPRESENTATION"

> Many audiences in the United States resist the idea that images have an ideological intent . . . image-making is political—that politics of domination informs the way the vast majority of images we consume are constructed and marketed.[51]

Bell hooks makes this insightful comment in her book *Black Looks*. She argues that images and representation can most usefully be understood as a specific signifying practice. In the same vein, Stuart Hall calls for our critical attention to the "politics of representation." "There is no escape from the politics of representation," he argues, "and we cannot wield 'how life really is out there' as a kind of test against which the political rightness or wrongness of a particular cultural strategy or text can be measured."[52] But it is Edward Said's theory of Orientalism that allowed film historians and scholars to make the shift from the former simplistic notion of imagery to representation in films as a means of political discourse. The concept of Orientalism has become a powerful analytical tool in the study of racial, ethnic, and gender representation in visual media (especially with regard to Asians and North Africans).[53] To put it simply, *Orientalism* helped to raise discussions on racism, colonialism, and Asian representation to new levels, concerning the question of power and systems of representation. According to Said, Orientalism is less about the Orient, as a particular geographical area, than about the historical experience of confronting and representing the other. "The Orient was Orientalized not only because it was discovered to be 'Oriental' . . . ," Said wrote perceptively, "but *made* Oriental."[54] As a Eurocentric idea, Orientalism promotes the differences between the familiar (Europe, the West, "us") and the strange (the Orient, the East, "them").

In his book, Said pointed out that "the Orient helped to define Europe (or the West) as its contrasting image, idea, personality, and experience."[55] The Orient became a sort of surrogate self for the West. That is where the conventional East/West dichotomy came from. Under this East/West, self/other polarity, Orientals are what Occidentals are not. In public perceptions (people's minds) Orientals and Westerners are binary categories defined always in reference to each other. For "Orientalism to make sense at all depends more on the West than on the Orient," Said argued,

> and this sense is directly indebted to various Western techniques of representation that make the Orient visible, clear, "there" in discourse about it. And these representations rely upon institutions, traditions, conventions, agreed-upon codes of understanding for their effects, not upon a distant and amorphous Orient.[56]

As a colonialist master discourse, Hollywood's movies perpetuate examples of Orientalism in their generic formulas, narrative conventions, and cultural assumptions. Hollywood's representation of Asians follows Rudyard Kipling's famous saying, "East is East and West is West, and Never the Twain Shall Meet."

Although Edward Said drew his primary evidence of Orientalism from academic writing, travel literature, and novels, there has been a growing body of literature on Orientalism in film published in the 1980s and 1990s.[57] As Matthew Berstein stated, "In *Orientalism*, Said expressed the hope that additional studies of other aspects of the phenomenon would follow his own, and indeed cultural critics and theorists have taken up Orientalism as an intriguing and compelling paradigm for the representation of race, ethnicity, and gender in the media, and particularly in film."[58] Three of the most recent books on Asian visual representation are exemplary works in this growing body of literature: Gina Marchetti's *Romance and the "Yellow Peril": Race, Sex, and Discursive Strategies in Hollywood Fiction* (1993), James Moy's *Marginal Sights: Staging the Chinese in America* (1993), and Darrell Y. Hamamoto's *Monitored Peril: Asian Americans and the Politics of TV Representation* (1994). Marchetti examines "the way in which narratives featuring Asian-Caucasian sexual liaisons work ideologically to uphold and sometimes subvert culturally accepted notions of nation, class, race, ethnicity, gender, and sexual orientations."[59] Similarly, tracing the history of representations of the Chinese, both on Broadway and in Hollywood, Moy's book "consists of ten readings, each a treatment of Euro-American strategies deployed in the staging of the Chinese in America."[60] Hamamoto contextualizes the "symbolic subordination" of Asian Americans on television, in the historical systems of racism, such as the ideology of "manifest destiny," U.S. military action in Asia, and the recent Japan-bashing movement. He writes: "Popular cultural forms such as network television programs are especially effective vehicles for the transmission of a racialized discourse that confers legitimacy to white supremacist social institutions and power arrangement."[61] Hamamoto skillfully frames the history of the representation of Asians on American television in a political, economic, and psychosocial color-caste system.

In this section, I will briefly discuss the representational strategies of Hollywood and how they operate and function as a powerful tool of social control with regard to Asian Americans.

Representational Strategies

The late Black film historian James Snead once wrote about Hollywood's strategies of Black representation, "My work on Hollywood film analyzes film stereotypes in terms of codes they form, and makes these codes legible, inspecting their inner workings as well as the external historical subjects they would conceal."[62] Specifically, he identified three devices used in Hollywood fiction on Black Americans. "Whenever you see blacks, in Hollywood movies especially," Snead suggested, "you should be looking for three kinds of operation: mythification; marking; and omission."[63]

A careful analysis of their formal properties reveals that similar schemes are deployed by Hollywood in representing Asian Americans. In Hollywood fiction Black mythification easily becomes Asian inscrutability. Indeed, Asians have long been stereotyped as "inscrutable Orientals." Asian characters in film can be good or bad, but they are always mysterious. "The anthropological gaze," as Moy explains, "the look that seeks to dominate, subjugate, and colonize," represents the mythification device Hollywood uses on Asians. Moy argues that the imperialistic gaze, as a representational practice, provides the means for the Anglo-American construction of "Chineseness." The gaze assumes the authority of pseudoscientific objectivity and authenticates the self/other differences. In films, often the gaze translates into manipulation of the mise-en-scène. DeMille's silent film *The Cheat*, shot on black-and-white film stock, is a good case in point. Lighting and shadows were skillfully manipulated to highlight Arakau's mysterious qualities. The kimono, the statue of Buddha, the rich silks, the figurines, and the incense burning created a perfect mise-en-scène of Oriental inscrutability. While it is difficult to describe inscrutability, some of the key elements are racial features (body shapes, facial features, and skin color), peculiar dress and hair styles, exotic eating habits, weird customs, and grotesque language accents.

In turn, marking (distinguishing racial traits), for Asian Americans, has been largely achieved by their racialization. The longtime Hollywood practice of racialization is played out through what Eugene Wong has called "yellow-facing," or racist cosmetology. This tradition not only allows the white actors and actresses to steal the show, but, like blackface, it helps dramatize Asian racial features (such as "slanted" eyes), to the extent of absurdity. For example, the title character in the Charlie Chan series was always portrayed by a white actor. Before his sudden death in 1938, Warner Oland performed the lead in some sixteen Charlie Chan films. He established the "good Oriental" detective type with his mysterious crime-solving ways. Oland's successors included Sidney Toler and Roland Winters. These white actors played the inscrutable Oriental detective Charlie Chan with taped eyelids and a singsong, chop suey accent. James Wong Howe, the famous Chinese American cameraman, was reported to call whites in Chinese roles "adhesive tape actors" because of this practice.[64]

This discourse of racialization also exists in the real world. A World War II–era *Time* magazine cover story provided the following "helpful" guide for the differences between the Chinese and Japanese:

> Japanese are likely to be stockier and broader-hipped than short Chinese. . . . Chinese, not as hairy as Japanese, seldom grown an impressive mustache . . . Although both have the typical epicanthic fold of the upper eyelid (which makes them look almond-eyed), Japanese eyes are usually set closer together . . . the Chinese expression is likely to be more placid, kindly, open; the Japanese more positive, dogmatic, arrogant. . . . Japanese are hesitant, nervous in conversation, laugh loudly at the wrong time. . . . Japanese walk stiffly erect, hard heeled. Chinese, more relaxed, have an easy gait, sometimes shuffle.[65]

In addition to the physical features, heavy Asian accents became another way of marking their differences. Elaine Kim, for example, did a careful analysis of the dialect of Charlie Chan, which is characterized by high-pitched, singsong tones; tortured syntax; the confounding of "l's" and "R's"; the proliferation of "*ee*"-endings; and the random omission of articles and auxiliary verbs.[66] This Charlie Chan dialect has become a recognizable feature of stereotypical "Asian" racial traits.[67]

"The death of Asia," a key narrative device in Hollywood fiction, has been discussed by several scholars as a way of omission (by killing off Asian characters). Dorothy Jones named the relationship between suicide, death, and sex "the death syndrome," while Maxine Hong Kingston called it the Oriental "suicide urge and suicide mode."[68] "There are a whole series of films," wrote Jones, "in which one of the lovers meets a tragic death before the match can be consummated."[69] James Moy describes "the death of Asia on the American field of representation" as a continuing motif in popular American culture.[70] Eugene Wong suggests that Asian life is portrayed by Hollywood as "cheap," or as less valuable than American life. In war genre movies between 1930 and 1975, according to Wong, an average of ten Asians was killed for every white.[71] The death syndrome is a constant Western-Asian theme and can be found as early as Cho-Cho-San in *Madame Butterfly*, around the turn of the century, and as recently as *Miss Saigon* in the 1990s. The device seems to provide the only possible ending to early love stories between an Asian and a Caucasian. In *The Bitter Tea of General Yen* (1933), for example, Megan (a captured missionary wife) falls in love with the general, but their love is never consummated, because Megan tells Yen how she feels only after he has poisoned himself and is dying. In *My Geisha* (1962), an American man praises Japanese women for "jumping into volcanoes" instead of suing for alimony like American women do.

Asian stereotypes and misrepresentations are not an incidental collection of innocent lies, but rather are by-products of a particular social order controlled by the "mind managers," a term invented by Herbert Schiller to describe media moguls and leaders of the educational establishment.[72] Thus, we should not only address how characters are depicted in our media, but also consider how they fit into social and ideological structures along the lines of race, class, gender, and ethnicity.

Controlling Images

In *Monitored Peril*, Darrell Hamamoto developed the concept of "controlling images"[73] when looking at the ideological context in which television images of Asian Americans are produced. For him, a controlling image is the practice of political, economic, and "psychosocial dominance" of subordinate groups through objectification.[74] Indeed, the most seductive and perhaps most powerful part of "the mind management industry," Hollywood images operate as powerful means of social control. Recently, the relationship between media stereotypes and their social impact has been a main topic of scholarly research on Asian film images. One useful approach scholars have taken lately has been to analyze the relationship between screen images and public prejudices. For example, when children in Georgia were asked their opinions about Japanese, the "majority who had never seen a Japanese before used the adjective 'sneaky,' no doubt strongly influenced by old Hollywood movies recently shown on TV about World War II."[75]

Stereotypes generated by the media serve the dual function of satisfying white self-fulfilling fantasies and blaming the victim. For example, Hollywood's glamorization of interracial romance between white males and Asian females serves some important ideological purposes. Gina Marchetti made an astute comment on the phenomenon: "Although Hollywood films have dealt with a range of interracial relationships between Caucasians and African Americans, Native Americans, and Hispanics, the industry, throughout its history, seems to have taken a special interest in narratives dealing with Asians, Pacific Islanders, and Asian Americans."[76] There is ample evidence to support the argument that sexual practice has been used repeatedly to enforce hierarchies of gender, race, and class in Hollywood industry. The assumption that Blacks are oversexed has served to justify their racial oppression. The similar idea that all Oriental women are utterly feminine and delicate has legitimized their subordination. This Hollywood-promoted fantasy easily translates into the real world. For example, when Japanese synchronized-swimming star and Seoul Olympics medalist Mikako Kotani dressed in a kimono to attend an International Olympic Committee meeting in Birmingham, Alabama, she was promptly described by a local reporter as a "geisha girl serving tea."[77] White men have also bought into the so-called yellow fever, with their fetish for exotic Oriental women. This fantasy has actually spawned an entire marriage industry. The Oriental mail-order bride trade has flourished over the past decade, with the Filipina wife particularly in vogue. American men order Asian brides from picture catalogues, just as they might buy a tool from Sears. It appears that many American men are seeking old-fashioned, compliant wives—the type of women they feel are no longer available in the United States.

Recently, several interesting studies have been done on the societal effects of media representation. It was discovered that the media's representation of the characteristics of a particular people helped to explain and excuse social problems in light of those characteristics (read: blaming the victim). A causal relationship between mass media stereotypes and anti-Asian violence has been persuasively articulated in a note in the *Harvard Law Review* entitled "Racial Violence Against Asian Americans."[78] According to statistics collected, Asian Americans suffer a higher per capita rate of hate crimes than any other racial minority. In the note, the author argues that stereotypes function as catalysts to violent crime committed against Asian Americans. "Despite the conventional wisdom that Asian Americans no longer face discrimination, many racial stereotypes continue to inform society's views of Asian Americans."[79]

Specifically, the note identified five major stereotypes. It points out that the perception that Asian immigrants are submissive, physically unaggressive, and politically docile may invite crimes. Asian Americans often become choice victims of street crime because they are deemed as unlikely to resist. Another stereotype of Asian Americans is that they are seen as foreigners, and this "animates a territorial response." "Because Asian Americans are different," the note suggests, "and because the difference is conceived as foreign—not in a cosmopolitan sense, but in the aberrant, un-American sense, they are denied the respect granted to fellow members of our national community."[80] This supposedly intrinsic foreignness promotes the "nativist" response. In the turf war against outsiders, a scapegoating response against Asian Americans goes hand in hand with turf protection. The tactic of classifying Asian Americans both as unfair competitors and as the model minority "amounts to interracial baiting that heightens resentment against Asian Americans."[81] Finally, the dehumanization of Asian Americans removes the social and psychological inhibitions against committing violence on a fellow human being. "For Asian American victims," the author notes, "the psychological process of dehumanization is achieved via the stereotype of foreignness, which denies them 'in-group' status, and that of fungibility, which strips them of individual dignity."[82] Indeed, the "foreigner" and "fungible" (racial lumping) stereotypes "transmogrif[y] Asian Americans into a faceless, deindividualized horde" and also "[bridge] national boundaries holding Asian Americans culpable for the deeds of Asian governments."[83] Clarence Spigner, in his article "Teaching Multiculturalism from the Movies: Health and Social Well-being," finds a correlation between Hollywood stereotypes about Asian Americans and the 1982 real-life death, at the hands of two assailants, of Vincent Chin in Detroit.[84]

Japanese American clinical psychologist Herbert Horikawa looks at the sociofilmic control from a clinical point of view.[85] As indicated by the title of his article, "Psychological Implications of Asian Stereotypes in the Media," Horikawa explores how racist stereotypes, as a special form of abuse, contribute to Asian Americans' developing "learned helplessness" (a psychological theory).[86] Because of the discriminatory information received from the mass media, Horikawa argues, Asian Americans develop the expectation of not having control over their lives. Accordingly, they tend to be less likely to try to exert control and power. Despite its limitations (for one, assuming the audience is a passive and uninformed Asian American one), the essay calls our attention to racism in visual media "as a special form of abuse in which the abused feels powerless."[87]

Misrepresentations not only justify the status quo by rationalizing racism, but they also create harm through "colonization of the imagination." Jessica Hagedorn, a Filipina American, wrote in *Ms.* magazine:

> Colonization of the imagination is a two-way street. And being enshrined on a pedestal as someone's Pearl of the Orient fantasy doesn't seem so demeaning, at first; who wouldn't want to be worshipped? Perhaps that's why Asian women are the ultimate wet dream in most Hollywood movies; it's no secret how well we've been taught to play the role; to take care of our men.[88]

Stereotypes also help develop cognitive associations between race and aesthetics. For Asian women, judgments of physical beauty and self-worth are sometimes internalized from culturally imposed expectations. Asian female anatomy has always been subjected to imposed ideals of physical beauty. Body shapes, facial features, and skin fairness are assigned value in a hierarchical manner. This mystique of Asian women is based on Western standards of exotic beauty, because the standard of beauty is not usually Asian, African, or Latino. The superstars in show business remain white and usually blond, though sometimes brunet. A different reading of the Nancy Kerrigan/Tonya Harding soap opera on ice proves the point. In the media glitz on the incident, Kerrigan was uniformly described as a "classic American beauty." Lucrative business deals were piling up for her. The skater reportedly flew to Disney, for an advertising contract, without attending the closing ceremony for the winter Olympics in 1996, in which she won the silver medal. In contrast, four years ago, Kristi Yamaguchi, who won two world championships and an Olympic gold medal in Albertville, France, in 1992, was never able to cash in on her championship. Yamaguchi was "cold-shouldered" by American advertisers because she looked Japanese, and not blue-eyed and blond-haired.[89]

John Fiske, in his analysis of Michel Foucault's *Discipline and Punish*, incisively wrote, "Foucault has revealed in detail the ways in which western societies have made the body into the site where social power is most compellingly exerted. The body is where the power-bearing definitions of social and sexual normality are, literally, embodied."[90] The ideologies of gender and race often place the Asian female body under the burden of conformity. Eugenia Kaw's essay "Medicalization of Racial Features: Asian American Women and Cosmetic Surgery" is a solid case study of the cosmetic alterations found among Asian American women in the San Francisco Bay Area (which includes nine counties).[91] Kaw presented well-documented findings on the most popular types of cosmetic surgery among Asian American women: eyelid restructuring, nose bridge buildup, and nose tip altering. Her research suggested that these women had internalized not only a gender ideology like other women, but also a racial ideology that associated their natural features with negative connotations. What was more, she discovered that the media industry and the industry of medicine had joined forces in promoting these racial and gender stereotypes.

This process of internalization does not stop there. It leads further to "flawed self-representation" (to borrow a term from James Moy). In his spirited analysis of "the establishment of a new order of stereotype, authenticated by its Asian American authorship," Moy has found that Asian American artists unconsciously participate in perpetuating and even institutionalizing Hollywood's false cinematic images. Moy makes the valid point that stereotypes have infiltrated and transformed the consciousness of Asian American artists as much as they have transformed the consciousness of the Anglo-American audience.[92] "Unfortunately for Asian America," Moy wrote, "most recent playwrights have located the struggle under the sign of greater racial authenticity. What better way to get behind the facade of the Chinese stereotype than to have a Chinese American guide?"[93]

Although his criticism is seriously undermined because of his reductive reasoning, in attributing popularity to a "complicitous desire" to "cater to Anglo-American expectations," Moy's argument brings to the forefront an important dimension of internalization. The dominant systems of representation have the power to represent and, by extension, to shape the consciousness of those who are the subjects of representation. Mira Nair's film *Mississippi Masala* (1991), for example, was criticized for its caricatures of Indian characters. Their mannerisms, "such as the bobbing of the head from side to side (an Indian way of saying yes)," to paraphrase Erika Surat Andersen in *Film Quarterly*, are exaggerated to the point of ridicule. "The Indian community is shown to be greedy, petty, and ridiculous," Andersen wrote. The men are drunks and the women are gossips. The hotel owner is greedy and hypocritical—paying lip service to people of color, displaying solidarity in one moment and disapproving of interracial romance the next. The bridegroom is depicted as effeminate, impotent, and ludicrous. In one of several bedroom scenes, he checks under his pajamas for an erection, and then hops on top of his bride (who emphatically rejects him), so finally he puts on headphones and watches TV instead. "If a non-Indian film-maker had portrayed such characters," Anderson speculated, "there would have been public outcry at the racist stereotypes. What does it mean for a film-maker to make such as film about her own people?" she asked indignantly. "Is it that she feels privileged to poke fun at her own kind? Are these scenes included purely for comic relief?"[94]

On the small screen, some critics have accused *All-American Girl* of being merely a multicultural spectacle for a white audience. This ABC domestic comedy, which premiered on September 28, 1995, was about a Korean American "Valley Girl" torn between her family's traditional values and the mall culture of Southern California. Gary Jacobs mentioned that *All-American Girl* was watched by 25 to 30 million people every week. "For many of them," he said, "this is probably the first time they are meeting an Asian American family."[95] However, the show caused some heated debates among its defenders and detractors. Guy Aoki, President of MANAA (the Media Action Network for Asian Americans), a media watchdog organization, was one of the show's star Margaret Cho's strongest supporters. "We feel 'All-American Girl' is positive," Aoki declared at an Achievement Awards dinner in honor of Cho, Janet Yang (the president of Ixtlan), and Russell Wong (star of the television series *Vanishing Son*), "because it is the first television series to feature an Asian American family. It is important for people across the country to see Asian faces every week, because in the past, we have been invisible or just purveyors of stereotypes."[96] Given the essentially conservative nature of network programming, most Asian Americans appreciated the first prime-time network series in television history with a primarily Asian American cast. But despite its stated goal to "crush Korean stereotypes (and find Cho a man)," the show was often cited by Asian American critics as an example of flawed self-representation.[97] In an interview Cho stated that "my character breaks all the stereotypes about Asian Americans. She's not good at math, she's lazy, she's rebellious, she's very outspoken. That sort of shatters all the stereotypes."[98] Many Asian American viewers and critics, though, regarded the show as offensive and misleading, for it emphasized cultural conflict instead of racism as the major theme, and it reinforced the model minority image. Their point is very well taken. Cho herself has compared her Asian American sitcom to the *Bill Cosby Show*. "The only thing I can possibly compare it to is the debut of 'The Cosby Show.' I'm Bill Cosby."[99] All in all, the small business–owning Kim family in the Cho show is presented as a showcase of the Asian success story. The show avoids any references to race and racism. As a reader of *AsianWeek* wrote, "'All-American Girl' is a banana—yellow on the outside, white on the inside. It tries too hard to be all-American. And it fails because it relies too heavily on stereotypes, while taking few risks."[100]

Although the postscript at the end of each episode credits the show as being based on Margaret Cho's standup comedy, critics believe the critical Asian American perspectives of the actress's routines is lost in the sitcom. Bill Wong observes that "none of Cho's razor-like observations on race, ethnicity and culture were included in her character's dialogue with her parents, siblings or workmates. Except for the obvious physical features of most of the cast, one would be hard pressed to even know this show had Asian sensibilities."[101] Even though Touchstone TV made a last-ditch effort to rescue the show from poor ratings (including firing both executive producer Gary Jacobs and the show's writers, and replacing most of Cho's TV Korean American family), it went off the air after only one season.

Because of the lack of specific data concerning public and individual responses to specific movies, much work still needs to be done to determine precisely how audiences receive, distill, and believe Asian film images. In short, the effect of cinematic Asian representation remains an elusive matter hidden in the biographies of many men and women, which calls for new research and interpretations. What is more, film texts should be viewed as sites of ideological struggle and contestation. Their reception is a dynamic and dialogic process. Stuart Hall, among many others, calls for critical attention to the operation of resistance and alternative readings among ethnic groups. In fact, ethnicity can function as "both imprisoning stigma and potentially liberating identity."[102] Independent Asian American cinema, as alternative media, serves as a good example for this struggle with mainstream media in contesting Asian film representation. As a result, replication of hegemony by the mainstream media is disrupted, and oppositional narratives provide important alternatives to Hollywood representation of Asians and Asian Americans.

ROLE PLAYING IN REPRESENTATION

When we discuss racial stereotypes, we tend to think about them in either a cultural or an ideological sense, and rarely do we give serious thoughts to mass media's institutional aspect of representing people of a certain race. Using ideas from Russian formalists and neo-Marxists, Eugene Wong's dissertation-derived book *On Visual Media Racism: Asians in the American Motion Pictures* provides a much-needed perspective, relating textual practices to the institution of production. Wong argues that although the motion picture industry's racism against Asians has its definitive individual and cultural proponents, it was the institutionalized nature of the industry's racism against Asians that was particularly humiliating.[103] Drawn from studio archives and personal documents, Wong's work points directly to Hollywood's institutional modes of representation. While Wong touches on all three aspects of cinema, including production (capital, talent, and creation), distribution (marketing, promotion, and reviews) and exhibition, I will focus on three industrywide racist practices in casting as a particularly important dimension of the racism embedded in institutional representation: role segregation, role stratification, and role delimitation.

Role Segregation

Segregating actors by roles seems to be reasonable, sometimes even desirable, when ethnic characters are cast. But the major problem is not role segregation per se, but the double standards used in casting. In the film industry, as Wong has carefully documented, Asians cannot cross into roles that are designated as white, yet Caucasian actors have the right to break the barriers of role segregation and cross freely into Asian roles (or Hispanic roles, and so on). This represents the discriminatory practice of one-way cross-over. Two historical reasons can be given for the persistence of this practice against Asian Americans. First, Asians cannot play white roles because of the two-tiered racial system in America. Contrary to our understanding as a people, America in the movies is not every color, but basically Black and white. This bifurcated system of representation is one of the root causes for Asian segregation on screen. Secondly, Asians cannot play whites because of the East/West dichotomy. Asians could play their "ethnic" or foreign roles, but not those of general Americans. The film industry will be reluctant to cast Asians as part of the mainstream of American life until Asians are accepted by the society at large.

It is interesting to note that, to maintain this double standard, Eurasian characters have become Hollywood's favorite creations. These mixed-race characters obviously allow white actors and actresses, with minimum makeup, to steal major roles from Asians. The best example is the Eurasian role in the TV series *Kung Fu*. Bruce Lee was rejected by Warner Bros. for the leading role despite his awesome martial arts expertise and Chinese ethnicity. Hollywood deemed it legitimate for the Eurasian role to go to white actor David Carradine. "This racial rejection by Hollywood," as Tiana (Thi Thanh Nga) recalls in a recent article, "Bruce told me, made him furious. It impelled him to leave the United States and return to Hong Kong, where, in two dizzying years, he became an international legend." The week before he died, Tiana remembers, Lee vowed to "outgross Steve McQueen and James Coburn," and so he did. Both McQueen and Coburn were Lee's students, and yet "each had told him that he [Lee] could never reach their star status because he was Chinese."[104]

The controversy over the musical *Miss Saigon* is probably the most recent example of this "Asian drag" practice. In the Broadway production of the musical, the furiously debated decision of casting Jonathan Pryce (a white British actor) as the lead role of a Eurasian male character allowed the British producer, Cameron Mackintosh, to literally practice the same tradition Hollywood had established for Asian characters. Under the guise of artistic freedom, Mackintosh's argument for color-blind casting could only serve to reinforce inequalities already in existence. Angela Pao's critical essay added one interesting dimension to the debate.[105] She drew our attention to how the cultural process worked in this case, specifically concerning gender and race. She argued that color-blind casting was impossible in *Miss Saigon*. The producer's decision to cast an Asian woman and a Caucasian man was *not* accidental. Rather, it had to do with the genre and the theatrical parameters: East/West tragic romance. Like *Madame Butterfly*, this Western maternal melodrama carried the following imperatives: the Asian prostitute, the "fallen woman," the maternal devotion to the child and to the lover, the desertion, and finally the suicide. To stick with these genre imperatives, the Eurasian role had to be played by a white man.

As for the implications involved when using cosmetics and wigs to "produce" a different race, Wong wrote:

> The industry's use of racist cosmetics is important in discussing institutional racism against Asians for three reasons: 1) The film industry has demonstrated its racist propensities by concentrating upon external racial differences, in this case the epicanthic fold. 2) The use of racist

cosmetics has been instrumental in the establishment of race freedom for white actors in the systems of role segregation and major/minor role stratification. 3) Racist cosmetology has been utilized as a means of justifying the continued displacement of actual Asian actors in the industry as a whole, particularly on the major role level, thereby preventing them from developing professionally within the industry.[106]

Furthermore, Wong emphasizes that, although this cosmetic treatment is not unique to Asians, "no one in this country would dare to put on 'black face' anymore," thereby offending Black racial sensibilities, causing a public scandal, and jeopardizing employment opportunities in the process. Yet, white "producers do not hesitate to allow non-Asians to use 'yellow face' (racist cosmetology)," even to this day.[107]

Role Stratification

Eugene Wong calls role stratification the vertical counterpart to role segregation in the racial politics of casting. While Asian actors and actresses are often cast primarily as background fillers and to create cinematic atmosphere as extras and "racials," he claims they are not considered competent enough to play leading roles. As indicated by D. W. Griffith's curious casting decision in *Broken Blossoms* (1919): "Most of the background characters are Chinese, but a role such as Evil Eye, which required acting talent, was entrusted to Edward Piel, who was all too obviously Caucasian."[108] Thus, opportunities for Asian American performers become fewer and the roles' scope even more minimal, as the importance of the Asian roles rise. The practice of role stratification is more pervasive in casting, but it is even involved in role creation. For example, as Wong has shown in the introduction to his book, the movie industry imposed a system of double standards with regard to interracial romance.[109] Antimiscegenation laws and the restrictive Motion Picture Production Code (which held sway from 1934 through the mid-1950s) had long forbade "scenes of passion," and expressly prohibited the filming of interracial sex or marital scenes and themes. However, the industry's double standards are based on the traditional racist assumptions in the white community concerning the "threat" of interracial sex and marriage. Despite such fears, white males are shown to easily transgress interracial sexual prohibitions on-screen. Such duplicitous standards have developed into the so-called phenomenon of "sexualization of racism."

In recent years, we have seen a new twist in the practice: leading roles are created for white actors or actresses in Asian American–themed productions. For example, when Alan Parker's *Come See the Paradise* (1990) was first released, some Asian Americans accused Dennis Quaid, a white actor, of stealing the stardom.

The movie was about the internment of Japanese Americans during World War II. Quaid played a guard who fell in love with a Nisei woman interned in the camp. Regardless of the moviemakers' intentions, the message conveyed was very clear to Asian Americans: a white lead was critical to make the movie acceptable for a mainstream audience. Mira Nair, director of *Mississippi Masala*, experienced similar problems with Hollywood in making her film. "People were disconcerted that we had no white characters [among the seventy-nine speaking parts] in the film," she recalls. One [executive] asked if I couldn't make room for a white protagonist. I said, sure, all the waiters in the film could be white," she recounted, laughing at her suggestion of casting whites as peripheral characters. Not bowing to the pressure, Nair made the movie independently with only $7 million and an independent crew—"an epic on a peanut," as Nair puts it. "We felt the story had to be told in the voices of the people it was about," she insisted. "It's about time one can see the world not necessarily through a white person's point of view."[110]

This phenomenon is perhaps not unique to Asian Americans. In a similar situation, Native American critics raised the same issue with Kevin Costner's blockbuster *Dances with Wolves* (1990). A drastic departure from the old "noble savage" image, the movie offered a more sympathetic portrayal of Native American peoples. But Indian media activists asked why the movie needed a white guide into Native American culture. Was it a white surrogate for the movie audience? To push the argument a bit further, were the Native communities merely offered up as a larger-than-life racial spectacle (in the same vein as graphic violence, alien encounters, car chases, and sex scenes) for the narrative development of the white male lead?

Role Delimitation

In addition, according to Eugene Wong, Asian Americans have experienced two kinds of role delimitations in the movie industry: numerical and dimensional. Looking over the entire history of mass media, in fact, one sees very few Asian roles in the first place. If we consider the airwaves today, Asians are almost absent, with some important exceptions. In the fall of 1991, the Media Coalition of Minorities and Women monitored fifty-eight TV shows, and reported that out of 555 characters whose race was identified, only three were Asian (or Asian Pacific) Americans. This lack of employment opportunities has often forced talented Asian Americans to change their careers early. So, to correct this wrong, in 1992 the Media Action Network for Asian Americans (MANAA) launched its so-called "Operation Primetime" campaign in an effort to increase the representation of Asian Americans on TV.

Besides the problem of invisibility or underrepresentation, the roles that Asian Americans have been offered come from a limited number of stereotypes—largely a patchwork of clichés. In on-screen portrayals, white actors and actresses have been depicted as representing the entire spectrum of social and human types, whereas the professional horizons for Asian actors are very limited. Very rarely are the Asian roles fleshed out as fully developed characters. This system of stereotypical delimitations has successfully prevented dimensional development and aesthetic continuity in the creation of Asian characters on the screen. Unfortunately, Asian American actors and actresses have to confront the moral dilemma between reinforcing stereotypes of their people and maintaining their own professional and sometimes economic survival. As Ruthanne Lum McCunn wrote, "These are the images casting directors have in mind at auditions, and they are so powerful that Chinese American actors and actresses sometimes become doubtful about who they are, affecting phony [Asian] accents and using eyebrow pencils to make their eyes more slanted."[111] Adrienne Telemaque, a Chinese American actress, recalled in an interview, "Finally, I did get myself a Suzie Wong wig. I hated doing it, but it's what they want. After buying the wig, I got the job I went out for."[112] This practice reminds us of Robert Townsend's autobiographial *Hollywood Shuffle* (1987), where the filmmaker satirizes Hollywood racial conventions by having white directors "teach" Black performers how to conform to white stereotypes about Black characters.

Left with little choice, some Asian Americans try to make the best of a bad situation. Lauren Tom, who played one of the daughters in *The Joy Luck Club*, said, "I don't want to be Pollyannaish about it, but my attitude is that you're aware of inequalities and the racism that goes on in the world of casting, but to just keep focusing on the positive has enabled me to get parts that are cross-over." Tom's latest role, in *Mr. Jones* (1993) with Richard Gere, was not originally written for an Asian American. It remains to be seen whether this practice is the rule or the exception.

In the past three or four decades, an increasing body of literature has accumulated on Asian cinematic representation. Scholars have approached the subject from various perspectives. While it is beyond the scope of this chapter to present a full-blown account of those works, a limited sampling of the literature has been given to contextualize Asian American films. It is against this backdrop of Hollywood's stereotypical, ideological, and institutional practices that the Asian American independent filmmakers are operating. From the beginning, the independents not only have confronted the daunting task of dismantling, transforming, and creating critical alternatives to those Hollywood screen images, but also they have had to improvise ways to work around the hurdles and obstacles within the movie industry. The significance of Asian American independent cinema could only be understood from the lives of creative artists, the economics of the movie industry, and certain forms of political intervention in the process of production, distribution, and exhibition. Accordingly, their achievements and limitations should be appreciated in view of contemporary as well as historical precedents in the institutions of cinema that both frustrate and engage their imaginations.

In conceptualizing the dynamics of media and culture, scholars such as Antonio Gramsci, Raymond Willliams, Mikhail Bakhtin, and Stuart Hall all have emphasized media texts as the sites of constant ideological struggles.[113] Bakhtin's concept of "dialogic imagination," for example, demonstrates how all texts are informed by the historical consciousness of both their authors and their audiences.[114] For my purpose in the book, Raymond Williams's elaboration of the dynamics of hegemony, Antonio Gramsci's idea of "common sense," and Stuart Hall's ideas of media and representation have proved most useful in the discussion of marginalized cultural production groups. For Williams, hegemony is a process in which dominant social values constantly struggle with subordinate values. Williams's three categories of dominant, residual, and emergent cultures were especially useful for this study's explorations of domination/subordination, center/periphery, and, above all, resistance/hegemony. While residual values can be oppositional, it is emergent culture that represents the most serious challenge to the dominant culture. To put it in Williams's words:

> By "emergent" I mean, first, that new meanings and values, new practices, new relationships and kinds of relationships are continually being created. . . . It is true that in the structure of any actual society, and especially in its class structure, there is always a social basis for elements of the cultural process that are alternative or oppositional to the dominant elements.[115]

Since the 1960s, social historians have already documented the creative and constructive responses to hegemony by various subordinate social groups. The values and traditions, or simply "common sense," to borrow a concept from Antonio Gramsci, are potential sources of counterhegemony. Artistic and cultural productions (including independent films), as one form of "common sense," perform an important function of counterhegemony in society.

The important theories Stuart Hall helped develop have also served as useful models for studying ethnic representation as it is related to film. One of the key concepts Hall created has served to reformulate our understanding of representation. In contrast to the "old" notion that representation merely "re-presents" meaning that is already there, Hall posits that there is no single fixed meaning of media images. To him, the signifier and signified in representation are not solely reflective, but "constitutive," a process by which the viewer is drawn into the image in an active way, through identification. Hall's new understanding of representation is a profound one, in the sense that it offers a new way of looking at how people perceive what is being represented. Hall's ideas also help to "deconstruct" the notion of the "subject/object" dichotomy in media representation. Thus, any film, seen as text, can be interpreted through a dominant, negotiated, or oppositional reading, or all three. The reception of visual texts then becomes a dynamic and dialectical process between the producers and the audience.[116] Even more useful for this study is Hall's discussion of how cultural studies can contest gender and racial stereotyping. Rather than creating "positive images," Hall advocates a different approach. He suggests that the viewer should "get inside" the image and ask questions about the very process of representation. The aim of this approach is to make the stereotypes, to use his own word, "uninhabitable."[117] As Gina Marchetti suggests, "Rather than looking at racial and ethnic media images as simply 'positive' or 'negative,' 'realistic' or 'racist,' 'progressive' or 'reactionary,' cultural studies view the ideology of ethnicity and race in film as contradictory, historical, and subject to a variety of changing interpretations."[118]

In studying independent media arts, some scholars have advocated the Third Cinema concept, which is complementary to, but different from, the counterhegemony model in cultural studies. The idea of a Third Cinema was first advanced in the late 1960s in Latin America, taking its inspiration from the Cuban Revolution.[119] Specifically, the term *Third Cinema* (also known as *alternative cinema* or *imperfect cinema*) was in fact coined by Argentine documentarists Fernando Solanas and Octavio Getino to designate a kind of filmmaking that opposes both dominant-industrial ("first") and independent-auteurist ("second") cinema.[120] To quote Solanas for a definition:

> First cinema expresses imperialist, capitalist, bourgeois ideas. Big monopoly capital finances big spectacle cinema, as well as authorial and informational cinema. Any cinematographic expression . . . likely to respond to the aspirations of big capital, I call first cinema. Our definition of second cinema is all that expresses the aspirations of the middle stratum, the petit bourgeoisie. . . . For us, third cinema is the expression of a new culture and of social changes. Generally speaking, Third Cinema gives an account of reality and history.[121]

Some Third Cinema critics have noted the differences between the European notion of counter-cinema—the French New Wave, for example—and the notion of the Third Cinema.

> The notion of counter-cinema tends to conjure up a prescriptive aesthetics; to do the opposite of what dominant cinema does. Hence the

descriptive definition of dominant cinema will dictate the prescriptive definition of counter-cinema. The proponents of Third Cinema were just as hostile to dominant cinemas but refused to let the industrially and ideologically dominant cinemas dictate the terms in which they were to be opposed.[122]

In the context of ethnic filmmaking (and since the 1979 Bard College Conference on U.S. Alternative Cinema), African American, Latino, and Asian American filmmakers have claimed a stronger presence in the Third Cinema movement. In this study, I would argue that the Asian American film movement, especially in its early stages, was a clear example of the Third Cinema movement. It shared some major characteristics with Third Cinema in that it was both opposed to Hollywood and different from the counter-cinema. For example, like Third Cinema, which was opposed to the technical perfection of Western cinema, early Asian American filmmaking carried a strong antislick tradition.[123] Following the Third Cinema model of "guerrilla filmmaking," community-based Asian American filmmakers also voiced their opposition to the auteur theory. As Robert Nakamura, one of the founding members of Visual Communications in Los Angeles, recalled:

> We wanted to work as democratically as possible, so we very purposely avoided the usual production staffing structure. You'll notice in our early films, you won't see credit lines. Except for a few crew members and outside contributors, you would never see specific credits like "Directed by," or "Edited by" or "Director of Photography." We would rotate crew positions in an attempt to share responsibilities equally.[124]

Even Wayne Wang, with his name recognition and increasing clout in the industry, told writer bell hooks in a recent interview, "I'm not an auteur in the sense that I have a specific artistic vision and say, this has to be exactly this way. . . . Cinema is a collaborative thing. That's why, in a sense, *Blue in the Face* [his latest production] is so exciting for me, because there was no authorship, so to speak. As a director, more than anything else, I feel like I'm always a facilitator. A traffic cop."[125]

This book will celebrate the growing power of Asian American cinema. It attempts to demonstrate how, as independent filmmakers, Asian Americans have used this medium to give voice to a socially pertinent discourse that both Hollywood and the auteur-based cinemas have excluded from their works. Instead of presenting their fellow Asian Americans purely in terms of "white" norms and practices, these Asian American filmmakers have begun to successfully articulate a different set of aspirations out of the raw materials collected from their communities in the United States, from Asia, and even from the Asian diaspora.

NOTES

1   The term *intertextual* is commonly used by literary critics and cultural scholars to describe the relationship between a given film and other earlier films in terms of meaning and interpretation.

2   Four major books and numerous articles deal with Hollywood stereotyping of Asians and Asian Americans. The four books are: Stuart Creighton Miller, *The Unwelcome Immigrant: The American Image of the Chinese, 1785–1882* (Berkeley and Los Angeles: University of California Press, 1969); Dorothy B. Jones, *The Portrayal of China and India on the American Screen, 1896–1955* (Cambridge, Mass.: Center for International Studies, MIT, 1955); Harold R. Isaacs, *Scratches on Our Minds: American Images of China and India* (New York: John Day Company, 1958); and Eugene F. Wong, *On Visual Media Racism: Asians in the American Motion Pictures* (New York: Arno Press, 1978).

3   Carlos E. Cortés, "What Is Maria? What Is Juan? Dilemmas of Analyzing the Chicano Image in U.S. Feature Films," *Chicanos and Film: Essays on Chicano Representation and Resistance*, ed. Chon A. Noriega (New York: Garland Publishing, 1992), 83–104.

4   Jones.

5   The better-known works include Christine Choy, "Images of Asian-Americans in Films and Television," *Ethnic and Racial Images in American Film and Television*, ed. Randall Miller (Philadelphia: Balch Institute, 1978); Richard A. Oehling, "The Yellow Menace: Asian Images in American Film," *The Kaleidoscopic Lens: How Hollywood Views Ethnic Groups,* ed. Randall Miller (Englewood, N.J.: Jerome S. Ozer, 1980); Dick Stromgren, "The Chinese Syndrome: The Evolving Images of Chinese and Chinese-Americans in Hollywood Films," *Beyond the Stars: Stock Characters in American Popular Film*, ed. Paul Loukides and Linda K. Fuller (Bowling Green, Ohio: Bowling Green State University Popular Press, 1990); and Renee Tajima, "Asian Women's Images in Film: The Past Sixty Years," *In Color: Sixty Years of Minority Women in Film: 1921–1981* (New York: Third World Newsreel, 1993).

6   Jones, 28–36 and 63–65.

7   Choy, 149.

8   Isaacs.

9   Stromgren, 61–77.

10   Isaacs, 63.

11   American writer Jack London, recently revealed to have had white supremacist views, worked as a war correspondent during the Russo-Japanese war. He wrote an influential essay entitled "The Yellow Peril" for the Hearst newspapers (which, perhaps not coincidentally, became tarred with the label "yellow journalism," implying stereotypes and unfair treatment), which helped advocate the yellow peril thesis. For more information, see Frank Gibney, *The Pacific Century: America and Asia in a Changing World* (New York: Maxwell Macmillan International, 1992), 479–511.

12   For a good overview and history of this yellow peril theme in Hollywood, see Oehling, 182–206.

13   Gina Marchetti, *Romance and the Yellow Peril: Race, Sex, and Discursive Hollywood Strategies in Hollywood Fiction* (Berkeley: University of California Press, 1993), Chapters 2–4.

14   Gary Hoppenstand, "Yellow Devil Doctors and Opium Dens: A Survey of the Yellow Peril Stereotypes in Mass Media Entertainment," *The Popular Culture Reader*, 3d ed., ed. Christopher D. Geist and Jack Nachbar (Bowling Green, Ohio: Bowling Green University Popular Press, 1983), 174.

15   Kevin Brownlow, *Behind the Mask of Innocence* (New York: Alfred A. Knopf, 1990). 347.

16   Ibid., 348.

17   Marchetti, 10.

18   Robert Lang, *American Film Melodrama: Griffith, Vidor, Minnelli* (Princeton, N.J.: Princeton University Press, 1989), 102.

19   Brownlow, 334.

20   John Dower, *War without Mercy: Race and Power in the Pacific* (New York: Pantheon Press, 1986), 9.

21   Oehling, 204.

22   William K. Everson, *The Bad Guy: A Pictorial History of the Movie Villain* (New York: Citadel, 1964), 130.

23   Colin Nickerson, "Senator's Comment Ignites Fury in Japan," *Boston Globe* (March 5, 1992), National/Foreign 2.

24   Lan Nguyen, "*Rising Sun* Presents Damaging Portrayal of Japanese, Asians," *Rafu Shimpo* (July 1, 1993), 3.

25   For more information, see "Japanese Offended by Bugs 'Toon," *Fort Collins Coloradoan*, (Feb. 5, 1995), C1.

26   Jessica Hagedorn, "Asian Women in Film: No Joy, No Luck," *Ms.* (Jan./Feb., 1994), 77–78.

27   Ibid., 78.

28   For more information on the history of that opera, see *International Dictionary of Opera* (Detroit: St. James Press, 1993), 784–786.

29   Endymion Wilkinson, *Japan versus the West: Image and Reality* (London: Penguin, 1990), 113.

30   Renee Tajima, "Lotus Blossoms Don't Bleed: Images of Asian Women," *Making Waves: Anthology of Writings By and About Asian American Women*, ed. Asian Women United of California (Boston: Beacon Press, 1989), 300–17.

31   I owe the idea about this Charlie character to Amy Kashiwabara's online essay "Vanishing Son: The Appearance, Disappearance, and Assimilation of the Asian-American Man in American Mainstream Media" [http://www.lib.berkeley.edu/MRC/Amydoc.html], 6–8.

32   Isaacs, 119.

33   Jones, 34.

34   Frank Chin, "Confessions of the Chinatown Cowboy," *Bulletin of Concerned Asian Scholars*, 4:3 (Fall 1972), 67.

35   See Randall Miller, *Ethnic and Racial Images,* 243.

36   Donald Bogle, *Toms, Coons, Mulattoes, Mammies, & Bucks: An Interpretive History of Blacks in American Films* (New York: Continuum, 1994), 223.

37   Chiung Hwang Chen, "Feminization of Asian (American) Men in the U.S. Mass Media: An Analysis of 'The Ballad of Little Jo,'" *Journal of Communication Inquiry* 20:2 (1996), 57.

38   Peter Feng, "Redefining Asian American Masculinity: Steven Okasaki's 'American Sons,'" *Cineaste* 22:3 (1996).

39   See David Henry Hwang, *M. Butterfly* (New York: Plume Books, 1988), 98.

40   bell hooks, *Black Looks: Race and Representation* (Boston: South End Press, 1992), 146.

41   Tajima, "Asian Women's Images in Film," 27.

42   Marchetti, 216.

43   Roger Daniels, *Asian America: Chinese and Japanese in the United States Since 1850* (Seattle: University of Washington Press, 1988), 317–320.

44   Christine Choy, "Cinema as a Tool of Assimilation: Asian Americans, Women and Hollywood," *In Color*, 25.

45   Somini Sengupta, "Charlie Chan Retooled for the 90's," *New York Times* (January 5, 1997), sec. 2, pg. 20, col. 1.

46   Ibid.

47   Herbert Schiller, *The Mind Managers* (Boston: Beacon Press, 1973).

48   Paul S. Cowen, "A Social-Cognitive Approach to Ethnicity in Films," *Unspeakable Images: Ethnicity and the American Cinema.* ed. Lester Friedman (Urbana and Chicago: University of Illinois Press, 1991), 353.

49   Robert Stam, "Bakhtin, Polyphony, and Ethnic/Racial Representation," *Unspeakable Images*, 251–76.

50   Ibid, 258.

51   hooks, 5.

52   Stuart Hall, "What Is This 'Black' in Black Popular Culture," *Representing Blackness, Issues in Film and Video*, ed. Valerie Smith (New Brunswick, N.J.: Rutgers University Press, 1997), 131.

53   Edward Said, *Orientalism* (New York: Pantheon Books, 1978).

54   Ibid., 5–6.

55   Ibid., 2.

56   Ibid., 22.

57   *Visions of the East: Orientalism in Film,* ed. Matthew Bernstein and Gaylyn Studlar (New Brunswick, N.J.: Rutgers University Press, 1997) has a selected bibliography at the back of the book, which is very helpful as a starter.

58   Ibid., 4–5.

59   Marchetti, 1.

60   James S. Moy, *Marginal Sights: Staging the Chinese in America* (Iowa City: University of Iowa Press, 1993), 5.

61   Darrell Y. Hamamoto, *Monitored Peril: Asian Americans and the Politics of TV Representation* (Minneapolis: University of Minnesota Press, 1994), xi.

62   James A. Snead, *White Screens/Black Images: Hollywood from the Dark Side* (New York: Routledge), 2.

63   Ibid., 143–49.

64   Brownlow, 325.

65   "How to tell Japs from the Chinese," *Time* magazine 38:33 (Dec. 22, 1941), 81–82.

66   Elaine Kim, *Asian American Literature: An Introduction to the Writings and Their Social Context* (Philadelphia: Temple University Press, 1982), 12.

67   Anyone watching the O. J. Simpson trial would agree that Judge Lance Ito spoke perfect unaccented English; still, some people felt free to assign him an exaggerated Japanese accent. On April 4, 1995, New York Senator Alfonse D'Amato, for example, used a distorted Japanese accent during an appearance on a radio talk show to criticize the presiding judge's handling of the Simpson trial. Replacing his R's with L's, D'Amato quipped, "He is making a disgrace of the judicial system. Little Judge Ito. For God's sake, get them in there for 12 hours; get this thing over. I mean, this is a disgrace. Judge Ito with the wet nose. And then he's going to have a hung jury. Judge Ito will keep us from getting televise[ed} for the next year." D'Amato's use of the mock Asian accent testifies to the power of this marking scheme. See Sam Fulwood III, "N.Y. Sen. D'Amato Apologizes for Using Japanese Accent in Parody of Judge Ito," *Los Angeles Times* (April 6, 1995), Section Part A.

68   Maxine Hong Kingston, *Tripmaster Monkey* (New York: Vintage Books, 1990), 319.

69   Jones, 17.

70   Moy, 82–94.

71   Wong, 241.

72   Schiller, 1.

73   I borrowed the term from Hamamoto's book. See its page 1.

74   Hamamoto, 2–3.

75   Wong, 9.

76   Marchetti, 5.

77   As quoted by Karen Ma in *The Modern Madame Butterfly* (Rutland, Vt., and Tokyo: Charles E. Tuttle Company, 1996), 17.

78   See *Harvard Law Review* 106:8 (June 1, 1993), 1926–1943.

79   Ibid., 1930–1931.

80   Ibid., 1934.

81   Ibid., 1936.

82   Ibid., 1937.

83   Ibid., 1938.

84   Clarence Spigner, "Teaching Multiculturalism from the Movies: Health and Social Well-being," *Shared Differences: Multicultural Media and Practical Pedagogy*, ed. Diane Carson and Lester Friedman (Urbana: University of Illinois Press, 1995), 106.

85   Herbert Horikawa, "Psychological Implications of Asian Stereotypes in the Media," *Ethnic and Racial Images in American Film and Television*.

86   Ibid.

87   Ibid., 162.

88   Hagedorn, 78.

89   Arthur Webb, "Not Quite Gold, The Strange Case of Kristi Yamaguchi," *The Journal of the American Chamber of Commerce* 30:4 (April 1, 1993), 56.

90   John Fiske, *Television Culture* (London: Routledge, 1987), 248.

91   Eugenia Kaw, "Medicalization of Racial Features: Asian American Women and Cosmetic Surgery," *Medical Anthropology Quarterly* 7:1 (March 1993), 75–89.

92   Moy, 126.

93   Ibid., 20.

94   Erika Surat Andersen, "Review: Mississippi Masala," *Film Quarterly* 46:4 (Summer 94), 25–26.

95   Carlos Mendez, "Melodramatic Margaret Minces the Media Mavens," *AsianWeek* (Dec. 23, 1994), 24.

96   See "MANAA's Media Awards Dinner to Honor Cho, Yang and Wong," *AsianWeek* (Nov. 4, 1994), 15.

97   Monika Guttman, "One-Woman Cho," *USA Weekend* (Sept. 16–18, 1994), 8.

98   Ibid.

99   John Carmen, "Margaret Cho Breaks Ground in Sitcom Role," *San Francisco Chronicle* (May 10, 1994), E-1.

100   Joann Faung Jean Lee, "Margaret the 'All-American Bust' of TV," *AsianWeek* (Dec. 2, 1994), 6.

101   As quoted by Darby Li Po Price, " 'All American Girl' and the American Dream," *Critical Mass: A Journal of Asian American Cultural Criticism* 2:1 (Winter 1994), 138.

102   Gina Marchetti, "Ethnicity, the Cinema and Cultural Studies," *Unspeakable Images: Ethnicity and the American Cinema*, ed. Lester Friedman (Urbana and Chicago: University of Illinois Press, 1991), 284.

103   Wong, 1–55.

104   Tiana (Thi Thanh Nga), "The Long March—From Wong to Woo: Asians in Hollywood," *Cineaste*, 21:4 (1995), 39.

105   Angela Pao, "The Eyes of the Storm: Gender, Genre and Cross-Casting in Miss Saigon," *Text and Performance Quarterly* 12 (1992), 21–39.

106   Wong, 40.

107   Oriental Actors of America to Actors Equity Association of New York, "Asian Roles for Asian Actors," *Bridge* 3:3 (June 1974), 4.

108   Kevin Brownlow, 327.

109   Wong, 21–29.

110   David Gritten, "Salaam Mississippi," *Los Angeles Times* (Feb. 9, 1992), Calendar Section.

111   Ruthanne Lum McCunn, "Adrienne Telemaque," in *Chinese American Portraits; Personal Histories 1828–1988* (San Francisco: Chronicle Books, 1988), 133.

112   McCunn, 133.

113   For a comprehensive account of the new cultural theories, see both Gina Marchetti, "Ethnicity," 277–307, and Andrea S. Walsh, *Women's Film and Female Experience: 1940–1950* (New York: Praeger, 1984), 8–11.

114   See Mikhail Bakhtin, "Discourse in the Novel," *The Dialogic Imagination* (Austin: University of Texas Press, 1981, trans. C. Emerson and M. Holquist). See also Tzvetan Todorov, *Mikhail Bakhtin: The Dialogical Principle* (Minneapolis: University of Minnesota Press, 1984).

115   Raymond Williams, *Marxism and Literature* (London: Oxford University Press), 123–24.

116   Stuart Hall, "Encoding/Decoding," *Culture, Media, Language,* ed. Stuart Hall et al. (London: University of Birmingham, 1980), 128–38.

117   See the video *Representation and the Media,* which is considered one of the landmark lectures delivered by Stuart Hall, available through Media Education Foundation in Northampton, Mass.

118   Marchetti, "Ethnicity," 254.

119   Four theoretical essays stand as landmarks in the Latin American film movement: Glauber Rocha's "The Aesthetics of Hunger" (1965); Fernando Solanas and Octavio Getino's "Towards a Third Cinema" (1969); Julio Garcia Espinosa's "For an Imperfect Cinema" (1970); and Jorge Sanjines's "Problems of Form and Content in Revolutionary Cinema" (1976). All four are included in *Twenty-five Years of the New Latin American Cinema,* ed. Michael Chanan (London: BFI and Channel Four, 1983).

120   The "auteur theory" in film emphasizes how great films come from great directors and underplays sociohistorical contextual analysis.

121   See Paul Willemen, "The Third Cinema Question: Notes and Reflections," *Questions of Third Cinema,* ed. Jim Pines and Paul Willemen (London: British Film Institute, 1989), 9; also Teshome Gabriel, *Third Cinema in the Third World—The Aesthetics of Liberation* (1982).

122   Willemen, 7.

123   Renee Tajima, "Moving the Image: Asian American Independent Filmmaking 1970–1990," *Moving the Image: Independent Asian Pacific American Media Arts,* ed. Russell Leong (Los Angeles: UCLA Asian American Studies Center, 1991), 21.

124   Robert Nakamura, "Visual Communications: The Early Years," *In Focus* 6:1, 9.

125   bell hooks, "The cultural mix: an interview with Wayne Wang" *Reel to Real: Race, Sex and Class at the Movies* (New York: Routledge, 1996), 139.

Documentaries As Social History

ALTHOUGH IT HAS BEEN THE DRAMATIC FILMS (mostly in the 1990s) that have earned Asian American filmmakers both popular and critical attention, documentaries have been, and remain, the predominant genre of Asian American cinema. It was a significant corpus of highly acclaimed documentary films (rooted in the collective memories, visions, and aspirations of Asian Americans) that first presented viable alternatives to Hollywood's stereotypes and made their impacts known. Loni Ding's *Nisei Soldier: Standard Bearer of an Exiled People* (1983) and *The Color of Honor* (1987), for example, helped make history when they were screened in the U.S. Congress during the successful Japanese American redress campaign. Tiana's (Thi Thanh Nga) *From Hollywood to Hanoi* (1994) was also shown to Congress in celebration of President Clinton's decision to lift the twenty-year-long trade embargo against Vietnam. Lee Mun Wah's *The Color of Fear* (1995) has been widely adopted across university campuses, as well as by government agencies and corporate America (for example, the Department of Defense, the U.S. Navy, the CIA, the U.S. Treasury, Hewlett Packard, and Levi Strauss) for public education and sensitivity training. In the 1980s, Arthur Dong's *Sewing Woman* (1982), Steven Okazaki's *Unfinished Business: The Japanese American Internment Cases* (1986), Lise Yasui's *Family Gathering* (1988), and Christine Choy and Renee Tajima's *Who Killed Vincent Chin?* (1988) won Academy Award nominations. More recently, Steven Okazaki's *Days of Waiting,* Freida Lee Mock's *Maya Lin: A Strong Clear Vision* and Jessica Yu's *Breathing Lessons* claimed Oscars in 1991, 1995, and 1996, respectively.

This chapter examines the nonfiction film, the earliest and most vibrant Asian American film genre. In the movie industry, feature films mean prestige and profits, while most documentaries earn neither money nor name recognition. As TV documentarist Anthony Chan wrote, "Life sure isn't cute when you're an Asian living in America. It's worse when you're doing docs about the Asian experience in America. . . . You'd make a better living selling real estate in Monterey Park 'cause making documentaries isn't money heaven."[1] Nonetheless, documentary films have become the dominant genre in Asian American cinema, and they continue to thrive today. In part, this documentary impulse is the result of limited funding and resources. "Even today," said Robert Nakamura, "it's the access to major funding to do feature films that's the root cause of it. Documentaries and short films are much more accessible in terms of financing."[2] To a certain extent, this preeminence of documentaries also reflects a conscious ideological commitment on the part of Asian Americna filmmakers. As discussed in Chapter 1, Asian American cinema, from its inception, assumed an irreverent (even subversive) role outside commercial mainstream productions.[3] As Luis Francia, a Filipino American film curator and critic, puts it:

> The documentary thus becomes an alter ego to the filmmaker's "I," probing for the parameters of what it means to be Asian American. It also becomes a way of subverting official history, to include the points of view that have been allowed to slip through the cracks. . . . In Asian American cinema the documentary has become the logical antithesis to the . . . mainstream view of Asian American culture and history.[4]

For many Asian American independents, the medium of documentary film is much more democratic than the commercial drama. "Documentaries have always been much more open-minded in the subjects that they explore," commented Kayo Hatta, "and feature films and dramatic films have been much more limited . . . less democratic and much more elite."[5] In an illuminating interview, Steven Okazaki offered similar explanations for the prevalence of documentary filmmaking among Asian Americans:

> Well, I think there are a couple reasons. One is that there was a need initially to sort of put the history down and say, "This is where we came from [and] this is our background," before "This is part of who we are." I think it's difficult to say, "This is who we are," without giving the background and that has kind of been done and now people want to work in more contemporary settings and within a dramatic setting. But there is also the economic factor that there are not that many dramatic or feature films, because those are harder to get funded and there's not a large theatrical audience for those films, yet.[6]

The majority of Asian American documentaries (mostly historical films) fall into three distinctive categories: personal diary films or family portraits, biographical histories, and social issue films. As indicated by the subheadings in this chapter, each subgenre is dictated both by a special purpose and by its intended audience. The diary films and portraits present Asian Americans as subjects of history; talking heads biographies are made to locate a new historical consciousness; and social issue documentaries provide information, urge change, and suggest solutions. My discussion in the following pages will center on three areas of their productions: the creative process in making the documentary (themes and contents), the composing and editing process (film forms and film language), and the aesthetic innovations involved.

HISTORY AS SUBJECT: PERSONAL DIARY FILMS AND FAMILY PORTRAITS

> Oftentimes, what is passed on as recorded history is what a certain group of people has chosen to remember. Ultimately, all history is point of view, and those that are in power are the ones who are above to record their view of past events. Clearly, the real histories of many people are either distorted or completely left out in such a process. It is the task of the *Pearls* television series to address one such history—that of Americans of Asian descent.[7]

Consequently, history has become one of the basic themes of Asian American documentaries. Traditionally, Asian American history was either celebrated, as a contributor of exotic customs to this country, or studied as a series of painful histories of victimization. Asian Americans in turn are portrayed as forever victims—in the words of historian Yuji Ichioka, portrayed as "objects" instead of as "subjects" of history. To address this problem, Sucheng Chan, in the preface to her textbook *Asian Americans: An Interpretive History*, called for a new vision in studying Asian American history, which "sees members of minority groups as agents of history—men and women who make choices that shape their lives, even when these may be severely limited by conditions beyond their control."[8]

In the last three decades, a large body of historical documentaries has been created to recover Asian American stories that have been left unwritten or omitted from the annals of official history. In 1989, Loni Ding spoke about her strategies as a Chinese American filmmaker. "As a producer, I have become more and more interested in developing new forms, new ways of telling the story. Mainly, I have been looking for more subjectivity, and searching for the first-person voice."[9] A veteran filmmaker who has been making TV documentaries since 1969, Ding's personal vision of subjectivity has helped establish a trademark of Asian American films. This strategy of seeking Asian American subjectivity should be viewed as a reaction to the mainstream media's imperialist and hegemonic gaze, as well as their attempt to position viewers within their subjectivity. Desire to resist that positioning drives independent filmmakers to have their own subjectivity represented.

This subjective approach often starts with the most personal, immediate, and direct stories—personal or family histories. As Noel Izon, project director of the TV series *Pearls* (1978), wrote, "Our approach has been to design what we call a personalized historical documentary. In each program, we focus on living people and attempt to combine the clarity of historical facts with the richness of these peoples' lives."[10] Interestingly, most of the early better-known Asian American films (and the number is still growing) are "personal diary films," or "family portraits," as Elizabeth Weis calls them, where the filmmakers' public and private lives intersect.[11] According to Weis, "There is a trend among independent filmmakers to make documentaries about their own families. . . . The urge behind these films comes from the filmmakers' desire to understand themselves through their origins—genetic and ethnic."[12] Prominent examples of this genre include both the classics and newer films, such as Eddie Wong's *Wong Sinsaang* (1971), Felicia Lowe's *China: Land of My Father* (1979), Arthur Dong's Oscar-nominated *Sewing Woman* (1982), Lisa Hsia's *Made in China: A Search for Roots* (1985), Lise Yasui's *Family Gathering* (1988), Christine Choy and Renee Tajima's *Yellow Tale Blues: Two American Families* (1990), Kip Fulbeck's *Banana Split* (1990), Rea Tajiri's *History and Memory* (1991), Sharon Jue's *My Mother Thought She Was Audrey Hepburn* (1991), Janice Tanaka's *Who's Going to Pay for These Donuts Anyway* (1992), Paul Kwan's *Anatomy of a Springroll* (1993), Wendy Hanamura's *Honor Bound: A Personal Journey* (1993), and Sokly "Don Bonus" Ny's *a.k.a. Don Bonus* (1995), to name some of the better-known.

A common characteristic of diary films is the personal voice. "The presence of the filmmaker as first person observer," John Esaki noted, "is a vital component of these films."[13] Unlike the self-effacing cinema vérité artists (who mainly played the role of provocateurs), the filmmakers turn the camera or tape recorder on themselves, as the ones who actually participated in the presented historical experience. Often they are very straightforward about their antihegemonic positioning and purpose for making the films. This practice of using documentary filmmaking as a vehicle of reclaiming cultural heritage and personal identity is especially common among Sansei (third-generation Japanese American) filmmakers. Lise Yasui, Rea Tajiri, and Janice Tanaka are three typical examples of such documentarians. As its title aptly indicates, *Family Gathering* is the story of a hidden family history excavated by filmmaker Lise Yasui, the daughter of a Japanese American physician father and a Caucasian mother. The film begins with this voice-over, "On December 12, 1941, five days after the Japanese attacked Pearl Harbor, my grandfather was arrested by the FBI." In her attempts to recover her family history, especially the story of her grandfather, Yasui discovered a family mystery about her grandfather's death. She learned from her father that twenty-eight years ago her grandfather had committed suicide. This personal inquiry into her family history takes Yasui back some fifty years, through three generations and across four states.

Similarly, Janice Tanaka made the poignant *Donuts* into a personal quest to locate her long-missing father, Jack Koto Tanaka, whom she had not seen since she was three years old. "After the death of my mother in 1988," the filmmaker narrates at the beginning of the video, "I began looking for my father." Shot in the interview format, the film begins with a shadowy, dark image of her father looming over the screen, symbolizing a blurred memory of a long-forgotten piece of her family history. After finding her father at a halfway house for the mentally ill in Los Angeles, the filmmaker finally comes to terms with her heritage. "When you have a past," as Janice Tanaka observes, "it's easier to believe the present has a reason . . . with this insight one can look to the future with hope."[14]

Although Rea Tajiri, in filming *History and Memory*, does not appear to convey a personal sense of urgency about her roots, she certainly shares the desire to find her own cultural identity through an exploration of her family's history. She poetically explains her feelings of uprootedness as a Sansei by saying, "I began searching because I felt lost, ungrounded, somewhat like a ghost that floats over terrain witnessing others living their lives and yet not having one of its own."[15] What emerges from her search for roots is a complex story of suppressed history, both personal and collective.

Similar themes are explored by filmmakers of other ethnicities. Chinese American Sharon Jue's film *My Mother Thought She Was Audrey Hepburn*, according to its catalog description, is "a freshing stream of consciousness autobiography." Using the name of Suzanne for the main character, Jue made the film into a personal statement about growing up Asian American in a 99.63 percent white community. Jue's mother was a pivotal figure in the process of exploring her personal identity. Her mother was proud to dress like Audrey Hepburn or Jackie Kennedy, thinking she could attain the American dream if only she modeled herself after them. Very early in her life, Jue was taught a "Chinese self-hatred" and whiteness admiration. By showcasing Asian faces, Chinese movie posters, and Chinatown streets, the film became a personal odyssey of cultural awakening for the filmmaker.

Shot by the central character himself and produced in collaboration with veteran filmmaker Spencer Nakasako, *a.k.a. Don Bonus* is the video self-portrait of a young Cambodian immigrant growing up in today's America. Back in 1979, three-year-old Sokly Ny and his family escaped from the Khmer Rouge on foot, traveling through the jungle and finally reaching San Francisco. Now an eighteen-year-old high school senior, Sokly "Don Bonus" Ny turns the camera on himself and looks into his own struggle in school and life in general. The intimacy of the mise-en-scène and the filmmakers' openness about their own experiences make the video into an emotionally compelling and stunningly honest film diary.

Turning the camera on his parents' interracial relationship, Kip Fulbeck's *Banana Split* is also a personal exploration of his own experience as a biracial child (half-Chinese and half-white). In a standard daily diary format, Fulbeck addresses biracial ethnicity, peer pressure, interethnic dating, and media stereotypes about Asian American men under the rubric of twenty-five stories (dated diary entries), ranging from "love story" and "street story" to "spiritual story" and "Zen story." The movie stills, family photos, and newspaper clippings, together with Chinese language and music, become the background for Fulbeck's fast-paced monologue. Close to the end, in one of the most interesting entries, Fulbeck writes a self-reflective comment, dated June 4, on self-enforced cultural essentialism among Asian Americans: "This piece [the film] gets rejected from an Asian American festival. An insider tells me to submit it under my Chinese name."

Vietnamese American filmmaker Paul Kwan co-wrote and co-directed *Anatomy of a Springroll*, which is based on his childhood sensory memories of cooking, eating, and sharing the most celebrated Vietnamese food, the spring roll. "Food is everyone's first language," as the voice-over states at the beginning. The film mythologizes Vietnamese food culture as a celebration of his ancestral spirit as well as a way to connect to his native land. Against the background of his family kitchen, and the food stalls and bustling markets in both San Francisco and Saigon, Kwan focuses the camera constantly on the hands, utensils, and various ingredients (peppers, cilantro, and chilies) used to make the spring roll. The process of making and enjoying the rolls is meticulously documented and nostalgically celebrated as his family history. The NAATA's distribution catalog states it well: "In America, cooking is often a solitary experience, but in Vietnam it is a family affair, with everyone cutting, chopping, and stirring while chattering." The difficulties of assimilation are symbolized by its commercialization. Two animated robots are shown working on an assembly line, mass producing boxes of spring rolls, which are humorously judged by a "crunch-o-meter." A huge American microwave spoils the taste of the century-old style of food. But the film ends on a positive note. After a trip to Saigon, sampling the rich and varied food of his homeland, Kwan returns to America, determined to carry on his family and community tradition by learning "the last recipe" from his now seventy-six-year-old mother.

Some film critics have recently highlighted the significance of autobiographical films that have flourished in American since 1968.[16] This type of film has challenged, in varying degrees, the traditional assumptions about autobiographies—a tactic of self-disclosure typically deployed by women and minorities.[17] Third Cinema critic Teshome Gabriel keenly observes in a different context:

Here I do not mean autobiography in its usual Western sense of a narrative by and about a single subject. Rather, I am speaking of a multi-generational and trans-individual autobiography, *i.e.* a symbolic auto-biography where the collective subject is the focus. A critical scrutiny of this extended sense of autobiography (perhaps hetero-biography) is more than an expression of shared experience, it is a mark of solidarity with people's lives and struggles.[18]

Indeed, this "multi-generational and trans-individual autobiography" often transcends the traditional genre limitations, because the cross-cultural life experiences cannot easily be contained within the limits of one single cinematic category. Such autobiographies often approach subjectivity by focusing on a variety of social relationships through such traditional institutions as the extended family, the kinship network, and religious rituals. Often, an intensely personal story is told in relationship to family and community, mixing both shared racial identities and a collective past in a nonlinear chronology. Arthur Dong's *Sewing Woman*, for example, is at once a personal story of the thirty-year survival fight Dong's own mother's waged in the garment factories, although her recollections are articulated through a fictionalized script based on oral histories.

These family portraits have become a natural outgrowth of the diary films. In her journey to reclaim family history in *Honor Bound* (the touching and emotional story of her father as a soldier in the famed 442nd Regiment), television reporter Wendy Hanamura narrates the story of the Nisei unit, which suffered the highest rates of casualty and became the most decorated military unit in American history. Based on her father's memoir, Hanamura's poetic voice that relates the story tells as much about her father as about his friends, his comrades, and the foot soldiers who died on the battle field. With pride and tears, the veterans recall how they rescued the "Lost Battalion" of 211 from the 36th Texas division at a price of some 800 killed or wounded. The ratio of four killed to every one rescued, according to Eric Saul, the on-screen military historian, was extraordinary. Another fascinating part of their story is the friendly fight and rivalry between the exuberant Hawaiian-born Japanese Americans and the more reserved mainland Nisei. However, the Hawaiian soldiers' first-ever visit to the internment camps during their training soon earned the mainlanders the highest respect from their Hawaiian brothers.

In re-creating her family's camp experience in *History and Memory*, Tajiri uses a myriad of both conventional and unconventional sources—personal diaries, private letters, family albums, artifacts, and amateur video footage from the National Archives. But her most important sources of historical information are oral histories. Utilizing direct interviewing techniques, Tajiri sought to excavate collective memory as a set of events stored, preserved, and shared in the minds of three generations of her family members. These personal memories are often scattered, sometimes nightmarish, and even contradictory. As the text in the prologue reads, "The spirit of my grandfather witnesses my father and mother as they have an argument about the nightmares their daughter has been having on the 20th anniversary."[19]

Two South Asian documentaries can also be loosely defined as family histories. Mira Nair's *So Far from India* (1983) and Indu Krishnan's *Knowing Her Place* (1990) poignantly paint portraits of extended Indian families pulled between two cultures. In *So Far from India*, Ashok Sheth moves alone to New York to seek a better life soon after his marriage. His pregnant wife, Hansa, is caught between the expectation of traditions and the Americanization of her husband. At the film's end, after Ashok Seth's visit back to India, Hansa and her son remain behind and Ashok returns alone to New York. The film details the rationale and ritual of his arranged marriage, his sheltered life in a small-town middle-class family, and the painful effect of separation between husband and wife. Indu Krishnan's film *Knowing Her Place*, shot over a period of three years, follows the life of Vasundara Varadhan, an Asian Indian woman who spent her early childhood in the United States and was then sent back to live in India. She entered an arranged marriage at the age of sixteen. The film traces the consequences of this union and her return to American life as a wife and mother of two sons.

In these personal, or family, histories, the "voice" more than the "face" assembles the stories in a subjective mode. Always passionate and personal, the voice in these films is generally in the first-person singular "I" or the plural "we," instead of the neutral or objective "they." This voice allows the filmmaker to speak with emotion and feelings, rather than in a disengaged, third-person tone of nonchalance (which has been the hallmark of older documentaries). Arthur Dong's *Sewing Woman* is based entirely on a monologue by Zem Ping Dong, the filmmaker's mother. She recalls how she was groomed for an arranged marriage at thirteen, and how she and her child remained in China while her husband went to America (he didn't return until after World War II). To join her husband in the States, she was forced to disown her first son and remarry her husband as a "war bride." After working in San Francisco's garment factories for over three decades, she was finally able to bring her first-born son to America. *Days of Waiting* (Steven Okazaki's Academy Award–winning biographical film on Estelle Ishigo, a gifted Caucasian artist who was interned with her Japanese American husband) is also narrated in a dramatic first-person monologue. The monologue takes the form of a letter to a fellow camp internee, based on Estelle Ishigo's book *Lone Heart Mountain*, giving the film its intimacy. This deep and passionate first-person voice changes to the third-person, but only when Estelle's own story comes to an end.

Camera angle and frame of the shots also contribute to the subjective dimension of the stories told. Tajima observes that "the great achievement of the Asian American documentary may be its intimacy. Cameras rarely stray far from the subject, and there is little of the visual remove of a wide-angle lens, or the attitude of remove of cinema vérité and old-style broadcast journalists."[20] Loni Ding calls this management of field size "camera's gaze." She reminisces about the origin of the idea:

> Someone once startled me with the proposal that if you were to gaze at anybody long enough, you could become enamored with them. Like the primal bonding of mother to infant. . . . Perhaps the gaze of the camera does the same, in the hand of someone who turns towards the camera subject with respect. . . . A human gaze is empowering; equally empowering is the camera's gaze.[21]

Specifically, Loni Ding uses the term *tableaux*, which means a creative intermixing between the props and subjective reflections and memories. As she explains, "A tableau is conceived as a still life or scene where objects are brought together that might not ordinarily be arranged in that particular way. They are not 're-creations' or simulations of the past, as in naturalistic 'flashbacks' or docu-drama, but are stylized representations of subjective reflections and memories."[22] Ding cites an example from *Island of Secret Memories* (1987), a documentary about eleven-year-old Joe's trip to Angel Island, in San Francisco Bay, where his grand-father was detained. "All the personal items—the bed, a bottle of Chinese pills, a Chinese-English dictionary, a pair of spectacles—compose a tableau." When the boy puts on his grandfather's glasses, "he 'sees' another tableau from the past: an interrogation is in progress, played in limbo—a young Chinese male is being questioned by the immigration officer."[23]

By focusing less on the events of history than on the impact of those events in human terms, the family portraits have bridged the gap between public history and private lives. Turning the camera inward allows the filmmaker to examine how the historical process affects individuals. As Sumiko Higashi remarks, Asian American documentary films have turned the "documentary filmmaking practice into an investigation of the intersection of family dynamics and history."[24] In other words, these films provide an emotional dimension that gives Asian American history a human face. Loni Ding's most recent TV series *Ancestors: Coolies, Sailors, Settlers in the Americas* (1996) is a good case in point. The strength of the film is its personal touch. It brings history to life through personal recollections, family photo albums, and historic film footage. The story told is not one of bland facts and figures, but rather one of human interest that relates a personal pride in the accomplishments of the main characters despite the many obstacles they faced. This emotional approach functions as an important corrective to the widely held stereotype of Asians and Asian Americans as stoic, emotionless people. The presence of the individual faces and voices in the films not only challenges the "objective" story of history, but also shows that how individuals and groups remember their histories (often in bits and pieces) is just as important as what "actually" happened. These documentaries testify to historian Michael Novak's bold assumption that different national experiences are evidenced less in "ideas" and "words" than in "affections and imaginations."[25] In short, these films rely on highly emotional appeals rather than on a cool and detached veneer of objectivity.

Ding summarizes the importance of documenting everyday life in her films. "I'm interested in stretching the documentary genre. I'm interested in the video diary, experimental documentaries, in films that are on one hand grounded in the world and in the faces of people that we recognize, those in our daily life. We use the streets, the sounds, the smells, the people that we actually encounter in real life."[26] Asian American films in general do not focus on politics or direct social action, "for that is only the tip of the iceberg, resting upon a less visible, but very real, politicized consciousness."[27] Rather, they look to the culture of everyday life, "where the contradictory interests of capitalist societies are continually negotiated and contested."[28] Diary and family portrait films have moved away from the "movers and shakers" in history and given voice to the "inarticulate." They have documented, so to speak, a positive Asian American history as opposed to the more familiar history of Asian victimization in America. In this sense, the films have served an oppositional function in historical discourse.

HISTORY AS CONSCIOUSNESS: BIOGRAPHIES AND COMMUNAL HISTORY

In his trenchant analysis of the "unmeltable ethnics," historian Michael Novak defines "the new ethnicity" as "a form of historical consciousness."[29] Some well-respected studies in social history have demonstrated how all ethnic groups have developed their own historical personalities and consciousness. Lawrence Levine, for example, in his seminal work *Black Culture and Black Consciousness*, called on historians "to expand their own consciousness by examining the consciousness of those they have hitherto ignored or neglected."[30] In his study of the Chicano experience, Richard Griswold del Castillo emphasizes that "since the late nineteenth century, Mexican American history has also been characterized by creative and constructive responses to changing circumstances."[31] John Modell, in his study of the Los Angles Japanese American community, rejected the tendency to view Japanese Americans as victims of majority culture. Instead, he argues, "Neither wholly autonomous nor simply passive recipients of the malign initiatives of majority Americans, minorities have evolved varied attitudes and institutions appropriate to their circumstances."[32] Until very recently, Asian American history was essentially faceless, with the story usually told in terms of an anonymous "they." As a counterpoint, one way to document the new historical consciousness is to create profiles of Asian American personalities and record communal histories. Clearly, in recent years, Asian American cinema is moving slowly from the realm of personal and family histories to biographies and communal histories. Film biographies of one kind or another and community portraits are produced in an effort to humanize people as individuals, rather than as types.

So many biographical films have been produced that it has become possible to treat them as a separate category of Asian American documentary. Film profiles have been created, and still are being made, for Asian American artists, writers, poets, musicians, political leaders, and ordinary citizens alike. Some selected titles include Alan Kondo's *I Told You So* (1974), on famed Japanese American poet Lawson Inada; Renee Cho's *Jazz Is My Native Language: A Portrait of Toshiko Akiyoshi* (1983); John Esaki's *Yuki Shimoda: An Asian American Actor* (1985); Joan Saffa's *Maxine Hong Kingston: Talking Story* (1990); John De Graff's *A Personal Matter: Gordon Hirabayashi vs. the United States* (1992); Ahrin Mishan and Nick Rothenberg's *Bui Doi: Life Like Dust* (1994), a profile of Ricky Phan, a Vietnamese American gang member who is currently serving an eleven-year sentence for armed robbery in a California state prison; Rea Tajiri and Pat Saunders's *Yuri Kochiyama: Passion for Justice* (1993); Keiko Tsuno's *The Story of Vinh* (1990), a touching, sad story of the biracial child of a U.S. GI and a Vietnamese mother; *Play It Again, Nam!* (1993), which looks at the life and art of renowned Korean American video artist Nam June Paik; and Freida Lee Mock's *Maya Lin: A Strong Clear Vision,* about the celebrated young designer of the Vietnam memorial wall in Washington, D.C.

A derivative form of film biographies profile groups instead of individuals. Among the better-known entries in the group biography category are Christine Choy's *From Spikes to Spindles* (1976); Allie Light's *Mitsuye and Nellie: Asian American Poets* (1981); Steven Okazaki's *Unfinished Business* (1986); Christine Choy's *Mississippi Triangle* (1984); Yuet-Fung Ho's *Eight-Pound Livelihood* (1984); Felicia Lowe's *Carved in Silence* (1987); Arthur Dong's *Forbidden City, U.S.A.* (1989) and his 1990 documentary *Claiming a Voice,* which chronicles the twenty-year history of Visual Communications; Steven Okazaki's *Survivors: Forty Years After Hiroshima* (1982), a tale of twenty atomic bomb survivors who endured four decades of physical, psychological, and social traumas; Valerie Soe's *Art to Art: Expressions of Asian American Women* (1993); Scott Tsuchitani's *Meeting at Tule Lake* (1994); and Loni Ding's *Ancestors: Coolies, Sailors, Settlers in the Americas* (1996).

To record people's life stories before they die, Asian American filmmakers are pressured "in a race to beat the chronological clock."[33] "The 1960s–1970s was crucial to Asian American history," in the words of Renee Tajima, "as the Manong [first-generation Filipino immigrants], Issei [first-generation Japanese immigrants], bachelor-society sojourners and other pioneers were beginning to age."[34] Christine Choy, the longtime documentary filmmaker (who has made about fifty films since 1972), told a group of Asian American youths about her purpose in making *Mississippi Triangle* (a film about a little-known, century-old Chinese community in the Mississippi Delta): "These people in the Delta are dying out and it's our responsibility to document their history. Your mother, father, grandparents—there's so much history to be told."[35] She felt compelled to carry out a rescue mission as she underscored the importance of community work:

> As an artist, I have a responsibility to my community. That's primary, and any other experience and work is secondary to me. It's important that in 1984 we portray our history and art even to contradictions in our community—interethnic prejudice, relations between men and women, generational problems. Those issues need to be done and have not been done so far. And no one is going to do them besides Asian artists.[36]

With very little written documentation, the process of filmmaking involves extensive original research and fieldwork. The behind-the-scenes production process becomes an extraordinary story itself. Often, the filmmakers' ethnicity does not necessarily guarantee their cameras' access into the community. Sometimes, because of the sensitivity and intimacy of the subject matter, the filmmakers encounter skepticism and, occasionally, even strong resistance from within. Arthur Dong recalled that when he started the *Forbidden City* project, about Chinatown's oldest nightclub, some older Chinese warned him against investigating the subject: "Forbidden City? It was a sleaze joint! Don't dig this up again!"[37] Some Asian American women activists reacted even more negatively. They bluntly demanded, "We've had enough problems trying to deal with that image—that sexy-Oriental-woman mystique, that 'mysterious' image. Why are you digging this up? Hide it! Bury it! We don't want to see it!"[38]

In filming *Mississippi Triangle*, Christine Choy and her crew were confronted with similar problems against "airing dirty laundry." For example, when they found Arlee Hen, an elderly Black Chinese woman, they decided that she was a subject of special sensitivity for the story. However, since Hen was completely isolated and ostracized by the Chinese American community, Choy and her crew had to sneak back into Hen's home, but only after feigning that they had left the day before. Naturally, by making a Black Chinese woman the major on-camera character, Choy exposes a topic that is usually considered taboo. After the film was shown, Hoover

Lee, the Chinese mayor in Louise, Mississippi, complained that the film spent too much time looking at the "down side of things—gambling, pool rooms, rundown stories."[39] Choy, the director, saw the issue differently. She asked for a more critical self-examination of Asian American communities.[40]

Like other independent filmmakers have been doing since the 1970s, Asian American film biographers have relied heavily on oral history, that is, direct interviews or personal monologues with very minimal narration. As a strategy and a form, the interview-based films privilege the points of view of those whose experiences are being portrayed, avoiding the mediation of an outside "expert." The "talking heads" carry the story with no third voice imposed between the subjects and the audience. This is a technique utilized in almost all of Choy's films, from *Mississippi Triangle* and *Who Killed Vincent Chin?* to her newest film, *Shot Heard 'Round the World* (1997). Without the intrusive narration or expert analysis, the subjects' recollections appear to direct or motivate the visual sequence. In *Mississippi Triangle,* for instance, instead of a narrator's voice guiding the viewer, what moves the film forward is a topical structure based on the social institutions in the area—the cotton industry, retail businesses, the family, the school system, the church, and various political organizations. "Each topic is dealt with by juxtaposing interviews with White, Black, and Chinese respondents, so that each perspective is not only voiced but also set off against the perspective of a community with which it is in conflict."[41]

By removing voice-over, the subjectivity of the historical experience also shifts somewhat from the filmmakers to the audience. Without narration, the viewers are placed in a "helpless" position to draw their own conclusions from a montage of impressions, opinions, and eyewitness accounts. Of course, this practice does not eliminate the subjectivity of the filmmakers' shooting and editing, but at least the audience is allowed more critical space to develop their own interpretations. In contrast to the hegemonic viewer positioning in most industry films, Asian American filmmakers have enlisted the viewers as active discursive partners in the creative process.

What is more, these biographical histories are organized around collective instead of individual points of views. Often a personal profile can easily become the frame for the story of a group. Take Christine Choy's *From Spikes to Spindles,* for example. Although the film was introduced by a New York Chinatown rally (in support of a Chinese American man unjustly accused of assault and resisting arrest) the film's focus is the history of Chinese immigrants in American labor from the railroads to the garment industry (hence the title *From Spikes to Spindles*). The plural voice in these films subverts the unifocal or bifocal point of view and gives credence to multiple perspectives. In the same vein, Steven Okazaki's *Unfinished Business* examines the legal cases of Fred Korematsu, Gordon Hirabayashi, and Minoru

Yasui, who challenged the constitutionality of World War II internment all the way to the U.S. Supreme Court. Although their stories are told through first-person accounts, their struggles are skillfully interwoven with the context of wartime hysteria through personal vignettes, vintage home movies, archival government film footage, and witty observations from other internees.

The most eloquent example of this collectivity is Christine Choy's *Mississippi Triangle*. This charming film provides different ways of framing a whole range of questions about race, class, gender, and age, and explores the way in which these issues relate specifically to the Chinese American community. In stressing both intra-ethnic and intra-Asian American community concerns, *Mississippi Triangle* comes to grips with the complexity of the Chinese American experience in the South. No one person monopolizes the voice, so there is no "official" story or point made in the film. There were also three different crews filming the project: a black crew headed by Worth Long, a black folklorist; a white crew led by Allan Siegel, a founding member of New York Newsreel and now Associate Director of Third World Newsreel; and an Asian American crew led by Christine Choy herself. The diversity of these collaborative views helped to map out the contours of different Asian American experiences in the South. In the style of cinema vérité, more than 500 people of different ethnic and class backgrounds were interviewed. "The theory of the melting pot is ludicrous," said Choy. "The races do not exist in harmony. So I wanted to look at those differences, and have each group express its own point of view. This concept made the process of the film very important. That's why we shot it with three crews: one black, one Asian, and one white."[42] Understandably, the three co-directors each look at Delta society from a different perspective, which accounts for a large number of viewpoints. As Gina Marchetti puts it precisely, "No single, unified point of view dominates; rather, a number of perspectives vie for the viewer's attention and support."[43] "The film doesn't tell you anything," Choy remarked in an interview. "It doesn't say go this way or that. If you try to look at individual issues or areas, you might not digest the recurring themes. I hope people see the film two or three times."[44] This film, because it presents a complex and multidimensional Chinese American community from a cross-ethnic and cross-class perspective, is an extremely rare piece of social history in American visual media.

In making biographies, one of the most difficult tasks is how to re-create the past now that the key players are no longer living. Asian American filmmakers have employed at least three useful strategies: filming in docudrama format, using other art forms, and intercutting dramatic episodes with actual documentary footage. To help overcome the difficulties of sources, they have resorted to docudrama (or what Joan Mellen calls the "fictional documentary"), where historical events are re-created in a documentary style, often using real people who are asked to reenact an activity in which they have actually participated. A good example of this format is Robert Nakamura's *Conversations: Before the War/After the War* (1986). The film re-creates the Japanese American internment experience through dramatic scenes staged by three former internees, using traditional on-camera interviews over voice narration. "By having community people play a character, and not themselves, and yet encouraging them to bring forth their own personal stories and experiences, they were able to disclose very real emotions and private feelings without revealing themselves," says Nakamura.[45]

Loni Ding's *Ancestors: Coolies, Sailors, Settlers in the Americas* is even bolder in its approach. According to its program brochure, the pilot program of her NEH-funded, four-part series for the Public Broadcasting Service has employed what the filmmaker calls the "docu-memoir" approach that "stretches the documentary genre to represent a remote and inaccessible past by combining narrative film structure to remembered history and historical records."[46] Drawing on sources from census tracts, newspaper accounts, birth and death records, archeological artifacts, folklore, and period literature, the documentary has brought to life a complex and nearly lost past of journeys that cross three centuries and span half the globe. Through the film's biographer, who bears the name Time Traveler Narrator (TTN), we meet Ho Qua, a Cantonese tea merchant and the world's richest millionaire at the time, who invested half a million dollars (in Mexican silver) in American railroads through his American colleague, John Forbes. We also meet Lau Chung Mun in his garden in Guangdong Province, China, where he tells how his grandfather and two great-uncles were sold to work overseas, "bought and sold like pigs." However, we receive more biographical information about ordinary Asian immigrants: "My name is Wong. . . . My name is Lee. . . . Chang. . . . Chiu. . . . I am part of the Americas because I have been voyaging there for centuries."[47]

Sometimes, with little or no on-location footage, a technique that helps bring the biographies to life is the photo-animation of historical graphics, photos, and paintings, then combining that with dialogue and music, in the style of Ken Burns's classic *The Civil War*. This cross-fertilization of different genres is exemplified in Valerie Soe's *Art to Art: Expressions of Asian American Women*. The documentary is a collective portrait of visual artists Pacita Abad, Hung Liu, Yong Soon Min, and Barbara Takanaga, plus video artists Christine Chang, Christine Choy, Karen Kavery, and Chuleenan Svetvilas. It demonstrates the extraordinary lives and artistic visions of these Asian American women filmmakers, painters, and sculptors by featuring and analyzing their creative works. Likewise, in Okazaki's *Days of Waiting*, Estelle Ishigo's drawings, paintings, and photographs have been joined with actual film footage of camp life at a detention center in Heart Mountain, Wyoming. Okazaki dissolves or cuts back and forth between archival footage and Ishigo's drawings chiefly for dramatic effect. Mostly in shades of black, gray, and brown, Ishigo's own works help dramatize "long lines of people waiting to be fed . . . icy winds and bitter cold, shabby, shivering people with patches on their clothes . . . people with nothing to do but watch the sunset."[48]

This mode of delivery, combining stills and other art forms, also helps the filmmakers solve specific problems of, for example, footage of patchy (broken) English. "Pictures, visuals, B-rolls and cutaways . . ." as Anthony Chan explains, "it all amounts to getting generic shots to cover those hesitant sound bites."[49] Chan cites a specific example from filming *Another Day in America* (1989):

> The Japan-born painter was shy, hesitant and wasn't all that fluent in English. But what he said made great copy for the story. Since my Filipino American shooter gave me plenty of painting footage, I solved this problem by cutting her sound bites—without the hesitation, without the ums and ahs—over visuals of the artist at work. That gave the story a great feel for the art and for her.[50]

Mise-en-scène also lends credibility to the stories that lack extensive live footage of the profiled characters. A careful reading of *Mississippi Triangle* reveals the special care Choy gives the details of her mise-en-scène. The business dealings in the grocery store, the mahjong games behind the counter, the weddings, the parties, and the funerals all become part of the props for the interviews. Tajima comments on Choy's use of mise-en-scène in establishing the frame:

> In composing interviews, Christine Choy . . . searches for and celebrates the clutter of Chinese American households to contextualize the subject. Like John Akomfrah of the Black Audio Film Workshop, who uses ornate and stylized backdrops to elevate the interview frame, Choy's composition employs a complex interplay of light and object in the backdrop. The camera, however, stays up-close probing the interior life of the subject resulting in a masterful economy of a single frame.[51]

Putting Asian American life stories on record only accounts for part of the film biographers' goals. Reshaping cultural memories and locating a submerged historical consciousness is also a critical step in documenting the Asian American experience. In recent years, when conceptualizing the dynamics of ideology and society, neo-Marxist cultural theorists placed special emphasis on the tactical maneuvers employed by varied subordinate social groups. As briefly discussed in Chapter 2, Antonio Gramsci's idea of "common sense" emphasized that ordinary people, even those with relatively little power, were actively engaged in constructing cultural meanings and modifying their social environments.[52] In defining Black genre films, Thomas Cripps made the distinction between Black genre films and so-called "blaxploitation" films. While the latter "redundantly depicts only what has been done *to* blacks, not *by* them," the former celebrates "the combination of triumph over adversity, fellow feeling, and moral superiority of the oppressed, known most recently as 'soul.'"[53]

A remarkable example of how Asian American films celebrate the ways in which Asian American actors and actresses get around the system of discrimination is Arthur Dong's critically acclaimed *Forbidden City, U.S.A.*, a story about San Francisco's Chinatown's oldest Chinese nightclub. Like the Cotton Club of Harlem, Forbidden City represented a unique showplace for Chinese American entertainers involved in all-American productions in the 1930s and 1940s. The tone of the film is set by Charlie Low, the owner of the club, in an on-screen interview. "I wanted to present the modern version of the Chinese girl; not the old fashioned way, all bundled up with four or five pairs of trousers. We can't be backwards all the time, we've got to show the world that we're on an equal basis. Why, Chinese have limbs just as pretty as anyone else!"

The film's producer does not emphasize what the performers were up against so much as how they overcame the difficulties. Through the recollections of several former entertainers, such as the "Chinese Fred Astaire," the "Chinese Sophie Tucker," and the "Chinese Frank Sinatra," the documentary pays tribute to the artists who fought against prejudice within the Chinese American community and racial barriers in the industry. Dancer Dorothy Toy reflects, "We had to be much better than the Caucasians, or else we wouldn't get the bookings." Noel Tay remembers that when applying for a job, she was asked if she ever spoke English, "No. Not a damn word. What do you want to know?" Mary Mammon, another dancer, tells her interviewers, "We heard people ask, 'Do Chinese dance? They don't have any rhythm. And their legs, they're terrible. They've got terrible legs'. . . . But we showed everyone we are as good as anybody else." Larry Ching, a singer, recalls, "Those white guys would come in and say, 'That Chink can't sing, that Chinaman, that slant-eyes.' Being in the business, we had to take some of that. We were supposed to take some of that. But we didn't."[54]

On the one hand, the film recognizes the weight of social power (in setting severe limits to the range of choices open to Asian American artists), while, on the other, it stresses the diverse strategies through which Asian Americans were able to achieve a larger measure of control over their daily lives. As Dong himself reflected, "[The performers] were an inspiration, with their stories of fighting against the system, fighting against what was expected of them, being ostracized, being looked down on because of their personal choices in life. It was inspiring."[55]

Felicia Lowe's elegantly crafted *Carved in Silence* (1987) offers another compelling example. Much less known to ordinary Americans than Ellis Island in

New York Harbor, the Angel Island detention center in San Francisco Bay incarcerated thousands of Chinese and Japanese in the early decades of the twentieth century. In the film, recollections of three survivors, blended with historical footage, become a collective testimony both to the indignities they suffered and to their tactics against the exclusion policy. Invented "paper sons," smuggled coaching messages, and powerfully moving Chinese verses carved on barrack walls offered proof of their ingenuity in fighting the injustice of the system.[56] This film affirms the adaptive capacities of the detainees by showing how they responded to the pressures of incarceration, and how they created instruments through which they could achieve a limited measure of success.

Although Asian Americans were discriminated against in the arts, it was the primary social institutions "that have been most proximate and immediate to human experience—family, church, workplace and neighborhood," that kept Asian Americans culturally resilient.[57] Unlike filmmakers of the past, who focused on marker events and paid little attention to the daily lives of ordinary people, Asian American filmic biographies document a variety of everyday human activities by individuals and communities. Rita Laboux's *Great Branches, New Roots: the Hmong Family* (1983) and Ritu Sarin's *The New Puritans: The Sikhs of Yuba City* (1985), for example, both explore the healing role of the family in the midst of crises. *Between Two Worlds: The Hmong Shaman in America,* produced by Taggart Siegel in 1985, is a touching story of the importance of folk religion for the Hmong community in Chicago.

On the surface, this kind of documentary history may not seem particularly political, yet it is in a rich analytical engagement with social issues. It pays special attention to the residual values of cultural or ethnic traditions. It implicitly recognizes the validity of visions outside the mainstream, endorses alternative cultural traditions, and celebrates the importance of Asian American struggles in history. Contrary to the popular image of Asian Americans as an undifferentiated mass, the documentaries have ascertained the vision, resolve, and actions of selected men and women in Asian American communities. Their historical consciousness is built around their daily struggles with their extended family, kinship networks, religious rituals, cultural customs, and immediate work environment.

HISTORY AS AGENCY:
SOCIAL ISSUE DOCUMENTARIES

Renato Constantino, a Third Cinema filmmaker, once said, "The past should not be the object of mere contemplation if the present is to be meaningful. For if the past were viewed as a 'frozen reality' it would either dominate and immobilize the present or be discarded as irrelevant to today's concerns."[58] Indeed, the importance of learning history is, of course, to know how to interpret the present, act on it, and thereby influence the future. Asian American documentaries, as a historical narrative, not only are concerned with the past, they also have developed an existential theme, a concern for present-day political and social issues. This contemporary orientation has helped develop an "advocacy scholarship," committed to the social practice of history, making it meaningful for the present.[59] Called advocacy cinema and enacted by members of Asian American communities, a lot of these films portray a journey from the past to the present by giving memories of past experiences, current contradictions, and potential sources for empowerment.

This last section examines the third subgenre of Asian American documentaries: films that reflect, draw attention to, and focus on contemporary political and social struggles. Starting in the 1980s, stimulated by some landmark legal cases, and thanks to a surge of research and publications, several dozen social issue documentaries have been produced.[60] Three topics seem to have received the most critical attention: films that smash stereotypes (for some years a central issue for documentarists), films that attempt to treat community issues, and films that attack racism head-on. These films are set apart from each other by form, content, or both, dictated in part by the film's purpose and intended audience. The main aim of this section is to consider in greater depth these three documentary areas in terms of their contemporary significance.

First, a number of films and videos were produced to remake Asian American images. Two outstanding examples are Deborah Gee's 1988 video *Slaying the Dragon* and Valerie Soe's *All Orientals Look the Same*. Built around a core of interviews by filmmakers, scholars, and critics, *Slaying the Dragon* surveys the history of Asian women representations through numerous clips from Hollywood movies. The dragon lady, the geisha girl, and the Connie Chung–style TV anchorwoman capture the essence of the Orientalist fantasies about Asian women. To defuse the racist and sexist intents of the images, critical comments by scholars, humorous reflections from Asian American artists, and mocking voice-overs are offered as interventionist or counter-strategies. *All Orientals Look the Same* (1986), a black-and-white short video (only one-and-a-half minutes long), offers a powerful critique of this racist myth. Using slide dissolves and a repetitive voice-over, producer/director Valerie Soe plays with the title phrase and presents a succession of portraits of Asian Americans and Pacific Islanders. The men and women, old and young, are positioned in different postures and displayed with distinct facial expressions. Depending upon their prior exposure to these diverse populations, viewers are challenged to confront their own deeply held prejudices and misconceptions.

The most recent works in this category have provided analytic and historical contexts for the issues they raise; thus, the boundaries between these works and film biographies can become somewhat blurred. Kip Fulbeck's seven-minute short *Game of Death* (1991), for example, looks at Asian male imagery in America through the Bruce Lee legend. "Using unedited footage from Bruce Lee's last (unfinished) film," goes the distribution catalogue, "Fulbeck examines the various roles he posthumously came to represent—from the filmmaker's own boyhood idol to an Asian American male icon." Fulbeck's more recent *Some Questions for 28 Kisses* (1994) goes a step further into challenging media stereotypes, focusing on interracial dating. "How many times have you seen an Asian man kiss someone on TV?" "Are Asian men socially inept?" "Why are so many newscasting teams white men and Asian women?" Fulbeck responds to these questions by exploring media images, cultural icons, and socialized dating patterns.

Like media stereotypes, diverse community issues involving labor, mixed racial identities, and homosexuality continue to be interesting subjects of documentary interest. The list of films on community issues is long. A selection of titles includes: Long Ding's *Nisei Soldier* and *The Color of Honor*, Richard Gong's *Children of the Railroad Workers* (1981), Curtis Choy's *The Fall of the I-Hotel* (1983), and Helen Liu's *Through Struggle and Strength* (1988). Although some of these works appear dated today (*The Fall of the I-Hotel* was revised), and much of the information they present has since become widely known, it should be noted that each of these works was relevant at the time, and several were enormously influential. Loni Ding's *Nisei Soldier* and *The Color of Honor*, as mentioned before, were part of the campaign to win Japanese American redress for their internment during World War II, a struggle that was won with the passage of The Civil Liberties Act of 1988 by Congress.

A recent topic explored in a number of films is racial classification, and what it is like to be racially unclassified in a society obsessed with race and racial categories. Roddy Bogawa's 16mm feature-length (seventy minutes) *Some Divine Wind* (1991) explores the identity issues for mixed-race Asian Americans through the perspective of an Amerasian youth. Very experimental in style (raw footage intercutting with paintings, cartoons, maps, and distorted portraits), the film confronts and questions the viewer's rigid understanding of racial and ethnic classifications of any sort and examines where those classifications come from (history, media, or government policies). The film's dark, grainy texture, the eerie music, the two voices (male and female), and the two languages (English and Japanese) all highlight the inner struggles of the Amerasian bicyclist constantly on the road. The scrolling texts from a book capture the film's theme: "We don't need 'Roots' to remind us that geneology exerts a strange fascination over people . . . the mixing of genes from two parents in each offspring allows the variability that Darwinian proceses require." In *None of the Above* (1993), filmmaker Erika Surat Andersen, whose mother is Asian Indian and father Danish American, tries to explore what she used to call her "own personal hangup" and find others in the same ambiguous category of multiracials. The film is organized around three central figures: Leslie, a young woman of Native American, African, and European ancestry; Curtis, whose mother is Japanese and father African American; and Henrietta, whose family has been mixed for at least six generations and defies categorization. *None of the Above* successfully addresses the complexities inherent in establishing a biracial or multiracial identity.

Historically, the cinematic image of the homosexual, which has only come into focus in the last two decades, has consistently suffered from stereotypical distortion, derision, and condescension. For some Asian Americans, it is even a taboo subject. Some filmmakers did take on the challenge to work on the subject. Nidhi Singh's *Khush Refugees* (1991), a documentary drama, was one of the pioneering works on the gay experience examined through the interracial gay relationship between Rhul, an Indian immigrant, and Dante, an ex-Marine from suburban Ohio. Pablo Bautista's *Fated to Be Queer* (1992) focuses on the lives of four Filipino gay men in the San Francisco Bay Area. Ming-Yuen S. Ma's *Toc Storee* (1992), according to NAATA's catalogue, addresses the issues of sexuality, subjectivity, tradition, and identity in an Asian gay context. New York video artist Mari Keiko Gonzales's *The Love Thang Trilogy* (1994) consists of three sensual four-minute vignettes portraying different aspects of Asian Pacific lesbian issues and concerns. Based on Allan Berube's groundbreaking book *Coming Out Under Fire: The History of Gay Men and Women in World War II* (1990), Arthur Dong's black-and-white *Coming Out Under Fire* (1994) takes a historical look at the experiences of nine gay and lesbian veterans in the U.S. military.

Of all the films that fall into this mode, the most provocative have been two videos (on one videotape): *Not a Simple Story* (1994) and *Out in Silence, AIDS in the Asian Pacific American Community* (1994). Both directed by Christine Choy, the two intriguing films present Asian Pacific Americans, gay and straight, male and female, who have courageously gone public about being HIV positive. They all speak out with a sense of urgency and a determination to dispel the myth that Asian Americans do not get AIDS. As a punchline from *Out in Silence* goes, "Silence is our culture. We uphold our traditions and family values even when our loved ones are stricken." *Not a Simple Story* profiles Robin, the widowed mother of a young child and the only Asian female in an activist group of AIDS educators. Still mourning her husband who died of AIDS, when Robin herself was diagnosed with HIV she began to worry about her daughter's future. We also meet Vince, an aspiring singer from San Francisco, in *Out in Silence*. He recalled how his initial realization of being gay led him to drop out of his community, leave his close-knit family, and drift to Hawaii and New York. He was shocked when he was diagnosed with HIV. He began to realize how little he, as an Asian American, knew about the disease. To help educate other Asian Americans, he now performs with a gay theater group and lectures to students. Even the act of appearing before a camera is an achievement by itself. Despite the clarion call to be "out of the closet," large segments of the gay Asian community fear that any sort of public exposure may mean loss of jobs, friends, or family support.

Arthur Dong's new award-winning (two awards at the 1997 Sundance Film Festival) documentary *Licensed to Kill* (1997) offers a daring exploration of anti-gay violence in contemporary American society. The film is based on a combination of crime-scene photos, interrogation videos, courtroom footage, and clips of such conservatives as Pat Robertson and Jerry Falwell spreading antigay rhetoric. But at the core of the film are the interviews by the filmmaker of seven convicted murderers (four white, two Black, and one of mixed heritage) serving sentences in state and federal prisons. All the seven killed gay men, and one of them, Sgt. Kenneth Jr. French, went on a murderous rampage, killing four people in a North Carolina restaurant after President Clinton announced plans to lift the ban on gays in the military. Dong has made the film out of a personal passion on the issue. On an evening in May 1977, the film director was attacked by four teenage boys while walking in San Francisco's heavily gay Castro district. "I was stunned," Dong recalls. "I was never attacked as an Asian man, and I'm obviously an Asian man. But I was attacked as a gay man."[61] However, Dong's message is much broader than a personal one. "This is not a gay film," Dong says in a telephone interview. "This is a film about heterosexuality and the institutions of heterosexuality. This is a film about straight people, and straight attitudes about homosexuality. Straight people need to see films about themselves, and how they think."[62]

In an additional subcategory are many films that address racism against Asian Americans in contemporary American society. For the filmmaker, the intent is twofold: to educate the public on Asian American civil rights issues, and to call for community empowerment. These films run the gamut of styles and techniques, from the well-documented history to newsreel TV programs to experimental-style documentaries. Among the best-known are Spencer Nakasako's *Monterey's Boat People* (1982), a piece on the racial tensions between Vietnamese American fishermen and their white counterparts; Sandra Yep's Emmy Award–winning *Perceptions: A Question of Justice* (1984), a Korean American Gregorio Cortez legend; and Taggart Siegel's *Blue Collar and Buddha* (1988), a dramatic documentary about a Laotian community in Rockford, Illinois, and the hostilities and terrorist attacks they endured from their working-class neighbors. Also in this category are Renee Tajima and Christine Choy's Oscar-nominated *Who Killed Vincent Chin?*; Choy's newest documentary *Shot Heard 'Round the World* (1997); Michael Cho's video documentary *Animal Appetites* (1991), a hilarious film about two Cambodian immigrants arrested and tried for killing their dog for food; Dai Sil Kim-Gibson and Christine Choy's *Sa-I-Gu: From Korean Women's Perspectives* (1993); Karen Ishizuka and Robert Nakamura's *Looking Like the Enemy* (1996); and Lee Mun Wah's *Stolen Ground* (1993) and *The Color of Fear* (1995).

Typically, in the "vindicationist tradition," to borrow a term from St. Clair Drake, these stories have an open-ended conclusion with a message. In these documentaries, history is often presented more as a process people live through rather than as a linear chronology. Tajima and Choy's *Who Killed Vincent Chin?* (the story of a twenty-seven-year-old Chinese engineer who was brutally murdered with a baseball bat by two white unemployed auto workers in Detroit), takes, for example, a process-oriented, as opposed to an event-oriented, narrative structure. Instead of viewing a straightforward anti-Asian racist incident run amok, the viewers are led on an eighty-seven-minute tour of Chinese immigration, the auto industry, the city of Detroit, and the international trade war. Central to the film, as a mode of organization, is the story of the Chin family and their trials and tribulations in a racist American society. The questions raised by the film are much larger than one man's guilt or one mother's loss. In many ways, the Chin family's story becomes the vehicle on which the viewers travel to the murder case, which in turn contextualizes the tension and conflicts that are to be the principal materials of the narrative. The linearity, or time sequence of the event, is broken repeatedly and the enactment of the crime and its causes are played out only as the background— mostly racial antagonism and the economic decline of the American auto industry—unravels itself. When Ronald Ebens walks away a free man after five years of struggle in the courts, and Lily Chin pleads haltingly for justice for her son, the audience is left with lingering questions about the case and its implications. In the film, Choy gives equal on-screen time to the views of Ronald Ebens, his adopted son, the two defendants, and their families and friends. The audience shares subjective responsibility for making connections between the Chin case and the latent racial and class conflicts.

The significance of these films lies particularly in the fact that they shift their frame of reference to incorporate new measures and criteria that "ran counter to the pragmatism that had informed traditional liberal histories" (in which social movements' significance was judged by goals achieved).[63] The films emphasize the historical process more than immediate results, affirming the significance of struggle, of decisions made, and of consequences accepted. Put differently, the films have provided Asian Americans with a sense of historicity in their current struggle for equality and justice. This theme corroborates immigration historian Rudolph Vecoli's account of a new ethnicity:

> The new ethnicity is not simply a form of therapy to soothe bruised ethnic egos. Rather the formation of a new historical consciousness, as in the case of Black Americans, is the very basis for concerted group action to correct traditional neglects and injuries.[64]

Perhaps operating out of this new historical consciousness, a group of Asian American filmmakers has taken up topical, often controversial, subjects. Consider *Sa-I-Gu: From Korean Women's Perspectives,* for example. During the Rodney King civil unrest in Los Angeles from April 29 to May 2, 1992, Korean American businesses were specifically targeted in the violence and suffered about half of the $800 million in property damages. Many community leaders and activists believe the mainstream media contributed to the destruction in the city's Koreatown. "When Korean-Americans were thrust in the spotlight in April 1992," says Elaine Kim, co-director of *Sa-I-Gu,* "the enormity of misunderstanding about them was brought into play. The media reduced Korean-Americans to images of screaming women and men on the roofs with guns."[65] To respond to mainstream media's biased coverage, three women of Korean background, Dai Sil Kim-Gibson, Elaine H. Kim, and Christine Choy, flew to Los Angeles to record the stories of Korean American women shopkeepers who lost their businesses and livelihoods. The result of their efforts is the thirty-six-minute documentary *Sa-I-Gu.* The film does not pretend to portray balanced and objective views on both sides of the conflict, but it offers a badly needed perspective from those Korean immigrant women on the riots, ethnic relations, and racism in American society. For the filmmakers themselves, the production was an eye-opening experience. As Kim recalls in an interview,

> The media's portrayal of the hatred between Koreans and African-Americans or between Koreans and Latinos isn't [accurate]. People are more complex, and so are communities. We went to Mrs. Song's store with her and her husband three months after the riots so we could film their rubble. When we were there, everyone—I mean everyone—came by to say, "Hi" to them. This black car with loud blaring music pulls up with these guys in tattoos and I thought, "Okay, this is it." But they rushed over and hugged Mrs. Song and said, "We are really sorry this happened to you." A lady had salvaged Mrs. Song's bible from the ashes and gave it to her. Everyone defied my expectations.[66]

Similarly, Karen Ishizuka and Robert Nakamura's *Looking Like the Enemy* (1996), a historical film about the wartime experiences of Japanese American veterans in World War II, Korea, and Vietnam, is often viewed under the contemporary context of the Bruce Yamashita case. Yamashita, a Sansei who fought a successful five-year legal battle in the early 1990s against the U.S. Marine Corps, claimed that he was victimized by racial discrimination during his training at Marine Officer Candidate School (OCS) in Quantico, Virginia. Acknowledging the discrimination charge, the Marine Corps granted Yamashita his commission and made sweeping changes in OCS training policies. The Yamashita case, hence hailed as a major civil rights victory, matches the story of David Miyoshi in the film. Miyoshi, who fought in Vietnam, describes an incident that happened in his Marine officer training. One day a drill instructor ordered Miyoshi to get up on the podium and stand at attention in front of his fellow trainees. Pointing in his direction, the instructor told the class, "This is what the enemy looks like. Kill it before it kills you." Turning around, he then told Miyoshi to "growl for me, gook." Many equally disturbing "looking like the enemy" incidents are given by the veterans in the film. Vince Okamoto told the story of an injured Japanese American soldier who was nearly thrown out of a helicopter in mid-air when the crew was ordered to "jettison the gooks." Unable to speak because of a fractured jaw and a heavy dose of morphine, the soldier was saved only by a more sensitive African American comrade who had identified him as one of their own. Although these filmed stories took place decades ago, well-informed viewers are fully aware of their contemporary relevance.

Lee Mun Wah, a Berkeley therapist and award-winning filmmaker, provocatively probes the impact of racism between and among ethnic groups in two emotionally charged social issue documentaries. In 1993, he co-directed *Stolen Ground*, a forty-three-minute film about racism toward Asian Americans. The documentary features six Asian American men in the San Francisco Bay Area who talk poignantly of white racism. "We wanted to put a human face on what racism does to people," explains producer Lindsey Jang. "We hope non-Asians will begin to understand what it is to be an Asian American who faces racism."[67] The director agrees: "This film was quite significant to bring out to the community because it broke the myth of the way Asian men talk—that we are not passionate, that we don't get angry, that we don't have a sense of humor."[68] Even more powerful is his second film, *The Color of Fear*, which won the 1995 Gold Apple Award for Best Social Studies Documentary at the National Education Media Competition. In this full-length documentary, nine men—two Mexican Americans, two Chinese Americans, a Japanese American, two African Americans, and two European Americans—are gathered in Ukiah, California, for a weekend of dialogue on racism.

At the beginning they all seemed nervous and vulnerable. David, one of the white participants, is baffled by the painful experiences of racism among the minorities in the group. In a state of denial, he constantly questions the statements of all the nonwhite members. "Why can't you just be American and not Chinese American?" And, "Why do these guys have such a problem with their color? Why can't they make a name for themselves?" One of the Chicano participants responded poignantly, "As a white man, he [David] doesn't have to think about his place in the world. He doesn't have to think about being a white person . . . they don't have to deal with it from day one. . . . They step into the world that is theirs." Victor, who is Black and the most articulate in the group, told David, "I won't trust you unless you can become transformed by my [Black] experience as much as I am transformed by your [white] experience every day." The turning point comes when producer, director, and participant Lee asks David, "What's keeping you from believing that this [racism] is happening to Victor?" In the film we see each individual's guard gradually go down. Out of this intimate and intense dialogue has emerged a deeper sense of understanding and trust. Every participant comes away believing that he can make a difference.

Lee successfully lends a raw and honest quality to the film. The men communicated so well that it seemed as if they were professional actors with scripted dialogue. "Steven Okazaki told me he wouldn't have the guts to do it," Lee recalled. "Even with a half a million dollar budget. He said the people would just clam up."[69] But Lee did not give up. "Race relations is hard work, and many want to give up," Lee said. "It requires a commitment." When his mother was murdered by an African American in 1985, he vowed to dedicate the rest of his life to dealing with racism and violence by leading workshops that tackle the issue head-on. "Most Americans are afraid of this type of dialogue, so I find it important to create safer environments in which parties can discuss the issues." Lee specifically intended the film for "a liberal American who may not use 'Chink' or 'Jap,' but doesn't do anything about racism." "Racism won't wait for us," Lee said. "Whites have the luxury to walk away from it; minorities have to deal with it every day."[70] Indeed, Lee continues to spread his message in a new film he is currently working on, entitled *Last Chance for Eden*, about racism and sexism in contemporary American society.

These films demonstrate how important it is to document current history and living people, and how historical referents can play powerful roles in people's current struggles. As George Lipsitz has noted, "We need to understand the past in order to make informed moral choices about the present, to connect our personal histories to a large collective history."[71] All these films perform a critical function by informing, agitating, and mobilizing action for social justice. The orientation toward community empowerment has come at least partially from the filmmakers' commitment to a tradition of activism back in the 1960s. Some Asian American filmmakers express their firm belief in the power of the media to effect social and cultural change. As one critic puts it, "The act of filmmaking is essentially an act of education for action."[72]

Having said all the above, it is interesting to observe that several Asian Americans who began as documentarians have moved into fictional filmmaking. The most prominent example is Steven Okazaki, who made several highly acclaimed documentaries before directing *American Sons* (1996), a dramatic film some critics categorize also as documentary drama. Trinh T. Minh-ha, known for her innovations in experimental films, has recently directed her first fiction film—*A Tale of Love,* based loosely on *The Tale of Kieu,* a classical Vietnamese poem. Likewise, Shu Lea Cheang made her foray into 35mm feature filmmaking through *Fresh Kill* (1994), a story based on a screenplay by Filipina American novelist and performance artist Jessica Hagedorn. Rea Tajiri has also made the move from experimental documentaries to feature films. Her first dramatic feature, *Strawberry Fields,* was premiered at San Francisco's International Asian American Film Festival in March 1997.

However, many Asian American filmmakers are committed to documentary filmmaking, as well as to making historical films. Even today, "We're still in a phase of trying to take care of our history as Asian Americans," comments Felicia Lowe.[73] As a powerful medium that is able to evoke emotions, shape ideas, and communicate a message, Asian American documentary films have performed an important function in re-visioning Asian American history. Although the format of the films tends to be repetitive (interviews spliced with documentary footage), they are based on a myriad of unconventional as well as conventional sources such as demographic data, private diaries, personal letters, anonymous writings, folk songs, family albums, religious rituals, and other artistic expressions and artifactual evidence. Utilizing the techniques of interviews and incorporating photographs, newsreel footage, newspaper clippings, and quoted journals, these films bring to life a mosaic of the Asian American experience. These artists have endowed Asian Americans with a cinematic voice and subjectivity rarely seen in conventional cinema. What is more, as a group, these works have provided the bedrock, both thematically and aesthetically, for the future evolution of Asian American cinema.

NOTES

1 Anthony B. Chan, "Rashomon Blues," *Moving the Image: Independent Asian Pacific American Media Arts,* ed. Russell Leong (Los Angeles: UCLA Asian American Studies Center, 1991), 228.

2 Interview with Katherine Leslie, April 1996.

3 Erik Barnouw, *Documentary: A History of the Non-Fiction Film,* 2d rev. ed. (New York: Oxford University Press, 1993), 262–94.

4 Luis Francia, "Asian and Asian American Cinema: Separated by a Common Language?," *Moving the Image,* 104.

5 Interview with Katherine Leslie, April 1996.

6 Interview with Katherine Leslie, April 1996.

7   Noel M. Izon, Introduction to *Pearls: A History of Asians in America* (TLC-TV Project, 1978), available from GPN Lincoln, Neb., iv.

8   Sucheng Chan, *Asian Americans: An Interpretive History* (Boston: Twayne Publishers, 1991), xiii.

9   Loni Ding, "Strategies of an Asian American Filmmaker," *Moving the Image*, 59.

10   Izon.

11   Elizabeth Weis, "Family Portraits," *American Film* 1:2 (Nov. 1975), 54–59.

12   Ibid., 54.

13   John Esaki, "Back to Real Asian American Filmmaking," *Moving the Image*, 35.

14   As quoted by Thomas Morley, "Japanese American Film Maker Explores the Legacy of Internment Camps," *Asian American Press* (June 18, 1993).

15   Rea Tajiri, *History and Memory* script, version 8/12/1991, available from Video Data Bank, The School of the Art Institute of Chicago, Chicago, Illinois.

16   Jim Lane, "Notes on Theory and the Autobiographical Documentary Film in America," *Wide Angle* 15:3 (1993), 21–36.

17   Indeed, Asian American literature, especially writings by Asian American women, such as Maxine Hong Kingston's *Woman Warrior* and *China Men*, blends several literary genres.

18   Teshome Gabriel, "Third Cinema as Guardian of Popular Memory: Towards a Third Aesthetics," *Questions of Third Cinema,* ed. Jim Pines and Paul Willemen (London: British Film Institute, 1989), 58.

19   *History and Memory* script, 1.

20   Renee Tajima, "Moving the Image: Asian American Independent Filmmaking, 1970–1990," *Moving the Image*, 23.

21   Ding, 48.

22   Ibid., 59.

23   Ibid.

24   Sumiko Hagashi, "Film Reviews," *American Historical Review* 98:4 (Oct. 1993), 1182.

25   Michael Novak, *The Rise of the Unmeltable Ethnics: Politics and Culture in the Seventies* (New York: MacMillan, 1972), xviii.

26   Interview with Katherine Leslie, April 1996.

27   John Fiske, *Understanding Popular Culture* (London and New York: Routledge, 1989), 159.

28   Ibid., 32.

29   Novak, xv, xviii.

30   Lawrence Levine, *Black Culture and Black Consciousness: Afro-American Folk Thought from Slavery to Freedom* (New York: Oxford University Press, 1977), ix, xi.

31   Richard Griswold del Castillo, *The Los Angles Barrio, 1850–1890: A Social History* (Berkeley: University of California Press, 1979), xi.

32   John Modell, *The Economics and Politics of Racial Accommodation: The Japanese of Los Angles, 1900–1942* (Urbana: University of Illinois Press, 1977), vii.

33   Tajima, "Moving the Image," 16.

34   Ibid.

35   Renee Tajima, "Intersection in the Delta," *Southern Exposure* (July/August 1984), 21.

36   Shirley Kwan, "Asian American Women Behind the Camera," *Anthology of Asian American Film and Video* (New York: Third World Newsreel, 1984), 35.

37   As quoted by Craig Seligman, "Forbidden' [sic] challenge," *San Francisco Examiner* (Nov. 15, 1989).

38   Ibid.

39   For details, see Adria Bernardi, "Heat in the Delta: Reactions to the Triangle," *Southern Exposure* (July/Aug., 1984).

40   Kwan, 35.

41   Gina Marchetti, "Ethnicity, the Cinema and Cultural Studies," in *Unspeakable Images: Ethnicity and the American Cinema*, ed. Lester D. Friedman (Urbana and Chicago: University of Illinois Press, 1991), 301.

42   Tajima, "Intersection in the Delta," 19.

43   Marchetti, 298.

44 Erick Dittus, "Mississippi Triangle: An Interview with Christine Choy, Worth Long and Allan Siegel," *Cineaste* 14:2 (1985), 40.

45 Karen Ishizuka and Robert A. Nakamura, "Conversations: An Experiment in Community-based Filmmaking," *Moving the Image*, 39.

46 "Ancestors in America," program brochure, 1.

47 Ibid., 2.

48 Okazaki, *Days of Waiting*.

49 Chan, 229.

50 Ibid.

51 Tajima, "Intersection in the Delta," 19.

52 Antonio Gramsci, *Prison Notebooks* (New York: International Publishers, 1970), 12.

53 Thomas Cripps, *Black Film As Genre* (Bloomington: Indiana University Press, 1979), 12.

54 All the quotes by the former entertainers are from Arthur Dong's documentary *Forbidden City, U.S.A.*

55 Seligman.

56 To work to overthrow the Chinese exclusion laws, citizens of Chinese descent fabricated "paper sons" (legal only on paper) who could come to the United States to join their Chinese "fathers."

57 The author quotes his adviser Clarke A. Chambers from his comments on the manuscript.

58 As quoted by Roy Armes in *Third World Film Making and the West* (Berkeley: University of California Press), 305.

59 Interview with E. P. Thompson, *Visions of History*, ed. Henry Abelove et al. (New York: Pantheon, 1983), 14–16.

60 I must admit that the term "social issue documentary" is imprecise or even misleading, because very few of the Asian American documentary films under study are for personal or entertainment purposes alone.

61 As quoted by Renee Graham, " 'Kill' takes look at anti-gay violence," *Denver Post* (July 6, 1997), 10D.

62 Ibid.

63 The author quotes his adviser Clarke A. Chambers from his comments on the manuscript.

64 Rudolph Vecoli, "Louis Admic and the Contemporary Search for Roots," *Ethnic Studies* 2:3 (Melbourne, Australia: Australia International Press and Publications, 1978), 29–35.

65 See *"Sa-I-Gu's* Dai Sil Kim-Gibson and Elaine H. Kim," *International Documentary,* 12:8 (Sept. 1993), 1.

66 Ibid., 15.

67 As quoted by William Wong, "Asian-American men confront effects of racism," from the *Stolen Ground* program package.

68 From Lee Mun Wah's lecture at Colorado State University, April 28, 1996.

69 Gerard Lim, "The Different Hues of 'The Color of Fear' " *AsianWeek* (Jan. 21, 1994), 9.

70 Ibid.

71 George Lipsitz, *Time Passages* (Minneapolis: University of Minnesota Press, 1990), 21.

72 Russell Leong, "Introduction: To Open the Future," *Moving the Image*, xviii.

73 As quoted in Kwan, 36.

1. *Hito Hata: Raise the Banner* (1980) crew (L to R): Nancy Araki, Takashi Fujii, Bob Omachi, Robert Nakamura, and Duane Kubo. Courtesy of Visual Communications, Southern California Asian American Studies Central, Inc.

2. Still from the documentary film *Forbidden City, U.S.A.* (1989) by Arthur Dong. Courtesy of DeepFocus Productions.

3. Sokly "Don Bonus" Ny in *a.k.a. Don Bonus* (1995) by Spencer Nakasako and Sokly "Don Bonus" Ny. Photo by Leland Wong. Courtesy of National Asian American Telecommunications Association.

4. Top left: Artist and architect Maya Lin from *Maya Lin: A Strong Clear Vision* (1995) by Freida Lee Mock. Photo by Eddie Marritz.

Top right: Director Freida Lee Mock. Photo by Adam Stoltman.

Bottom Center: Director Mock filming Maya Lin fabricating the Civil Rights Memorial.

All stills and photos courtesy of American Film Foundation.

5. Still from *Surname Viet Given Name Nam* (1989) by Trinh T. Minh-ha. Courtesy of Women Make Movies, Inc.

6. Still from *History and Memory: For Akiko and Takashige* (1991) by Rea Tajiri. Courtesy of Women Make Movies, Inc.

7. Still from *Two Lies* (1989) by Pam Tom. Courtesy of Women Make Movies, Inc.

8. Poster for *Double Happiness*, © 1995, Fine Line Features. All rights reserved. Poster courtesy of New Line Productions, Inc.

9. Jade (Sandra Oh), Mom (Alannah Ong), Dad (Stephen Chang), and Pearl (Frances You) in *Double Happiness*, © 1995, Fine Line Features. All rights reserved. Photo by K. Tougas. Photo courtesy of New Line Productions, Inc.

10. Stills from *Chan Is Missing* (1981), a New Yorker film release, by Wayne Wang.

Top: Henry (Peter Wang). Photo by Nancy Wong. Courtesy of Wayne Wang, New Yorker Films and Photofest.

Bottom: Steve (Marc Hayashi) and Jo (Wood Moy). Photo by Nancy Wong. Courtesy of Wayne Wang, New Yorker Films and Photofest.

11. Vincent Chin in *Who Killed Vincent Chin?* (1988) by Christine Choy and Renee Tajima. Courtesy of Filmakers Library, Inc.

12. Still from *Sally's Beauty Spot* (1990) by Helen Lee. Photo by Rick McGinnis. Courtesy of Women Make Movies, Inc.

13. Still from *Slaying the Dragon* (1988) by Deborah Gee. Courtesy of Women Make Movies, Inc.

The Family Dramas

AS DISCUSSED IN THE PREVIOUS CHAPTER, while Asian American independent filmmakers have widely adopted the genre of documentary, they have also increasingly pursued the more creative dramatic format.[1] In the wake of Wayne Wang's *The Joy Luck Club* in 1993, many more Asian-directed dramas have achieved broad theatrical distribution. Some have even won honors in the industry. Taiwanese American Ang Lee's *The Wedding Banquet* (1993), for example, was nominated for an Academy Award as best foreign film, and it won the prestigious Golden Bear grand prize at the 1993 Berlin Film Festival. Hawaii-born, New York–based Japanese American director Kayo Hatta's *Picture Bride* (1994) was the winner of the Audience Award at the 1995 Sundance Film Festival. The Asian American cinematic breakthrough provides further proof that the Asian American perspective is as entertaining as it is distinctive. *Time* magazine dubbed the critical success of Asian American films as "China Chic," and *CineVue*, the newsletter of Asian CineVision (the largest Asian American media center), proclaimed that finally "Asian American cinema has arrived."

It is quite telling to note that virtually all Asian American–directed independent features, from Wayne Wang's mother-daughter sagas *Dim Sum: A Little Bit of Heart* (1985) and *The Joy Luck Club* to Ang Lee's "Father knows best" trilogy *Pushing Hands* (1992), *The Wedding Banquet,* and *Eat Drink Man Woman* (1994), can be broadly defined as family dramas. Grounded in intimate personal and family lives, these movies almost invariably deal with the trials and tribulations of the Asian American family, exploring both the bond of strong kinship ties and troubling domestic tensions across racial, gender, generational, and class lines.

This chapter examines this rapidly growing rank of Asian American dramatic feature productions. First, it asks what the significance is of the family narrative for Asian American filmmakers, and it inquires into how the special dynamics in Asian American family formation, mandated by longtime exclusionist policies and racism, became the thematic focus for Asian American artists. Second, it explores the major thematic problems concerning an intratextual dialogue on race, ethnicity, and gender that is debated in these family genre films, and it asks how these family stories subvert the notion of monolithic identities by emphasizing the process of "becoming" rather than "being." Finally, it considers whether the films' narrative strategies—their discursive innovations that the filmmakers have employed—differ from the structural and formal patterns in Hollywood's films. In sum, this chapter discusses the Asian American aesthetic elements that help define the parameters of this emergent Asian American film genre.

HISTORICAL SPECIFICITY AND FAMILY-ORIENTED NARRATIVE CINEMA

In researching this chapter, I have found that historical and anthropological research on Asian Americans often emphasizes their old-country traditions. Topics such as extended families, arranged marriages, filial piety, and concubinage, for example, are often cited as the main characteristics of traditional Asian families. Although patriarchal Asian cultures provide the subtle contexts, Asian American family dramas are fully embedded in the historical specificity of the Asian American experience in this country. U.S. immigration laws, as well as state and federal policies, have shaped and reshaped Asian American communities.[2] Families, the important social institution within those communities, experienced heartwrenching disruptions, and happy reunions as well. "You always have this theme of searching for identity and exploring family history," comments Vivian Huang, an organizer of the Asian American International Film Festival in New York City.[3] Steven Okazaki agrees, "The family is an interesting traumatic situation for most Asian Americans, and that is where the drama is."[4]

In this first section, I will explore how the longtime exclusionist policies, and their later liberalization, helped define the thematic focus for Asian American movies and influence their storytelling strategies. As Renee Tajima writes, "Let's say your drama centered on the Japanese American concentration camps, or Filipino and Chinese bachelor societies of California, or war brides, picture brides and the like. Apart from plot points, character development, and all the business of making cinema, you had to carefully explain all the details and factual implications of this specific sociohistorical event. Because the audience simply had no clue. This could put a mighty crimp into your storytelling style."[5] My discussion of the historical themes will be organized around three broad, sometimes overlapping, subcategories of historical dramas: women's odysseys, immigrant family sagas, and "green card" romances.

Women's Odysseys in Bachelor Societies

The first Asian immigrant group, the Chinese, landed in America in the mid nineteenth century and was predominantly men. Restrictions set by U.S. exclusion laws prohibited the immigration of Chinese women, even wives of Chinese American residents. The series of laws, beginning with the Page Law of 1875, which barred the importation of Chinese prostitutes, the Chinese Exclusion Act of 1882, and the subsequent immigration restriction laws in 1924 created a unique characteristic in early Chinese American family history: a dramatic gender imbalance. For years, the ratio of men to women was about twenty-five to one and aging bachelors were the rule in Chinatowns. This longtime shortage of Chinese women did not begin to change until after World War II. Because of the antimiscegenation laws in California, the home of most of the early Chinese immigrants, Chinese men were virtually deprived of the rights of marriage and children. While the cinema window rarely opens into this world of men, the pathos of the so-called bachelor societies is, ironically, often revealed in the stories of prostitutes, picture brides, and war brides. At least three women-centered movies produced in the late 1980s and early 1990s offer insightful glimpses into this little-known Asian American history: Nancy Kelly and Kenji Yamamoto's *Thousand Pieces of Gold* (1991), Kayo Hatta's *Picture Bride* (1994), and Wayne Wang's *Eat a Bowl of Tea* (1989).

Based on a namesake novel by Ruthanne Lum McCunn, *Thousand Pieces of Gold* tells the true story of a young Chinese pioneer woman named Lalu Nathoy (Rosalind Chao). The film opens on a morning in the 1880s in Northern China. Lalu, an adolescent girl, is pulled out of her bed and sold to a marriage broker by her impoverished father. She is then shipped, bound in chains, across the Pacific to San Francisco's Chinatown and auctioned off, naked, as a prostitute. She is bought by a Chinese cowboy by the name of Jim (Dennis Dun), who delivers her up north to Warrens Diggens, an Idaho mining town. Her new owner/husband, an ex-railroad worker turned bar manager, Hong King (Michael Paul Chan), intends to let her work off part of her debt as a saloon prostitute. But Lalu, nicknamed China Polly now, would rather kill herself than become a sex slave. Her fate begins to change when she is won in a poker game from King by Charlie Bemis (Chris Cooper), King's business partner. Much to Lalu's surprise, Bemis teaches her to stand up for her rights by saying, "No whore! No for you!" He even gives her a kitchen knife to defend herself with, "in case they don't get the message." Unlike most other Chinese women who were brought to the West in the 1860s and 1870s, Lalu narrowly escapes a life of sexual slavery intended for her from the outset. The film's title symbolically refers to her father's term of endearment, "my qianjin, my thousand pieces of gold," which is a double metaphor for both her courage and early Chinese immigrants' vision of America as the "Gold Mountain."[6]

The movie, despite its clichéd plot in the "white man possessing yellow woman" formula, can be read largely as a portrayal of a little-known aspect of American pioneer history.[7] Or, for that matter, the movie provides an enlightened view of early Chinese American life. With the discovery of gold, a wave of Chinese laborers arrived to work on the transcontinental railroads and in the gold mines in the West. A significant Chinese community worked and lived in Idaho. In the state of Idaho as a whole, Chinese Americans comprised almost one-third of the total population in 1870 (4,272 out of 14,999). The town of Warrens Diggens had 367 Chinese residents and 243 whites, along with three Native Americans and two African Americans. Although welcomed at first, these Chinese immigrant laborers soon became victims of racism as well as easy scapegoats for economic recessions. From the late 1860s on, many Chinese laborers were massacred and lynched in the Idaho territory. By the 1890s, they were completely driven out and then excluded from much of the inland West.

This chapter of Chinese American history is captured in *Thousand Pieces of Gold* through some vivid, vulnerable, and multidimensional characters. Jim, the Chinese cowboy, is handsome, gentle, and very attractive. He falls in love with his love-cargo (Lalu) and strives to claim her as his own. He is absent in the novel, but a significant addition in the movie, and his nickname, "Li Po," the name of the most famous Tang dynasty lyric poet, lends a strong aura of romance to their relationship. In contrast to the asexual Asian male stereotype Hollywood usually provides, Jim is portrayed as a very romantic man with sexual prowess. He even succeeds in making love to Lalu in Hong King's back rooms. He pulls himself out of the relationship only after he finds she has been "keeping house" with Charlie and falsely assumes they are already sexually involved. However, Jim's image of sensitivity is blemished by the fact that he turns his back when Lalu desperately tries to explain the situation, a scene that resonates well with one at the beginning when Lalu's father turns his back on her pleas not to sell her. Even the most unsympathetic Chinese character, Hong King, seems to be humane, because his greed is seen largely as an extension of the surrounding forces beyond his control. The movie draws to a dramatic close when Lalu turns her horse around toward Warrens Diggens to join Bemis, as all the other Chinese Americans are violently expelled from the mining town by a white mob.

The Japanese—the second oldest, and for a long time the largest, Asian American community—did not experience the same sexual imbalance as the early Chinese laborers, because of the immigration of a significant number of "picture brides." The 1907 Gentlemen's Agreement, signed between the United States and Japan, prohibited the free entry of Japanese laborers to the U.S. mainland; yet those who were already residing here could send for their wives or picture brides (wives acquired through letters and photographs). As a result of this policy, although male Japanese immigrants were no longer allowed free entry, Japanese women could join the men already in America. The saga of the picture brides was picked up by Kayo Hatta, a Sansei (third-generation Japanese American) woman filmmaker. Inspired by the real-life stories of Hawaii's early Issei (first-generation Japanese) immigrants, Hatta's award-winning *Picture Bride* (1994) tells the moving love story of Riyo (Youki Kudoh), a seventeen-year-old Japanese girl who moved to Hawaii to become wife of Matsuji (Akira Takayama), a sugarcane worker. Despite the fact that the newlyweds' only previous knowledge of each other was via pictures and letters, and that they both lied in their self-disclosures (Riyo found Matsuji was twenty-five years older than she was told), their lives were transformed by hardship and struggle into enduring affection for each other and their new homeland. As director Hatta stated in a phone interview, "It [*Picture Bride*] has to do with more universal themes of the redemptive power of love, the power of friendship between women, the search for family, and the desire to belong."[8]

The Immigration Law of 1924 literally stopped trans-Pacific migration as a whole. From then on, until the end of World War II, Asian immigration slowed to a trickle. Japanese and Chinese "war brides" were the first significant group of Asian women who arrived in the United States since the 1920s. These war bride stories are documented in several family dramas, among which Wayne Wang's *Eat a Bowl of Tea* is perhaps the best-known. With a screenplay by scriptwriter Judith Rascoe based on Louis Chu's 1961 novel, the movie offers a realistic portrait of the pathos and conditions of Chinatown. Set in 1949 in New York City, the movie begins with a series of vignette shots of the Chinatown district: Chinese men gathered in game rooms and in barber shops and restaurants, as well as waiting in line outside the apartment of a prostitute. A gravely voiced Wah Gay (Victor Wong) explains in a voice-over narration how American immigration laws at the turn of the century allowed only the men to emigrate from China, because of the high demand for cheap labor in the United States. Living in a dying community of aging bachelors, he talks of the despair and frustration of having been separated from his wife for more than twenty years.

The main story line traces Wah Gay's efforts to arrange a marriage for his son Ben Loy (Russell Wong) with Mei Oi (Cora Miao) from China.[9] Taking advantage of the War Brides Act, passed in 1945, war veteran Ben Loy goes to China to marry Mei Oi, daughter of Lee Gong (Lau Siu Ming), his father's close friend in Chinatown. On their return, the newlywed couple comes under tremendous pressure from the father to produce offspring for the family. All the drama results from the father's high expectations of a grandson, and the son's inability to deliver. In one hilarious scene, Wah Gay corners Ben Loy at work, grabs his own groin, and asks,

"Do you know what to do with this?" Symbolically, by submitting to his father's authority, Ben Loy lost not only his individuality but also his sexual prowess. Although the son had no trouble leading an active sexual life before his marriage, pressed by his father's desperate expectations for a grandchild, he finds himself impotent on his wedding night. Frustrated and lonely, Mei Oi is forced to find consolation with a local dandy named Uncle Ah Song (Eric Tsang Chi Wai). Only by the end of the film, when the couple relocates to San Francisco's Chinatown, away from his father's dominance and treated with a comforting bowl of herbal tea imported from China, does Ben Loy regain his sexuality.

Contrary to Hollywood's often facile portrayals of Chinese immigrant life, the movie succeeds in revealing, in an extremely funny way, the details about a rich Chinese immigrant culture that struggles for its survival and transformation. Especially fascinating is its presentation of traditional folkways, such as arranged marriages, elaborate wedding ceremonies (which would be expanded upon in depth and subtlety by Ang Lee's *The Wedding Banquet* years later), and community involvement in personal relationships in a geriatric male immigrant enclave that was 96 percent male and only 4 percent female. Despite its melodramatic plot, the movie is already an accomplishment in bringing to the large and small screen (produced by PBS's American Playhouse) an ignored and now rediscovered novel by a Chinese American writer, Louis Chu (1915–1970).

While not many feature films are made solely about Asian Americans, fewer still are made about their longtime history in this country. Viewed from a women-centered perspective, these movies have woven a touching and complex narrative of early Asian American experience. Steeped in historical specificity—in this case, the Exclusion laws—the stories offer a penetrating look into the complexities of early Asian American communities. The most fascinating aspects of these women's odysseys are the haunting details of the pathetic conditions of the closed "bachelor societies," and the painful process of adapting to circumstances. Like vivid photo albums, the movies replace clichéd Hollywood images of remote and even sinister Asian American characters with earthy and pragmatic individuals who are passionate as well as spiritual. "No sanitized exoticism," the stories represent, as Renee Tajima writes about *Eat a Bowl of Tea*, "a long-sought testament to what we'd all been searching for: Asian-American soul."[10]

Immigrant Family Sagas

In 1965, the Hart-Celler Act, passed by Congress, fundamentally reformed U.S. immigration policies. It changed the basis of admission from national origin to personal qualifications based on the principle of equality. Concurrently, most federal and state anti-Asian laws were struck down, and immigrants from Asia, for the first time in American history (at least, on paper), began to enjoy the same immigration and naturalization rights as other ethnic groups. With family reunification being a high priority in U.S. policy, chain migration became the new pattern for the Asian communities. The original gender imbalance was gradually being corrected. Universal themes such as assimilation, generation gaps, cultural conflicts, and identity issues are experienced, in one way or another, in Asian families all over America. A group of movies I will call immigrant family sagas has begun to address these issues. Some of the better known works include Wayne Wang's *Dim Sum, The Joy Luck Club*, and *Chan Is Missing*; Peter Wang's *A Great Wall* (1986); Michael Uno's *The Wash* (1988); and Pam Tom's *Two Lies* (1989).

Wayne Wang's *Dim Sum* is a typical mother-daughter story, focusing on the generation gap between the assimilated Geraldine Tam (Laureen Chew) and her tradition-bound widowed mother, Mrs. Tam (Kim Chew). The film begins as the Chinese New Year approaches and Mrs. Tam, who will soon be sixty-two, grows increasingly concerned that Geraldine will not marry Richard (John Nishio), her physician boyfriend from Los Angeles. Mrs. Tam's anxiety heightens considerably after being informed by a fortune teller that she will die in her sixty-second year. This news makes her even more desperate to see Geraldine settled, and after some forty years in America, she wants to pay her last visit to her homeland, China. Dutiful but independent, Geraldine is constantly pulled between conflicting wishes of having a life of her own and taking care of her mother. This mother-daughter relationship is complicated further by Uncle Tam (Victor Wong), the family's "surrogate father" (a position he has held since his brother's death fifteen years ago). He wishes to free Geraldine from filial duty and marry his brother's widow. Failing to tie the nuptial knot for Geraldine, Mrs. Tam flies to China (after passing her long-delayed exam for American citizenship). To everybody's surprise, she returns in good humor, for another fortune teller informed her that it is only the first cycle of her life that is over.

Similar in theme but much broader in scope, Wang's *The Joy Luck Club* is a four-fold multigenerational version of the mother-daughter saga. Adapted by Amy Tan and Ronald Bass from Tan's best-seller, the movie opens on a gathering of the Joy Luck Club, a mahjong-playing group of four Chinese women, Suyuan (Kieu Chinh), Lindo (Tsai Chin), Ying Ying (France Nuyen), and An Mei (Lisa Lu), who live in San Francisco with their daughters: respectively, June (Ming-Na Wen), Waverly (Tamlyn Tomita), Lena (Lauren Tom), and Rose (Rosalind Chao). At this particular meeting, Suyuan, one of the members, has died and been replaced at the table by her daughter June. She is planning a trip to China to meet her two sisters, who her mother thought had died as infants. It is at June's farewell party that the other three women and their daughters reminisce about their experiences in both China and America.

The tragedies, dramas, and occasional lighter moments are so close to real life that they touched the hearts of the cast, as well as millions of moviegoers. One of the most moving scenes is June's reunion in China with her two older sisters. "When we were filming the scene," as director Wang recalls,

> what was amazing was that during the rehearsal the whole row of extras could hear the dialogue. They were completely in tears. An older woman came up to me later and told me she had had to leave her baby during the war and had never found it again. She really broke down. There's a lot there that the Chinese can identify with. Chinese-Americans in their own way can identity with this daughter, June, because her story is going back to your own roots, going to your home, and finally doing something for your mother.[11]

June's childhood failure as a pianist is another one of the many plotlines that struck a chord with the actresses. "Oh—the piano playing was a big thing," Rosalind Chao comments. "Walk up to any Asian-American and you'll find a pianist. My mom was so into it that she told my little brother that if he learned to play the piano, he'd get a suit like Liberace."[12] Lauren Tom agrees. "My character is a little bit invisible and shy and I was in that space also when I was very young. Just your basic kid stuff—people calling me names. We were the only Asian family in Highland Park, Ill. And my dad was like, 'You have to marry an Asian or I'm going to disown you.' I am like, 'Dad, who?' There wasn't anybody for me to even look at— give me a break."[13] This strong sense of empathy is broadly shared by the moviegoers, and delivers tremendous emotional power.

Not as well-known, Pam Tom's *Two Lies*, another mother-daughter story, approaches the subject from a very different angle. This black-and-white featurette provides a disturbing and eerie look into identity issues from the perspective of Mei-Ying (Sala Iwamatsu), a Chinese American teenager concerned about her mother's cosmetic eye surgery.[14] Doris Chiu, the divorced mother, has been dating white men and plans to boost her self-image by undergoing double eyelid surgery. This mutilation of her face causes a serious identity crisis for the elder daughter. To Mei-Ying and Esther, the younger daughter, their mother represents their cultural heritage, and she (the mother) initially seems so proud of Chinese culture. At the beginning of the film, we see the mother telling the girls that "everything was invented in China," and she often scolds the teenagers for their bad American manners and wishes she had kept them in Chinese schools. However, all of a sudden the mother tries to deny her Chinese heritage by undergoing plastic surgery to try to attract Caucasian men.

As the film progresses, the family's trip to an Indian pueblo museum symbolically raises the question of authenticity. A guide tells the visitors how "Cabal loved the Indian people and had [an artist] carve the two-faced white man—a white man smiling out of one face and cheating out of the other." Mei-Ying sees that the pueblo is fake and tells her mother, "They shouldn't advertise it as an authentic Indian pueblo." Agitated, the mother says carelessly, "Don't ruin this trip for your sister—who the hell cares if it doesn't look like one!" This question of authenticity dramatizes the intense identity crises faced by the two Chinese American girls as they struggle with their mother's cultural denial. Toward the end of the movie, inside the darkened pueblo, the jumpy editing and erratic movements of the camera dramatize the partial blindness of the mother and her disorientation, while Mei-Ying tells her mother, "I was telling you what they call it in school: two eyes—two lies." This domestic drama, simple in plot and unpretentious, tackles one of the most sensitive topics among Asian American women: plastic surgery and personal identity.

This theme of familial conflicts is represented in not only "vertical" but also "horizontal" relationships. Michael Toshiyuki Uno's *The Wash*, drawn from a screenplay by Philip Kan Gotanda based on his namesake play, explores the dilemma of conjugal responsibilities and individual happiness. Set in the Japantown of San Jose, California, the movie provides a touching and sensitive look at the disintegrating marriage of an aging Nisei couple in the 1970s. Masi (Nobu McCarthy) and Nobu (Mako) met and courted in a internment camp during World War II and have been married for forty years. Months before the film begins, Masi has left Nobu, after many years of neglect and psychological abuse by her husband. Soon, she meets a widowed local pharmacist Sadao (Sab Shimono) and starts a tentative affair. He opens her eyes to what a loving husband can do for a wife. He plans their outings, makes picnic lunches, and takes her to a movie (*My Life as a Dog*). During a trip to Lake Tahoe, Sadao teaches her how to play blackjack. He gives her a gift-wrapped rod and reel and shows her how to cast. Not once in forty years has avid angler Nobu ever thought of taking his wife fishing. Most important of all, Sadao listens to Masi and responds enthusiastically when she wants to make love. Meanwhile, Nobu occasionally flirts with a middle-aged waitress by the name of Kiyoko (Shizuko Hoshi) at a neighborhood restaurant. It is obvious that Nobu goes to the restaurant more because of the free tempura she cooks him than his feelings for her. Back at his house, Nobu maintains the same lifestyle he always has: watching TV amid dirty piled-up dishes and crafting another kite (the same kind of kite he has made his whole life). In contrast, Masi is presented as a complex woman full of tender emotions and compassion. Although their marriage is in turmoil, Masi still goes back to Nobu's place, doing daily chores and washing his laundry (hence the film's title). Lonely and injured in pride, Nobu is cold and rude to her on these visits.

Despite common complaints about its resemblance to a staged play, the movie exposes American viewers to the inner depths of Japanese American family life—a rare experience in the visual media. For example, Sadao's comments about the trauma of growing old is particularly touching. "There's nothing good about growing old," he laments. "Most of the time you spend taking medicine and going to doctors. The rest of the time you spend going to funerals of friends who are taking the same medicine and seeing the same doctors." However, at the heart of the film is human sexuality and the question who is capable of being attracted and of making love. It is an eye-opening and daring move for the film to explore the sexuality of elderly people, especially among the allegedly "stoic" Japanese Americans. The three main characters are all, in fact, sexual beings. Sadao's bedroom comment to Masi rings true for many elder people: "Can you imagine what the kids are thinking? It embarrasses the hell out of me." Even the most unaffectionate Nobu is said to read girlie magazines. Renee Tajima responds from her experience to the love scene between Masi and Nobu (when briefly reunited). "Although I grew up surrounded by Japanese Americans, I've never in my life seen a *nisei* couple (my parent's generation) kiss, much less get naked. In Michael Uno's *The Wash* it's most jolting to see the sixtyish mom, Masi (Nobu McCarthy), bed down with her own husband, Nobu (Mako), then with another man. I mean, did *my* parents really do it?"[15]

Stories of their two grown Sansei children, Marsha (Patti Yasutake) and Judy (Marion Yue), form the movie's interesting subplots. Judy, the younger and rebellious daughter, is completely alienated from the father. She married a *kurochan* (Black man) and had a baby boy, angering Nobu so much that he disowned her forever. At one point, she complains about her father, "Can you imagine spending your whole life with a man who has the vocabulary of a cow?" In contrast, the much more traditional Marsha is trying to get her parents back together without realizing what she is doing. Ironically, the man she is dating, a yuppie writer, is very much like her father, who is more interested in her typing skills than anything else. When Masi must decide whether to ask Nobu for a divorce, the story comes to a quiet climax. For the most part, this story shatters the "trouble-free" image of Japanese American family life by exploring its characters' marital and sexual problems.

Peter Wang's *A Great Wall*, often referred to as a cross-cultural comedy, tells a transnational tale of two families, the upper-middle-class Fangs of San Francisco and the middle-class Chaos of Peking. The plot revolves around a brother, Leo Fang (Peter Wang), and a sister who have been separated for thirty years. The brother Fang, now forty, is a computer expert living in San Francisco. He has a lovely Chinese American wife Grace (Sharon Iwai) and a typical American teenage son Paul (Kelvin Han Yee). The sister (Shen Guanglan) in China is married to a retired bureaucrat, Mr. Chao (Hu Xiaoguang), who has a teenage daughter, Lili (Li Qinqin). Parental friction with the teenage children forms the main plot for the film. A few minutes into the movie, Leo Fang, for example, is shown as being deadly opposed to Paul's relations with his Italian American girlfriend Linda (Jeannette Pavini). "You don't like Linda because she's not Chinese," cries the bewildered son, who himself can't speak a word of Chinese. Embarrassed both by his failure to win parental approval and at being caught during a rendezvous at his parents' house, Paul bitterly complains, in front of his father, "All Chinese parents are racists." While in China, Paul is also outraged to learn that his cousin Lili's mother routinely opens and reads Lili's mail. "Haven't you ever heard of such a thing as privacy? I guess there is no such thing in China," he shouts indignantly. With Paul's encouragement, Lili confronts her mother. "It's not right to read other people's mails," she says. Madame Chao shouts back, "You're not other people; you're my daughter. What is this thing 'privacy'?" Impatient, Lili explains that "privacy" cannot be translated into Chinese. "Oh, so you're trying to hide things from your mother and use western words to trick her," her mother protests.

This generational gap is also being highlighted by contrasting attitudes toward America: the older generation's cultural anachronism juxtaposed with their children's eagerness to embrace American pop culture. Some of the funniest moments in the movie are Mr. Chao's preconceived notions about American culture. For example, he is constantly confused about U.S. venereal disease statistics. "Is it true," Mr. Chao asks in a whisper to Fang, "that everyone in America has V.D.?" When he sees Paul's nubby jacket with the patches on the sleeves, Chao immediately assumes that their in-laws must be in such poverty that they cannot afford new clothes for the boy. "The latest Calvin Klein," Paul says, trying to defy the language barrier and explain in English. "Fashion. It is the fashion," Chao's better-informed daughter proudly announces with gestures. However, to Mr. Chao, Paul's prefaded and fashionably short pants are further proof of their in-laws' financial difficulties. His American nephew has to continue wearing pants he has already outgrown.

Cultural critics who look at such movies as they investigate the interplay of cultural identity and ideology have posed a crucial question about the relations between the construction of identities and representation or lack of representation. They have argued convincingly that our identities are formed largely through representation. Asian American dramas, most of which have a familial theme, explore critical issues of identity formation within the context of the family (that is, domestic) life. The immigrant family dramas discussed above transcend the clichéd constructions of Asians in Hollywood. For one, they upset the notion of a homogeneous Asian people in America by exploring different cultures' particular problems in America. Rooted in specific historical experiences, the family sagas deal with the crises of assimilation for new immigrants; the destructively divisive political passions based on old-country ideological loyalties; and the heartbreaking gap between the older, foreign-born immigrants and their American-born children. Although these are common themes shared by immigrants from other countries, these films offer American viewers fresh cultural perspectives and rare Asian voices. More important, these dramas create something far greater than just compelling stories—it is through them that we can begin to fill in another gap in immigrant history: that of the Asian American.

"Green Card" and Interracial Romances

In recent years, Asian American communities have begun experiencing dramatic changes in their demographics. First, they have become the fastest-growing segment of the American population, with a growth rate that is double that of Hispanics, six times that of African Americans, and twenty times that of European Americans. This tremendous growth can be largely contributed to new immigration, which has significantly diversified the composition of the population. What is more, with the removal of the antimiscegenation laws, intermarriage rates for Asian Americans increased sharply in the 1960s and exploded in the following two decades. Intermarriage, both among Asian Americans and between Asians and non-Asians, has become a major factor in reshaping Asian American culture. There is a 17 percent rate of intermarriage for Asian Americans alone, versus a 2 percent rate for all Americans. This higher-than-average "outmarriage" rate among Asian Americans has created an increasing number of biracial households and children.

Motivated by all these changes, Asian American filmmakers have begun to tap into new themes of interracial dating and biracial families. The pursuit of a green card (a permanent residency visa) by a new Asian immigrant, whether legal or undocumented, has become a popular subject. The Yonemoto brothers' videotape *Green Card: An American Romance* (1982), Steven Okazaki's *Living on Tokyo Time* (1987), and Tony Chan's *Combination Platter* (1993) are three examples of these Asian American bittersweet romances. Historically, interracial affairs involving Asians are rare in mainstream movies except for the Madame Butterfly genre discussed in Chapter 2. More recently, there has been some loosening up of the taboo against on-screen interracial relationships between Asians and other groups. Among Asian American productions, interracial romance serves as either a primary or a secondary plot in Ang Lee's *Pushing Hands*, *The Wedding Banquet*, and Mira Nair's *Mississippi Masala* (1992).

The third installment of their "Soap Opera Series," the Yonemotos' *Green Card* is a fascinating exploration of mass media representation and private human relations. On the surface, the video's plot is uninspiring and trite. Faced with the expiration of her student visa, and the consequence of returning to Japan, Sumie, a Japanese artist studying in the United States, arranges her own marriage to an American surfer-filmmaker so that she can stay legally in America. Soon after their wedding, Sumie and Jay become the victims of their own making. While the green card marriage is a business arrangement, Sumie and her friends feel it is real. She acts out the role of the housewife—cooking, cleaning, and waiting for Jay, who by their nuptial agreement remains a free man. To Sumie's dismay, Jay's freedom means noncommitment and quickly leads to promiscuity. Finally, when Jay regrets his behavior and tries to make their romance real, a disheartened Sumie turns away from him and articulates the movie's motif. "We're living a lie. . . . Can't you understand that the way we see family, friends, relationships, even love is mass media propaganda?" This remark by Sumie, herself a victim of media propaganda, is a powerful critique of media-invented romantic fantasies of the good life in America. It is also a self-exposé by the Yonemoto brothers, who "grew up believing completely in the American Dream as televised," and were encouraged to be "more American than Americans" and "to negate the Japanese thing as much as possible."[16]

Living on Tokyo Time, directed by Steven Okazaki, tells a more sophisticated version of a similar story. The movie opens with a shot of the virtuous Asian face of Kyoko (Minako Ohashi), a nineteen-year-old Japanese immigrant. In heavily accented English, she explains that she has deserted her family and fiancé in Japan, and has fled to San Francisco in search of an "independent experience." However, life does not turn out to be easy for her. Struggling with her very rudimentary English, Kyoko works in a restaurant and finds shelter at the YMCA. In desperate need of a green card, she enters into a blind marriage with native-born Ken, a talentless rock guitarist who speaks no Japanese and works as a janitor. Their cultural differences soon get this mismatched couple in trouble. Ken is so out of touch with his own cultural roots that he can only seize on a stereotype to understand Kyoko. While Kyoko is a far cry from the Madame Butterfly mode (being clearly a stronger and more independent Japanese woman), the Americanized Ken is the opposite of the stereotypical superachiever Asian American man. By the end of the film, which is strikingly similar in plot to *Green Card*, when Ken truly falls in love with his green card wife, Kyoko leaves him, expressing no sense of nuptial devotion.

A similar plot for a green card romance of a biracial nature runs through Tony Chan's *Combination Platter*, a hit at the 1993 Sundance Film Festival. Set in Queens, New York, the story revolves around Robert (Jeff Lau), an illegal immigrant from Hong Kong, and his guilt-ridden green card romance. Having been in

America for only two months, Robert hopes to marry an American woman, get a green card, and stay here permanently. When negotiations for an arranged match with an Asian American woman collapses over price (he offers $25,000, but she wants $50,000), Andy (Kenneth Lu), Robert's friend, introduces him to Claire (Colleen O'Brien), a lonely white woman. They meet and date, but it is an awkward situation from the outset. First, Robert is a shy introvert who can hardly make eye contact with Claire. To make matters worse, he understands English just enough to be confused about everything she says. With a guilty conscience, Robert is too decent to deceive a unsuspicious and innocent woman for long. Their relationship abruptly ends when his innate honesty compels him to confess his motive. Unfortunately, he reveals his secret just at the point where the barriers between them are beginning to break down and genuine intimacy seems possible.

The topsy-turvy world of generational conflicts intermixed with interracial relations is the subject of two of Ang Lee's early family films: *Pushing Hands* and *The Wedding Banquet.* The title phrase "pushing hands" refers to the martial art practice of Tai Chi, which teaches the art of maintaining your balance while trying to unbalance your opponent. Set in a suburban community outside New York City, the story focuses on the tensions between a Caucasian wife and her Chinese father-in-law, with the son caught in the middle. Retired Tai Chi master Mr. Chu (Sihung Lung, one of Taiwan's most well-known film actors) has come from Beijing to live in America with his only son, Alex (B. Z. Wang), a computer wizard. Problems quickly arise between Martha (Deb Snyder), Alex's Caucasian wife, and the elder Chu. The father's presence unavoidably clashes with the daughter-in-law's lifestyle and routine. Contrasting habits in food, dress, and recreational activity are viewed with mutual disdain. Worse still, the language barrier prohibits any communication between the two. Martha's Chinese is limited to *shay shay* (thank you), while Chu speaks not a word of English. The stress soon begins to wear on the family. Alex is torn between his desire to fulfill his filial responsibility and his anguish over his wife's resentment.

Lost in his new surroundings, Chu finds that practicing Tai Chi becomes his only means to maintain his identity. The turning point comes when he meets Mrs. Chen (Lai Wang), a cooking teacher at the Chinese community center where he teaches a Tai Chi class. Hoping to bring some resolution to his father's loneliness and to the conflict in his home, Alex attempts to play matchmaker. But things get out of hand and his father is left feeling even more out of place and unwanted than before. Out of frustration, Chu runs away from home and gets a dishwashing job in a Chinatown restaurant. The story comes to a climactic close when Chu stands up to his abusive boss and becomes a hero in the New York Chinatown community.

A deceptively easygoing satire of East/West culture clashes, Lee's *The Wedding Banquet* explores not only a biracial but also a homosexual relationship. Chinese American Wei Tung (Winston Chao), a yuppie real estate agent, lives peacefully with Simon (Mitchell Lichtenstein), his Caucasian male lover in New York's Greenwich Village. Because of his father's failing health, Wei Tung's parents increase the pressure on their son to get married and beget children. We learn in a voice-over in the opening scene that his mother in Taiwan has been using a long-distance computer-aided dating service for her New York–based son for years. To conceal his homosexuality from his parents, Wei Tung instructed his mother to pick an almost impossible ideal bride who is "5 feet 9 and an opera singer with three Ph.D.s, one in physics." But when the parents call to announce their unexpected visit, Simon persuades Wei Tung to enter into a marriage of convenience with Wei-Wei, an illegal Chinese mainlander immigrant. While it has, at its center, a gay couple, the movie is not about being gay alone. It is also about an interracial relationship that turns upside down. Contrary to the stereotypes, it is Simon, the "rice queen," who plays the role of the "woman," who cooks, cleans, and throws out the trash.

Mira Nair's *Mississippi Masala* breaks new ground in telling the story of an Indian/Black interracial romance, a bold adventure rarely attempted by Hollywood. The story opens with a prologue set in Uganda in 1972. Dictator Idi Amin has come to power and ordered all non-Blacks to leave the country. A liberal native lawyer, Jay (Roshan Seth), who is an descendant of the Asian Indian slave trade, is forced out with his wife Kinnu (Sharmila Tagore) and their six-year-old daughter Mina. With a slow pan shot across a world map, the film takes us through years and continents to the heart of the American South, in Greenwood, Mississippi. Mina (Sarita Choudhury), now eighteen, works as a maid at the motel where the family lives. She is expected to become a bridal prize for Harry Patel (Ashok Lath), a wealthy and snobbish Indian expatriate. However, plans for the arranged marriage are derailed when Mina rear-ends a carpet-cleaning van driven by a handsome young Black man named Demetrius (Denzel Washington). They fall in love at first sight and their affair sets off a chain reaction of racial intolerance on both sides of the communities. When word gets out they are having an affair (the lovers are caught during a liaison in Biloxi), Demetrius finds his cleaning contracts canceled by his mainly Asian Indian clients. In retaliation, Demetrius threatens to sue over the earlier auto accident. Overwhelmed by community pressures, the lovers flee the town in search of a new life together.

All the family dramas introduced in the chapter are fully embedded in the historical experience of their communities. In a phone interview with the *Denver Post*, director Nair explained her purpose in filming *Mississippi Masala*. "I was drawn to the South initially by the documentary reality that Indians had taken over the motel business there, and the trick of history that here were Indians once again in the heart of segregation, once again between black and white. That was the theme I was pursuing, the hierarchy of color."[17] Similarly, director Wayne Wang is both a product and a strong advocate of Asian community issues. Having studied experimental filmmaking in the San Francisco Bay Area in the 1960s, he went back to Hong Kong to make television programs. When he came back to the States, he worked as a community organizer in Chinatown. This community experience was crucial to his artistic development. As Wang puts it himself, "[A] lot of that community work was much more important than what I learned in film school."[18] Clearly, these domestic dramas have become the perfect vehicle for Asian American artists to address the varied historical experiences of Asian immigrants. Drawn from ordinary people and everyday lives, they have contributed to our understanding of immigrant families and cast new light on the many new issues Asian Americans face today.

"BECOMING ASIAN AMERICAN": SUBJECTIVITY AND MIXED IDENTITIES

Asian American family dramas are groundbreaking in the sense that they boldly transgress the boundaries of race and ethnicity. In her often-cited essay "Heterogeneity, Hybridity, Multiplicity: Marking Asian American Differences," Lisa Lowe discusses identity issues in Asian American films and videos. Her major thesis is that those works argue forcefully against an essentialized Asian American identity and "emphasize the dynamic fluctuation and heterogeneity of Asian American culture." Indeed, critique of fixed notions of Asian American racial, cultural, and sexual identities stands as the trademark of these Asian American narrative dramas. Trinh T. Minh-ha raises the ultimate question in a different context: "What if the popularized story of identity crisis proves to be only a story and nothing else?"[19] The interrogation of the relationship between Asian American cinema and identities is the focus of this section. Three important themes have informed this important discussion.

Identity As a Social Construct

Asian American dramas explicitly question identities as naturally given in a primordial sense. Mira Nair's *Mississippi Masala*, for example, provides a rare, skeptical view into identity politics. Both groups portrayed in the movie, African Americans and Asian Indians, are obsessed with race and nationality, although their understanding of each other's culture is rather shaky. One local white is totally convinced that Mina's people are Native American Indians, while Demetrius's half-deaf uncle takes

Mina for a Black girl "from Indiana." In a family-dinner scene, Nair deftly exposes the dubious notion of any prescribed cultural identities. Demetrius brings Mina home for his father's birthday supper, where she explains that her own people were brought to Africa by the British to build railroads. "You just like us," says Demetrius's younger brother Dexter. "We from Africa, but we never been there, either."

According to North American racial configuration, identity boundaries are not naturally given, but instead are socially constructed and politically negotiated. Asian American dramas challenge those prescribed boundaries. In *Living on Tokyo Time*, for instance, the characters' ancestry does little more than define their ethnic affiliation. Nor is their ethnicity a major factor in formulating their identity. In fact, Ken's thoroughly Americanized sister gets along much better with her Caucasian husband than Ken does in his relations with Kyoko. In this case, cultural differences are more important than genetic makeup in defining who they are and where their loyalty goes. The heroine in *Thousand Pieces of Gold* has a multifaceted identity, too. She is not at home in either the white community or among the Chinese Americans on the other side of town. According to author McCunn, Lalu's detachment from other Chinese immigrants might be partially due to the fact that she is Mongolian (as her non-Han name would indicate) and partially because she spoke a different dialect of Chinese than the Cantonese spoken by the majority of nineteenth-century immigrants from southern China. Tony Chan's *Combination Platter* succeeds best with its exposure of the mixed allegiances of the Chinese beneath the surface of ethnic solidarity. Any sense of unity, if there is one, is marked by a pecking order among the Szechuan Inn employees themselves. The young and affluent "ABC" (American-born Chinese) cashier cannot read the Chinese menu. Because of this language incompetence, she becomes the object of taunts among the Chinese staff. A cook complains bitterly because his son is marrying a Chinese woman who speaks a different dialect. The members of the restaurant's serving staff, who are primarily from Hong Kong, and speak Cantonese, are deadly opposed to the kitchen staff, who are mostly from the mainland and speak Mandarin. This film presents a complex and multidimensional Chinese American community from a cross-ethnic and cross-class perspective, a very rare case in American movies. Personal identities for the characters can also be defined by other cultural reference points. For example, in *Dim Sum*, Wang creatively employs the "film within a film" technique to conceptualize and articulate the characters' different cultural positioning. Auntie Mary (Ida F. O. Chong), the next-door neighbor, is a *Dynasty* fan, but Mrs. Tam watches Hong Kong soap operas. When Geraldine's fiancé Richard comes to visit, he watches Kung Fu movies. As for Uncle Tam, Frank Capra's *You Can't Take It with You* is his favorite.

History teaches us that while personal and cultural identities can be externally imposed, they are usually negotiated successfully in our daily lives. The movies help illuminate the processes and strategies by which Asian Americans construct and articulate their personal sense of identity. Nair in *Mississippi Masala* demonstrates clearly how Asian Indians assume changing identities under different circumstances. In Greenwood, the Indians occupy an ambiguous middle ground. The white middle class applauds their work ethic but discreetly excludes them from full social fellowship. In one scene, for example, we see a white Southerner sharing with Mina's relative over the phone his deep racial prejudice against Black people, as if the Indian immigrant were one of his own. "Are y'all havin' nigger troubles?" he comments, referring to the relationship between Mina and Demetrius. In another, we witness two white shop clerks make racist comments about a noisy Indian wedding nearby. The older man says, with a strong Southern drawl, "I wish they'd go back to the reservation." Local Blacks resent the Indians' business success, clannishness, and "white" airs. As Demetrius complained to Jay bitterly, "I know that folks can come to this country and be as Black as the ace of spades, but soon as they come here they start to act white—and treat us like their doormats." While misjudged by both groups, the Indians are highly color-conscious themselves. They are shown exploiting their positions to their own advantage. Politically, they align themselves with the whites, claiming to be people of color only when it is expedient.

In a positive light, Mina manipulates her own identity in a variety of scenes. She is shown to be close to her parents, and is an accepted member of the Indian community. She is also comfortable in the African world, as evidenced in Uganda by her knowledge of Swahili and her affection toward Okelo (Konga Mbandu), a Black Ugandan and her father's best friend. In Mississippi she is at home in the Black disco, and enjoys spending an afternoon with Demetrius's family. She does not feel out of place at all while attending an elaborate Indian wedding ceremony. However, when meeting Demetrius's kin, she calls herself an African (from Uganda). Mina's character is multidimensional and flexible, in contrast to most other films dealing with interracial love, in which the identity emphasized for each of the characters does not go beyond racial categorization.[20]

By challenging fixed, essentialized Asian American identities, these dramas attempt to redefine personal and cultural identity not as a matter of simple inheritance, but as an active cultural construct as well. To borrow Lisa Lowe's words, it is "a much 'messier' process than unmediated vertical transformation from one generation to another."[21] Indeed, the films promote a cultural syncretism and ethnic multiplicity of Asian American identities. This cultural hybridity is based on a multiple and much more balanced understanding of the process of identity formation: that is, that ethnic identity could be inherited and invented at the same time. It involves personal negotiations as well as social construction. This type of identity constructed in the movies fits perfectly David Hollinger's vision of a postethnicity that is contingent and instrumental in nature.[22]

Identity As Mélange

Historically, racial formation in America has been and continues to be Black and white. In this dualistic matrix, people of other colors fall through the cracks. As Mira Nair explains to *Mother Jones* magazine, "People think of racism as black versus white, but there's a different kind of consciousness of color within minority groups as we equate beauty with fairness and ugliness with darkness."[23] For her film crew, their six-week filming experience in the South in the summer of 1990 testifies to power relations residing in the shades of color. Sarita Choudhury, of Indian descent, told a national TV audience on *The Arsenio Hall Show*, "I was hanging around with a little boy who was black, and they wouldn't let him come into restaurants I was allowed into. Things like that happened all the time."[24] Choudhury's experience was not atypical in the Mississippi Delta. For example, the New Orleans *Times-Picayune* reported responses to the movie by some local Indians in the Deep South. A twenty-three-year-old, Suresh Chawla, recalled his experience as a freshman at Greenwood High School in the early 1980s. White students sat on one side of the room, and Black students on the other. A Black student urged Chawla to sit on his side, but the teacher put the confused Chawla with the white students. "Can you imagine being asked whether you are black or white?"[25] For Mina's family in Greenwood, Mississippi, it is the second time they have found themselves in the middle of a Black/white racial divide.

The Hindi word *masala* refers to a mix of spices used in Indian cooking. For Nair, it is a perfect metaphor for the racial and cultural mixture in the movie. "What struck me really deeply," Nair said, "was the commonality that I saw in the rhythms between the black community and the Indian community. . . . Particularly in the connectedness of families, the fact that everybody knows everybody's business in a way, yelling out names from stoops and street corners and the emphasis on religion."[26] Indeed, *Mississippi Masala* captures on film the unusual racial stew of Black, brown, and white cultures that awkwardly mixed together. Nair states confidently: "I believe strongly that to be a Masala, to be mixed, is the new world order. So many of us think in one language and are forced to speak in another. . . . The alliance of the future is that between black and brown."[27] This point of view is a reflection of Mina's own life experiences—an Indian woman, born in Uganda, having lived in England, and settled in the United States. The film celebrates intermingling and cross-fertilization by being hybrid in almost every dimension: the music, the scenery, even the actors, who came from all traditions. Some, like Sharmila Tagore, are from Indian musicals; Roshan Seth is from the Royal Shakespeare Company; others, like Denzel Washington, are from Hollywood; and there is Sarita Choudhury, who had never acted before.

But nobody embodies a character of mixed identity better than Mina. One provocative dimension of her identity may escape viewers' attention: that is, Mina's relationship with Okelo, the Black Ugandan. It may not be apparent to every spectator on first viewing, yet there are unmistakable hints that Okelo could be Mina's biological father. It is noteworthy that on their way to exile, for example, Kinnu, the mother, picks up a photograph of Okelo and Mina and looks at it wistfully before placing it in her purse. She later places this photograph in a prominent position in the liquor store she runs in Greenwood. The farewell scene at the bus station in Uganda is equally suggestive of a relationship between Okelo and Kinnu, who share an intimate embrace, and who get a somewhat hostile look from Jay when he happens on them. What is more, Mina and Okelo's parting is affectionate and their faces are nose-to-nose in the frame, suggesting their similarity in physical appearance. Mina's complexion, a shade darker than that of her parents, supports the assumption that she is half African and half Indian. This alternate reading of Mina's biological identity adds to her mixed heritage and gives intriguing depth to the movie's subtext.

British scholar Homi Bhabha is interested in the margin of hybridity and the borderline experience, "where cultural differences 'contingently' and conflictually touch."[28] Asian American film productions address cultural identity as a mixture of all different elements put together. The dramas portray layers of multiple and even contradictory identities that defy any dogmatic notion of purity. Viewers learn from the characters that identities do not have to be fixed in a single geographical or cultural space. The identities explored do not fall into the familiar categories of national, cultural, and religious identity. Indeed, what bell hooks says about Wayne Wang's *Blue in the Face* applies to Asian American dramas in general: "In a very careful way the film . . . contests all sorts of construction of pure identity; it reminds the viewer that so much is mixed, and that it's in the mixing and sharing that the magic rises."[29] George Woo (professor of Asian American studies at San Francisco State University in real life), playing the part of the director of the Newcomers' Language Center in Wang's *Chan Is Missing*, points to an apple pie baked by the Sun Wah Ku bakery as a metaphor of Chinese American identity. "It is a definite American form, you know, pie, okay. And it looks just like any other apple pie, but it doesn't taste like any other apple pie, you eat it. And that's because many Chinese baking technique has gone into it, and when we deal with our everyday lives, that's what we have to do."[30] Although Woo's metaphor presents a very depoliticized image of cultural assimilation that does not address any power relations, it does celebrate the hybrids or mixtures in Asian American cultural identities.

In defense of his controversial novel *The Satanic Verses*, which brought a fundamentalist threat to his life that has him still in hiding, Salman Rushdie declares:

> It celebrates hybridity, impurity, intermingling, the transformation that comes of new and unexpected combinations of human beings, cultures, ideas, politics, movies, song [and that] rejoices in mongrelization and fears the absolutism of the Pure. *Mélange*, the hotchpotch, a bit of this and that is how newness enters the world. This is the great possibility that migration gives the world and I have tried to embrace it.[31]

This is an equally fitting commentary on Asian American family dramas, which explicitly counter any limiting and prescriptive notions of ethnic identity and celebrate cultural hybridity and diasporic sensitivities.

Identity As a Process of Becoming

In his essay "Cultural Identity and Cinematic Representation," Stuart Hall talks about identity as "a matter of 'becoming' as well as 'being.' It belongs to the future as much as to the past. It is not something which already exists, transcending place, time, history, and culture . . . like everything which is historical, they undergo constant transformation. Far from being eternally fixed in some essentialized past, they are subject to the continuous 'play' of history, culture and power."[32]

Indeed, identity politics, as presented in the dramas, is taken only as a point of departure rather than closure. So identity is presented as a contingent, constantly changing, flexible concept rather than as a fixed notion. The main character, Alex, in *Pushing Hands* shows convincingly that he is very Americanized, and he even marries a Caucasian novelist. But when his father comes to visit, he wants to be a good filial son and goes back to Chinese culture. Only after a confrontation between his wife and his father does he have to make a hard choice between the two. He decides to return to his American way of life, and lets his father go out to find a wife of his own. The movie does not attempt to posit any easy answers to Alex's problems, for to suggest any solution would have been *no* solution.

To illustrate the process of becoming, travel or movement and transnationalization serve as important tropes in these dramas. In any of these films under discussion (*The Wedding Banquet, Mississippi Masala, Chan Is Missing, Pushing Hands,* and *The Joy Luck Club*), key characters are uniformly either migrating or traveling. The chase and search for Chan Hung, who never appears in *Chan Is Missing*, is a metaphor for the Chinese American identity. As discussed in Chapter 1, Jo and

Steve went around Chinatown for seven days, asking a whole range of people to tell them where Chan Hung was. Instead of locating Chan in a single place, they received conflicting information on his whereabouts. Some people said Chan was a communist spy in hiding. Others said he was a robber who cheated their friends and fled to mainland China. A big question mark lingers in the minds of the audience at the end of the film. No closure seems to be available for Chan Hung's true identity, because he lends himself to so many different possibilities.

In *A Great Wall*, Leo Fang packs his family off to China. For him it is a journey home to visit his sister and to rediscover his cultural heritage—a quest for self-definition. It is a dream that comes true for Fang, since he is able to draw much nourishment from the traditional culture. He returns to America with a wealth of artifacts and a new cultural identity, signified by him switching from jogging to the practice of Tai Chi. However, for his wife, Grace, and his son, Paul, who portray second- and third-generation Americans, the trip to China is a visit to a foreign land where they are just tourists. Thus, the movie presents an eloquent example of a fluid cultural identity for its characters through traveling. As Lisa Lowe states it well, the director alternates between shots of Beijing and Northern California, "in a type of continual filmic 'migration' between the two, as if to thematize in its very form the travel between cultural spaces."[33]

In these migrations or movements, the movies explore the notions of homeland, displacement, nomadism, and people's alternating identities. Mira Nair told Andrea Stuart that in her film *Mississippi Masala* she was trying "to explore exile, memory, nostalgia, dislocation: This thing we call home."[34] Interestingly, in the movie a feeling of displacement does not necessarily imply having experienced an actual displacement, or travel. Rather, it may simply mean a sense of marginalization or a longing for the so-called "imagined communities." For example, both the African Americans and the Indian immigrants have a mythic notion of Africa and India as their ancestral homelands. Although Mina and Demetrius are generations away from Africa and India as native lands, they are deeply aware of where they can claim their ethnic heritage. Further, the hope of "returning home" implies very different meanings for the characters. For Mina's family, both the mother Kinnu and daughter Mina have easily taken America as their new homeland and settled successfully. In contrast, Jay, the father, is so bitter about his forced departure that he cannot adjust to his life in America. By cherishing the dream of a lost homeland, he is unable to use his education and talents to grow in his new home. As Nair reflected in an interview years ago, "I would have to admit that I have always been drawn to stories of people who live on the margins of society—on the edge, or outside, learning the language of being in-between, always dealing with the question: what, and where, is home?"[35]

As such, these dramas should be read as powerful texts that contest the usefulness of the category "Asian American" for present and future generations. They suggest the contingency of Asian American subjectivity and highlight the contradictions of Asian American identities. As a result, the movies have shifted the discourse on identity politics from the moot question "Who are Asian Americans?" to the critical issue of "What are the different ways of becoming Asian Americans?" Lisa Lowe's interpretation of Peter Wang's *A Great Wall* serves as the best conclusion to my discussion in this section: "In keeping with the example of *A Great Wall,* we might consider as a possible model for the ongoing construction of ethnic identity the migratory process suggested by Wang's filming technique and employment: we might conceive of the making and practice of Asian American culture as nomadic, unsettled, taking place in the travel between cultural sites and in the multivocality of heterogeneous and conflicting positions."[36]

ASIAN AMERICAN AESTHETICS

Films are, after all, works of art, so it is important to know how Asian American films tell stories not only overtly, through different points of view, but also through different film forms and styles. What is more, structures and forms can be used "as metaphors for points of view."[37] "The form contains much of its content," as Bruce Yonemoto once said in an interview, "and so we try to deal with that content in terms of form."[38] In this last section of the chapter, I would like to offer some observations on the structural similarities or specific formal properties among the films discussed in the previous pages.

Narrative Strategies

In narrative structures—an important formal element in film—Asian American family dramas adopt very different strategies with regard to subject positions and textual development. For one, the story is often told more as a process (the telling of the story) than as a linear chronology. *Chan Is Missing*, for example, can be interpreted as a parody of a Charlie Chan film. Indeed, the marketing of the videocassette release of the film refers to Jo and Steve as "two 'gumshoes'" who are "[w]alking self-mockingly in the footsteps of Charlie Chan and his Number One Son." Despite this "self-mocking" label, the film's narrative structure breaks away from the Hollywood norm. In contrast to the typical classic Hollywood detective drama, which pursues and ends up with a solution, *Chan Is Missing* offers no resolution to the mystery. This open-ended plot challenges the generic expectations of a Charlie Chan film.

Wang's second feature, *Dim Sum,* is noted for the ellipses in its narrative structure. At one point, for example, Mrs. Tam is being coached in American history for her long-delayed citizenship examination. The next thing we know, a cake decorated with the stars and stripes is brought in. Wang's direction conveys this crucial event in her life in a single stroke of narrative ellipsis. Also, because of an elliptical style, the complications of Geraldine and her mother's relationship are often left unsaid. As a *Newsday* critic comments, nothing seems to be clear-cut in the plot, which drifts along in simplistic repetitiveness of the narrative structure.[39] Interestingly, the Yonemotos have achieved a multilayered structure in *Green Card* through soap opera parodies and clichéd dialogues. While the video is based on the straightforward true story of Sumie Nobahara, the high-sounding dialogues about art and romance between the two main characters create conscious ruptures in the narrative; for example, "Hold me, never let me go," and "Make her see your love is strong enough for the both of you." As a reviewer points out, these "are clichés which click in the viewer's memory without identifying themselves."[40] "In memory," Sumie says incisively in the video, "there is no way you can tell one reality from another."

The Joy Luck Club, perhaps more than any movie in the group, should be noted for its circular textual structure. It is commonly known that films with more than four central characters often begin to lose their structural cohesion. How can one follow the interlocking collection of sixteen separate stories, about eight Chinese American women, told in Amy Tan's best-seller? The movie, like the novel, is structured like a mahjong game, with full repeating patterns and pieces. Using voice-over and multiple crisscrossing flashbacks, Wang successfully focuses on one mother and daughter at a time in rhythmic juxtapositions, going back and forth between the past and present. The first flashback, for example, concerns June and Suyuan. It shows June as teenager falling short of her mother's expectations by performing poorly at a piano recital. The next pair of flashbacks, set in China and America, contrasts Lindo's arranged childhood marriage with her daughter Waverly's interracial union with a Caucasian man. In the third pair, Ying Ying's similar unhappy early marriage in China becomes a mirror for her daughter Lena to reflect upon her own unhappy marriage. The last pair of flashbacks comes between An Mei and her daughter Rose. Following her own mother's example (who committed suicide to better her position in an extended family), An Mei helps Rose to control her own destiny in her family. Finally, through another set of flashbacks, we learn more about Suyuan and how she abandoned her babies in China. With June's visit to China, where she reunites with her long-lost sisters, Wang completes the stories, bringing the interlocking vignettes to a touching conclusion.

Characterizations in these films also help reinforce their multiple narrative structures. Robin Wood, in a review article, describes *Combination Platter* and *The*

Wedding Banquet as "ensemble" films, "in which the spectator's interest and sympathies are divided among a number of divergent yet interacting characters rather than focused upon a particular protagonist or single narrative line."[41] Indeed, we may find our empathy goes in divergent directions at different moments screening *The Wedding Banquet.* Sometimes our feelings go with the elder parents, other times with the bride in the marriage of convenience, and still other times with the gay couple. Often in these film narratives, there are times of nonmovement for the characters, according to bell hooks, who comments on this phenomenon in Wayne Wang's newest film. "In *Blue in the Face*, there were those perfect moments when the characters were almost not moving. . . . It was very uncharacteristic of American films in that it uses the pause in a very skillful way. There are moments of silence, in which you are actually able to reflect on what is happening. Most films are moving us forward, and you don't have that pace."[42] Indeed, this rarely used film device (in standard Hollywood-style filmmaking) reflects Wang's trademark indirection and the film's laid-back mood. It also invites audience participation by slowing things down and making viewers reflect on what is going on.

No matter what the story line is, whether "Mama knows best" or "Father knows best," there are no easy answers or pat endings to the stories. Presco's rain-puddle metaphor in *Chan Is Missing* best summarizes the nature of this nonclosure. Twice in the movie, Presco asks Steve and Jo to look in the puddle for the missing Chan Hung. "You guys are looking for Mr. Chan," asks Presco, "why don't you look in the puddle?" By the end of the film, while Jo is brooding over the case and losing hope of ever finding Chan in his apartment, Presco repeats the same advice to Jo: "You guys got to look in the puddle." By looking into the puddle, Steve and Jo will realize that Chan's identity does not adhere to a single or polar structure. Because of water's fluidity, every time they look, the puddle will be always differ in shape and size. What an evocative metaphor for the film's open-ended textual style.

Mise-en-Scène

In addition to their distinctive narrative strategies, another important stylistic feature of Asian American dramas is their significant use of mise-en-scène.[43] A film frame is filled not just with Asian "images," but with the visual texture of Asian American cultures, including angle of framing, locale, family decoration, and emblematic imagery. Reflecting on the production of *The Joy Luck Club*, for example, Wayne Wang cites the principle of Chinese paintings in his framing decisions. "If you look at Chinese landscape painting," he said, "[the point of view] is usually either parallel to the plane of action or it's very high up. The reason for being parallel is that everything is equal in that frame. There's no focal point or center of attention. There's no foreground or background."[44] Further, Wang attributes the film's camera work to this Chinese influence. "I kind of used that [principle] as my guidance for looking at the world. A non-emphasizing camera position. In *The Joy Luck Club*, when we're sort of medium or close up, I always put the camera parallel to the plane of action. When we were farther away, I always put the camera really high up."[45]

With her skillful eyes, Mira Nair in *Mississippi Masala* sets skin hues and varieties of dress against backgrounds that are exotic and commonplace at the same time. For example, at the movie's beginning, the viewers note the brown Indian skins contrast with the darker pigmentation of native Africans, and the greens of the vegetation below the Indian family's villa glow with a dry yellow dirt road. The diverse musical lines of several cultures, scored by L. Subramaniam, play rhythmically and melodically against one another. "The whole strength of the film," said the movie director, "is that it's genuine hybridization, a genuine *masala* where people are cast and wear clothes and listen to music that defines *them*. They're not all smoothed out at the edges."[46]

In terms of milieu, the foyer of shoes (*Dim Sum*), the mahjong table (*Dim Sum, The Joy Luck Club*), the restaurant (*Chan Is Missing, The Wedding Banquet, Combination Platter*), the motel (*Mississippi Masala*), and the family kitchen (*Eat Drink Man Woman*) have become the most common settings for Asian American stories. The props and set designs inside Szechuan Inn become synonymous with the lifestyles and customs of the Chinese characters in Tony Chan's *Combination Platter*. The decorations of the backdrop seem authentic to mature eyes. In fact, the whole film was shot in Chan's parents' restaurant in Flushing, New York. It was photographed from 10 P.M. to 10 A.M. and Chan had to clean up before the place opened for the lunch trade the next day. Similarly, according to *Dim Sum*'s production notes, the filming took place almost entirely in Mrs. Chew's house, with few changes in the setting. The filming process was so informal (and natural) that children of the household literally moved from room to room just one step ahead of the camera. The location provides a touching true-to-life quality, as though we are watching real life through a hidden camera. For example, anyone familiar with Chinese American household customs would not miss the evocative image of a row of shoes displayed in the doorway or stairway (all family members take off their shoes and put on slippers before entering the house, and even guests are politely asked to do so). Terrel Seltzer, who wrote the screenplay for *Dim Sum*, emphasizes the metaphorical meaning of "the older woman's orthopedic shoes next to her daughter's Day-Glo sandals, the traditional and the modern worlds side by side." For another example, it seems so familiar for Chinatowners to see Mrs. Tam converse with her neighbor across the clotheslines amid the close-standing houses and narrow yards. In a word, Wang frames his characters in private spaces (the every-day houses in the hilly streets of the Richmond district of San Francisco). These inti-mate locations and private spaces allow the viewers a rare entrance into the inner lives of Chinese American families.

Joining a cinematic world of food fetishism, the motif of Chinese delica-cies is represented through mise-en-scène in a number of films.[47] The movie titles—*Dim Sum*; *Combination Platter;* and *Freckled Rice* (1983), by the late Stephen Ning—are directly taken from the regular menu of Chinese restaurants. In both Wayne Wang's *Dim Sum* and Ang Lee's *Eat Drink Man Woman*, food serves as a metaphor for the primal human connections of family and love. Three world-class chefs worked on the production of *Eat Drink*, including food consultant Lin Huei-Yi, daughter-in-law of China's leading food expert, Fu Pei-Mei. Huei-Yi coached the actors on physical preparation of dishes, and special choreography was devised to mimic traditional chefs' movements.[48] Likewise, Ang Lee, in *The Wedding Ban-quet*, exposes the audience to a world of Chinese American customs seldom acknowledged by Hollywood. The wedding itself is the best set piece—a colorfully wacky procession of drinking games, fertility rituals, and Chinese etiquette and attitudes toward sexuality.

Given the cultural differences that shaped their historical experience, Asian American films have handled the mise-en-scène with a cultural sensitivity that cannot be expected in Hollywood dramas. The emotional texture of the films gives the viewers an empirical dimension to their life experience. Writer bell hooks comments that it is Wayne Wang's "ordinary details, the dailyness of life" that make his work so appealing. "Wang's work is not documentary realism," hooks wrote; "instead, he works to capture the meditative spirit of stillness and reflection that is often present in all our lives but goes unnoticed. He takes the fascination with small details, ordinary tasks that hint at a larger metaphysics."[49] Although, as some critics point out, Wang's preoccupation with inanimate objects echoes the great Japanese director Yasujiro Ozu, his cultural sensitivities are largely shaped by the Asian immigrant experience itself.

Montage

Every film, according to John Grierson's much-quoted definition, is "a creative treatment of actuality."[50] Thus, in each film there always exists such dialectics of what the camera sees and what the filmmaker selects. Since history concerns place and time, filmmakers' editing is of special importance in constructing meanings. Like the mise-en-scène, the montage in Asian American films is also worthy of our critical attention. In this respect, Wayne Wang is the most original in creating alternatives to standard Hollywood-style filmmaking. He plans his camera shots very carefully and gives a great deal of thought to composition. Following the philosophy of Chinese painting, he summarizes his editing in *Chan Is Missing* in several progressive stages:

> I originally started cutting it in the structure of the evolution of the Chinese written word. For example, I was interested in making a mystery where in the beginning there are only images, because the first stage of the evolution is just pictures of things. The second stage is called "pointing to the situation." If (in Chinese writing) you have a picture of a knife, how can you express the edge of the knife? You put a dot to indicate the edge. The third stage is called "the meeting of ideas." If you have a knife and a heart together—this is the montage theory—you have "patience." The fourth stage is the introduction of sound to the image. There are three or four other stages, but they got really abstract so I put them aside. . . . [It interests me] to build a mystery using that structure as its basis rather than thinking of a story first.[51]

In this case, principles in Chinese writing allow Wang to try an editing scheme that deemphasizes the standard mystery formulas. In many other cases, the shaping influence over his film style comes from the sociohistorical particularities in the Chinese American experience. In *Dim Sum*, Wang places special importance in the meanings of silent and still frames. Within Mrs. Tam's immaculate house, the camera often remains static and pauses for "empty frames." Wang does not attempt to create a continuous flow of action. Rejecting a shot/reverse shot structure, he moves the narrative forward through a montage of meticulously composed empty shots. In these silent still frames, we see just curtains swaying in the breeze, water rippling under the sun, or shoes huddled at the foot of a stairway. These sophisticated visual ideas do not block the overflow of the plot, but rather they help capture the essence of the characters' lives in delicate touches. Each of the director's quiet camera shots conveys a tranquil, rich mood and atmosphere for the movie.

In a recent interview with Wang, bell hooks asked the director about the special significance of empty space in his works. Wang explains:

> A lot of people ask why I'm so obsessed with the environment, with empty rooms, with inanimate objects. . . . And the details of how they organize the space are really important. A friend of mine used to do research on how the elderlies in Chinatown organized the space. They usually put their beds against the wall, the long side of it, and then they would put newspaper along the wall, because the newspaper would somehow cut the cold, the *ying chi*, that's coming off the wall. Those little details are culturally very important to me. . . . It goes back to the whole theory of montage.[52]

Drawing from his own bilingual and bicultural background, Wang's montage often displays the hallmarks of a hybrid sensibility.[53] When asked about some of the formative influences on film style in *The Joy Luck Club*, Wang cites Japanese director Yasujiro Ozu, Indian director Satyajit Ray, and British filmmaker David Lean as inspirations. He says, "Ozu and Satyajit Ray were two who portrayed human emotions in such a simple, truthful way. David Lean was a third one, because a part of this movie is very epic and very big." Wang believes "*The Joy Luck Club* had elements of these three directors."[54]

Sound

In the BBC television series *Ways of Seeing*, British cultural scholar John Berger uses photographs, as well as oil paintings and their reproduction (through the invention of the camera), as materials for cultural analysis. He demonstrates how powerful a factor silence and sound (among other techniques) can be in changing the meaning of an image (from Van Gogh's "Wheatfield with Crows" to British TV commercials).[55] In film production, the soundtrack is always built up and manipulated separately from the moving images. Thus, the cueing of sound effects and music as a technique is *not* of secondary importance for Asian American filmmakers. In *Picture Bride*, for instance, the director, Kayo Hatta, placed the "hole hole bushi" songs that women sang in the fields at the center of the film. She told an interviewer:

> "Hole hole bushi" songs are very expressive and very direct emotional expressions of what the women were going through. Some of them are bitter, some are very passionate. They give an interesting glimpse into Issei women who were thought to be reticent and stoic. Instead, these were earthly, country women singing sometimes bawdy, sometimes poignant and sad songs of daily life. Some were passionate love songs for their husbands saying, "My love for you burns brighter and hotter than the fires of the volcano, Hale Mau Mau."[56]

Similarly, the soundtrack of *Mississippi Masala*, as Gwendolyn Foster notes, "is a pleasurable mélange of African, Indian, African-American, and worldbeat music that provides bridges across Black and Brown cultures. The audience is treated to African chorals and instrumentals, African-American blues and rap music, Indian wedding songs and reggae music."[57]

The use of language in the movies deserves our attention, too. Like a number of Chicano/a independent feature films (*Ballad of Gregorio Cortez* and *El Notre*), many of these Asian American dramas are bilingual and require full or partial subtitling for the American audience. Linguistic differences also figure significantly in the dialogues, which slip easily between English and a native language of the community. In the film script for *Chan Is Missing*, English translation of scenes spoken in Chinese, and Chinese character text of scenes spoken in Chinese, had to be provided as an appendix. What is more, language often becomes a metaphor for cultural conflicts in the film. A few minutes into the movie, we see Jo and Steve at a table listening to a young Asian American woman lawyer rambling about "the legal implications" of a cross-cultural misunderstanding in view of Chan's case:

> At any rate, at this the policeman became rather impatient, restated the question, "Did you or did you not stop at the stop sign?" in a rather hostile tone, which, in turn, flustered Mr. Chan, which caused him to hesitate answering the question, which further enraged the policeman, so that he asked the question again, "You didn't stop at the stop sign, did you?" in a negative tone, to which Mr. Chan automatically answered "No." Now, to any native speaker of English, "No" would mean, "No, I didn't stop at the stop sign." However, to Mr. Chan, "No, I didn't stop at the stop sign," wasn't "No, I didn't stop at the stop sign." It was "No, I didn't not stop at the stop sign," in other words, "Yes, I did stop at the stop sign." You see what I'm saying? He was, um, correct in the Chinese because the answer has to match the truth of the action. However, English speakers, native American English speakers, tend to work more from a grammatical mode.[58]

Language defines communities, preserving and protecting certain traditions and values. Screenwriter Terrel Seltzer describes her experience with *Dim Sum*: "We did a lot of interviews. We talked to Laureen about the cake she gives her mother when the mother's friends are playing Mah Jongg. 'What kinds of things would they say to you?' we asked her. It was out of those conversations that I found lines like 'When are we going to eat your cake, Geraldine?—the one that smells so sweet and makes your mama so happy.' I couldn't make up lines like that. I don't know the idiom."[59] She added, "I love to listen to that kind of half-English, half-Pidgin talk. It's always so funny and heartwarming when friends are talking Chinese among themselves and suddenly there's a word of English and the listener 'gets' it."[60] Translators are crucial figures in Asian American dramas such as these. Often bilingual characters become our point of entry into the Asian American cultural world. Leo Fang, the only bilingual person among the two families in *A Great Wall*; Geraldine, Auntie Mary, and Julia in *Dim Sum*; and the mothers and daughters in *The Joy Luck Club* all bring that bilingual, bicultural dimension to their roles.

What constitutes an Asian American aesthetic may be the subject of endless debates, and I have never intended to arrive at any closure (read: definition). However, I do hope that, through a close reading of the narrative and aesthetic strategies deployed by the family drama film, I have succeeded in outlining its discursive parameters. To recap it briefly, an Asian American film aesthetic is grounded in historical specificity (content), subjectivity (perspectives), and formal properties (style). These alternative narrative and formal strategies may include, but are not limited to, textual structure, camera technique, editing styles, and film sound. Often at odds with Hollywood norm, they reflect Asian American filmmakers' efforts to develop an oppositional film practice that could only be interpreted in the historical and cultural context of the Asian American experience. Understanding and recognizing Asian American aesthetic sensitivities is critical as a step forward to help move the discussion of Asian American films beyond a racialized framework.

NOTES

1   See, for example, Tamio Spiegel, "Horror! Sci-Fi! Action! Asian American Genre Filmmakers," *CineVue* 8:2 (July 1993), 4.

2   For details, see Bill Ong Hing, *Making and Remaking Asian America Through Immigation Policy, 1850–1990* (Stanford, Calif.: Stanford University Press, 1993).

3   Somini Sengupta, "Asian-American Films Speak a New Language of Multicultural Variety," *New York Times* (July 28, 1997), B4.

4   Phone interview with Katherine Leslie, April 1996.

5   Renee Tajima, "To Be Asian American," *Cinemaya* 25–26 (1994–1995), 44.

6   The film does not indicate the origin and meaning of the title phrase, leading viewers to falsely believe that it may come from the price for which she is sold.

7   I want to again acknowledge Darrell Hamamoto for his thoughtful reading of my manuscript. His critique of *Thousand Pieces of Gold* as another example of "white man possessing yellow woman formula, as in *Come See the Paradise*" has changed my original interpretation of the movie.

8   Phone interview with Katherine Leslie, April 1996. In the interview, Hatta told Leslie that she was currently working on a book-derived film called *Floating World* (a road film about Japanese Americans after the camp experience). It is a story about how these former internees have traveled across the country looking for work, community, and a place to start all over again.

9   Lisa Lowe, "Heterogeneity, Hybridity, Multiplicity: Marking Asian American Differences," *Diaspora* 1:1 (Spring 1991), 34.

10   Renee Tajima, "Eat a Bowl of Tea," *Village Voice* (Aug. 1, 1989), 67.

11   John C. Tibbetts, "A Delicate Balance: An Interview with Wayne Wang about *The Joy Luck Club*," *Literature Film Quarterly* 22:1 (1994), 5.

12   As quoted by Blaise Simpson, "Stories from the Heart," *Los Angeles Times* (Sept. 5, 1993), C10, 105.

13   Ibid.

14   See director's note in the unpublished film synopsis.

15   Renee Tajima, "The Wash," *Village Voice* (Aug. 23, 1988), 61.

16   As quoted by Bill Horrigan, "Bruce and Norman Yonemoto: Assimilated," *Art and Text* 55 (Oct. 1, 1996), 56.

17   Howie Movshovitz, " 'Masala' explores hierarchy of color," *Denver Post* (Feb. 20, 1992), F4, 23.

18   Diane Mei Lin Mark, "Interview with Wayne Wang," *Chan Is Missing* (Honolulu: Bamboo Ridge Press, 1984), 105.

19   Trinh T. Minh-ha, "Difference: A Special Third World Woman Issue," *Feminist Review* 25 (March 1987), 5–22.

20   For example, many critics have made favorable comparisons between *Mississippi Masala* and Spike Lee's *Jungle Fever*.

21   Lowe, 27.

22   David Hollinger, *Postethnic America* (New York: Basic Books, 1995).

23   Peggy Orenstein, "Salaam America! An Interview with Director Mira Nair," *Mother Jones* (Jan./Feb. 1992), 60.

24   Steve Waiton, " 'Mississippi Masala' actors see racism in Delta," Jackson, Miss., *Clarion-Ledger* (Feb. 29, 1992).

25   David Snyder, "Indians say 'Masala' plot unlikely," New Orleans *Times-Picayune* (Feb. 28, 1992).

26   Movshovitz.

27   As quoted by Andrea Stuart, "Mira Nair: A New Hybrid Cinema," *Women and Film: A Sight and Sound Reader,* ed. Pam Cook and Philip Dodd (Philadelphia: Temple University Press, 1993), 212.

28   Homi Bhabha, *The Location of Culture* (New York: Routledge, 1994), 207.

29   bell hooks, "The cultural mix: an interview with Wayne Wang," *Reel to Real: Race, Sex, and Class at the Movies* (New York: Routledge, 1996), 134.

30   *Chan Is Missing* script, from Diane Mei Lin Mark, *Chan Is Missing,* 50.

31   Salman Rushdie, "In Good Faith: A Pen Against the Sword," *Newsweek* (Feb. 12, 1990), 52.

32   Stuart Hall, "Cultural Identity and Cinematic Representation," *Framework* 36 (1989), 68–81.

33   Lowe, 38.

34   Stuart, 210–16.

35   Manjula Negi, "Mira Nair," *Cinemaya* 25–26 (1994–1995), 27.

36   Lowe, 39.

37   Michael Nash, "Bruce and Norman Yonemoto," *Journal of Contemporary Art* 3:2 (Fall 1990), 77.

38   Ibid.

39   Joseph Gelmis, *Newsday* (Aug. 9, 1985), Part III, 7.

40   Howard Singerman, "Bruce and Norman Yonemoto, 'Green Card': An American Romance, Long Beach Museum of Art," *Artforum* 21:2 (Oct. 1982), 76.

41   Robin Wood, "Little Movies/Large Pleasures," *Cine ACTION* 33 (1993), 65.

42   hooks, "The cultural mix," 135.

43   For my purpose here, the concept of mise-en-scène refers to four major elements of the shot: setting, lighting, costume, and the behavior of the figures. I have used the definition given by David Bordwell and Kristin Thompson: "All the elements placed in front of the camera to be photographed: the settings and props, lighting, costumes and make-up, and figure behavior." See their book *Film Art: An Introduction,* 4th ed. (New York: McGraw-Hill, 1993), 495.

44   Howie Movshovitz, "Indirection plays key role in films of Wayne Wang," *The Denver Post* (July 16, 1995), 12F.

45   Ibid.

46   Movshovitz, op. cit.

47   Some of the food movies include *Like Water for Chocolate* (Mexico), *Babette's Feast* (Denmark), *Tampopo* (Japan), *The Scent of Green Papaya* (Vietnam), and *Fried Green Tomatoes* (United States).

48   Brooke Comer, "Eat Drink Man Woman: A Feast for the Eyes," *American Cinematographer* (Jan. 1995), 62.

49   hooks, "The cultural mix," 124–125.

50   John Grierson, *Grierson on Documentary*, ed. Forsyth Hardy (London: Faber and Faber, 1966), 145.

51   Movshovitz, "Indirection plays key role in films of Wayne Wang," F-1.

52   hooks, "The cultural mix," 131.

53   Wang's father was a fluent English speaker and had a keen interest in American movies.

54   Tibbetts, 6.

55   John Berger, *Ways of Seeing* (London: British Broadcasting Corporation, 1987).

56   Lillian Kimura, "Aloha, Issei! *CineVue* Interviews *Picture Bride* Director Kayo Hatta," *CineVue* 10:1 (May 1995).

57   Gwendolyn Audrey Foster, *Women Filmmakers of the African and Asian Diaspora: Decolonizing the Gaze, Locating Subjectivity* (Carbondale and Edwardsville: Southern Illinois University Press, 1997), 126.

58   Film script from *Chan Is Missing,* 18–19.

59   As quoted by Brooke Jacobson, "A Great Wall," *Film Quarterly* (Winter 1986–1987), 48.

60   Ibid.

Hybrid Cinema by Asian American Women

IN HER BOOK *Woman, Native, Other* (1989), Vietnamese American filmmaker Trinh T. Minh-ha explores the meaning and nature of popular memory, story-telling, "truth," and history for women of color. In the tradition of oral history, she identifies a nonlinear, open-ended approach to history and knowledge. "The story never really begins nor ends," she proclaims, "even though there is a beginning and an end to every story, just as there is a beginning and end to every teller. . . . It appears headless and bottomless for it is built on differences. Its (in)finitude subverts every notion of completeness and its frame remains a non-totalizable one."[1]

A new hybrid cinema, experimental films and videos produced in the last few years, both by and about Asian American women, exemplifies the dynamics of the different kind of story-telling described by Trinh T. Minh-ha.[2] Among the most innovative and critically acclaimed are Valerie Soe's *New Year: Parts I and II* (1987) and *Picturing Oriental Girls: A {Re}Educational Videotape* (1992), Lise Yasui's *The Family Gathering* (1988), Janice Tanaka's *Memories from the Department of Amnesia* (1991), Shu Lea Cheang's *Color Schemes* (1989), Trinh T. Minh-ha's *Surname Viet Given Name Nam* (1989), and Rea Tajiri's *History and Memory: For Akiko and Takashige* (1991). "There was a space for opening up, for other kinds of stories to break through," Rea Tajiri reflected on a recent film panel in San Francisco, "and it was time to sort of seize the opportunity. Just pick up the camera and . . . start telling the stories that have been missing for so long."[3] Indeed, utilizing unconventional techniques and provocative cultural practices, these sophisticated experimental works by Asian American women address important issues of racial representation and challenge the conventions of commercial (especially the Hollywood variety) filmmaking in ways rarely possible in documentaries or dramatic features.

For a long time, experimental films were largely overlooked by critics. This neglect may be explained both because of the films' topics and themes and because of their formal properties. Within the white- and male-dominated Hollywood tradition, Asian American women suffer, so to speak, a "double marginality." Being independent and Asian, not only are the artists outside of (and going against) the mainstream, but also they are often pigeonholed into dealing only with ethnicity and gender-specific subjects. In contrast to Hollywood's sexist and exotic stereotypes of "Oriental" women, the Asian American women filmmakers' works focus on their personal history, families, and everyday lives in the United States. In the audience-driven movie industry, these kinds of works are viewed as lacking broad public appeal. Furthermore, traditionally, the avant-garde film is often interpreted purely as a "personal" work of art, with its significant social dimension largely overlooked.[4] Avant-garde film criticism, according to P. Adams Sitney, usually focuses on visual aesthetics but rarely engages discourses on gender, race, and ethnicity.[5] Although he made the observation more than twenty years ago, in 1974, Sitney's statement still holds true today. As bell hooks writes about the situation among Black filmmakers, "Avant-garde/experimental work is central to the creation of alternative visions. Yet when black filmmakers embrace the realm of the experimental, they are often seen as practicing elitism, as turning their backs on the struggle to create liberatory visions."[6]

Minority filmmakers who attempt to use the experimental medium often find the criteria used in defining the avant-garde too restrictive. For Trinh T. Minh-ha, for example, a film might be considered avant-garde "because it exposes its politics of representation instead of seeking to transcend representation in favor of visionary presence and spontaneity, which often constitute the prime criteria for what the avant-garde considers to be Art."[7] Although sharing some common discursive ground with the avant-garde tradition, these films and videos directed by Asian American women have created alternative narrative techniques and cut across the constricting boundaries of political, experimental, and documentary genres. Further, in contrast to the avant-garde tradition, this new hybrid cinema allows the films to become vehicles for the filmmakers' political statements.[8] Shu Lea Cheang commented on her personal experience:

> Experimental film and video work expands the boundaries of conventional forms, using unusual structures or visual language, or approaching unlikely topics or themes. . . . By balancing an unusual formal structure with more immediate conceptual concerns I've been able to create accessible yet challenging work.[9]

But the diversity of their experiences, techniques, and cultural practices poses a serious problem of acceptance.[10] As a result, they are largely excluded from Eurocentric experimental film criticism.[11] However, it is "by their marginality," as Trinh T. Minh-ha puts it nicely, that "they contribute to keeping the notion of 'experimental' alive, hence to resisting modernist closures often implied in the very label of 'avant-garde.' "[12]

Taking this contradiction as a point of departure, this chapter examines Asian American women's experimental filmmaking as a new subgenre in the Asian American cinematic discourse. It proposes that these Asian American experimental films and videos have subverted a major convention of mainstream filmmaking—its "realism"—and opened up new discursive practices in the revision of the Asian American experience. They have "deconstructed" several key elements in filmmaking, such as the symbolic order of time and space, especially in documentaries (which allegedly possess a sense of objectivity because of visible evidence like eyewitness interviews). In the end, the alternative discourse of avant-garde filmmaking has been turned into a different form of story-telling.

AVANT-GARDE FILM AS HISTORY

Traditionally, discussions of historical film rarely take into account the experimental format. This neglect can be explained by both film criticism and historiography. "While films may be documentaries or fiction," film historian Malcolm Le Grice writes, "their essential form and language has been evolved to tell stories."[13] Like other story-oriented media—the short story, the novel, the play, the opera— movies are judged mainly on the basis of how well they tell a story.[14] Experimental film, from its early beginnings in the French avant-garde tradition, has developed a cinematic form quite different from film drama, the dominant mode of cinema. Since our popular conceptions of meaning and critical language are derived from literary habits, most major cinema critics have a strong bias toward theatrical dramas, while overlooking the nonnarrative format.

Furthermore, consciously or unconsciously we think of history ("his {mankind's} story") as a narrative. In the historical analysis of film, as Robert Rosenstone states, what probably comes to mind are the "historical romances" or historical documentaries. In both cases, these films share some common narrative conventions, in that they attempt to "compress the past to a closed world by telling a single, linear story with, essentially, a single interpretation."[15]

Although Hollywood narrative and the standard documentary are the most common forms of filmed history, the avant-garde has effectively engaged historical processes as well. In his analysis of "the individual period" of the American avant-garde (1946–1966), Fred Campter stresses the social dimension of experimental filmmaking. These "personal" works of art had a much broader agenda, Campter argues, and constituted a social challenge to the mass culture conformity of the post–World War II decades.[16] "It is no accident, for instance," writes Campter, "that a large proportion of the founding filmmakers were gay men, in an era

when being publicly gay was itself considered an anti-social act of major propor-
tions."[17] Campter's insights illuminate the existence of a radical American avant-
garde cinematic tradition, but the appreciation of its significance requires a new
critical approach. In his book on film history, French film historian Pierre Sorlin
calls for the reading of significant "structural patterns" in historical films concerning formal techniques and their relations. "Structural analysis is not a pure for-
malism," Sorlin points out, "nor a self-sufficient system: the structures do not exist
by themselves, at least when we are working on a limited object like a film; they
are conceptual models which help us in describing the organization and mutual
relations of a particular complex whole."[18] Although the "historical films" referred
to by Sorlin are not necessarily avant-garde films, Sorlin's semiotic and structuralist emphasis on textual production is useful for our understanding of experimental
films as history. It helps shift our critical attention from a film's historical accuracy
or authenticity to its mode of representation.[19]

Nowadays, one crucial question posed by contemporary cultural theoreti-
cians, from Louis Althusser to Fredric Jameson, has to do with the specific relation
of cultural artifact to historical truth. So, how is one to account for the disparity
between history and its representation, or between history and its *lack* of representation? The objectivity question, as Peter Novik calls it, has dodged historians since
the beginning of the profession. In a similar way, documentary filmmakers have
been preoccupied with "authenticity" since Flaherty and Grierson. Also, it is
assumed that filmed or written history can be objectified and reified through
"data" and "evidence." But the pursuit of objectivity in history often privileges the
powerful at the expense of the powerless, since traditional history texts often
reduce the "voiceless" subordinate communities and groups to "objects" of policies
and "references" of the main stories.[20] This approach is similar to Stuart Hall's idea
of "taking representation apart" (opening up the practice of representation), to recognize how ideology and power attempt to fix meaning in a particular direction,
and for particular ends and interests.[21]

In the following pages of this chapter, I intend to examine seven hybrid
films and videos by Asian American women: Valerie Soe's *New Year: Parts I and II*
and *Picturing Oriental Girls*, Lise Yasui's *The Family Gathering*, Janice Tanaka's *Memories from the Department of Amnesia*, Shu Lea Cheang's *Color Schemes*, Trinh T. Minh-ha's
Surname Viet Given Name Nam, and Rea Tajiri's *History and Memory*. These "reflexive"
film texts will be analyzed to show how their avant-garde style violates the temporal and spatial conventions of commercial cinema, and subverts the seductive power
of realism, the bedrock of any narrative. Specifically, they have challenged the cinematic language of cuts, fades, frame composition, and camera movement, and have
succeeded in creating their own forms of expression in re-presenting history.

TIME AND SUBJECTIVITY

In the Judeo-Christian tradition, time has been conceived as the medium of sacred history, and it has long assumed its own "objective" existence and linear character.[22] As Johannes Fabian put it, "Time, much like language or money, is a carrier of significance, a form through which we define the content of relations between the Self and the Other. . . . Time may give form to relations of power and inequality under the conditions of capitalist industrial production."[23] Along the same line of argument, Mary Louise Pratt notes that the way anthropologists tend to represent racial and cultural "others" is as if they were living outside time, in a realm of spatialized stasis.[24]

Under this reductionist logic, the Orient, conceived in Western discourse, is stagnant, passive, and feminine; it fulfills its role as the other to the West.[25] The duality of Asian primitivity, or backwardness, and Western modernity has been invented and recycled numerous times in Hollywood's representation of Asian Americans. A statement from the white cop Stanley White (Mickey Rourke) in *Year of the Dragon* (1985) can illustrate this point. At the beginning of the movie, White scolded a group of horrified Chinatown bosses, "I'm tired of Chinese this and Chinese that. Does the fact that bribery, extortion and murder have been going on for a thousand years make it kosher? Well this is America, which is 200 years old, so you'd better adjust your clocks." Abuse of women, arranged marriages, and other alleged Asian traditions are used by Hollywood as instances of an Asiatic anachronism. "The linear way in which we [Asian Americans] are taught to accept Eurocentric historical definitions and processes," Russell Leong writes, "also appears in the linking of our culture and history primarily to the experience of western domination."[26]

In conceptualizing Black film aesthetics, Teshome Gabriel supports the idea of a subjective nomadic time of Black cinema, where "time is seen, observed and experienced as 'subjective'. . . . The central orientation points toward a 'cyclic' system wherein several time frames occur simultaneously."[27] This so-called traveling aesthetics, or "migrant sensibility" as Salman Rushdie terms it, is not unique to Black cinema, but informs Asian American films as well.[28] In the form of personal, family, and community histories, each of the works under discussion rejects the linear narrative and validates a traveling aesthetics, a subjective experience of time, in various ways. Rea Tajiri's impressionistic experimental video *History and Memory*, for example, explores the gaps in both personal and popular memories. "I began searching for a story, my own history," Tajiri twice told her viewers in the video, "because I had known all along that the stories I had heard were not true and parts had been left out."[29] Here, her own subjectivity is infiltrated by Hollywood images. In recovering and reinterpreting her and her mother's memory, time in the film is compressed, expanded, and reversed at different points. For example, while her mother chose to "forget" Poston, Arizona, where she was interned during World War II, Tajiri is haunted by ghost-like memories of the site she has never been to. "There was this place that they knew about I had never been there," said the voice-over, "yet I had a memory for it. There was a time of great sadness before I was born. . . . I had not [sic] idea where these memories came from . . . yet I knew the place."[30]

Lise Yasui employs a strikingly similar technique in *The Family Gathering.* In the film's beginning, we hear her speak on the soundtrack nostalgically about a favorite childhood memory about her grandfather (the major family member she investigates): how he comes to visit her family, and how she stays up late, listening to him talk. But minutes later she openly admits, "Later, I learned that my grandparents never made such a visit, that I never met my grandfather at all. The memory was one I'd made up, a creation drawn from all the stories I'd heard and the images on my father's home movies." By playing with personal memory, "[Yasui] introduces the idea that memory can be fabricated, made up of a patchwork of events and feelings which may or may not correspond to what actually happened."[31]

This emphasis on personal memory, over "historical" time, coincides with the shift in focus (observes the French poststructuralist philosopher Michel Foucault) from traditional history to genealogy. Traditional history, according to Foucault, produces continuities that "link events into a united, coherent story. . . . Writing genealogy, on the other hand, involves the recognition of disparity, of the dispersion of origins, and links, of discontinuities and contradictions."[32] Organized around memories (themselves a patchwork of events and feelings) the "stories," or genealogical narrative in Foucauldian terms, are often elliptical, fragmented, and sometimes even disruptive. Flashback, backtracking, repetition, and other cinematic strategies are used to break the sequential order. Valerie Soe's two-part video *New Year*, for example, is supposed to be a progressive coming-of-age story. With first-person narration, accompanied by storybook drawings, the slow-paced progression of her childhood memory is twice disrupted by intertitles: "Ching Chong Chinaman sitting on fence/trying to make a dollar out of five cents," "Chinese/Japanese/Dirty Knees/Look at these Chinese Japanese/Dirty Knees." This disjunctive structure in the first part of the video breaks into a topical structure in the second part, based on Hollywood's five stereotypical representations of Asian Americans: "Japs, Slopes, and Gooks," "Fortune Cookie Philosophers," "The Worldwide Empire of Evil," "Geisha Girls and Dragon Ladies," and "Masters of Kung Fu." Each of these scrolling titles is followed by excerpts from various Hollywood movies, wartime documentaries, television shows, and comic books. "The scenes and caricatures are shuffled, repeated, and run together without identification," writes Carole

Gerster, "indicating that they are recycled stereotypes with interchangeable parts."[33] The narrative structure of *The Family Gathering* is also highly elliptical. Instead of unfolding in a clean and linear order, the film corresponds to the complex and meticulous process of her own investigation of her family history, which involves "false starts; backtracking to pick up what was originally overlooked; re-evaluating; and, ultimately, progression."[34]

In recent years, counter-memory, or popular memory, as some scholars call it, has become a powerful concept in cultural studies. Michel Foucault discusses counter-memory in terms of genealogy. According to Faucault, genealogy "must record the singularity of events outside of any monotonous finality; it must seek them in the most unpromising places, in what we tend to feel is without history— in sentiments, love, conscience, instincts."[35] George Lipsitz, in *Time Passages*, offers a different interpretation by emphasizing the oppositional nature of counter-memory. Counter-memory, Lipsitz asserts, "focuses on localized experiences with oppression, using them to reframe and refocus dominant narratives purporting to represent universal experience."[36] In studying the aesthetics of Third Cinema, Teshome Gabriel demonstrates how popular memory negates an official history that "claims a 'centre' which continually marginalises others." "For popular memory," Gabriel argues, "there are no longer any 'centres' or 'margins', since the very designations imply that something has been conveniently left out."[37]

Despite the apparent differences in emphases, the three scholars agree that as an alternative way of remembering and forgetting (rooted in the personal, immediate, and particular), counter-memories create an autonomous cultural space for marginalized social groups, which hegemonic narratives cannot totalize. In other words, counter-memory calls our attention to the fact that history is multi-leveled and plural-voiced narration and that often a single level or voice is privileged, depending on the preferences of the writer. It is precisely the notion of counter-memory that problematizes this easy writing of history and opens up new critical spaces, allowing for the marginalized and silenced voices to be heard. Thus, personal memories have become an interventional tool for negotiations and mediations. As a victim of incarceration in relocation camps, for example, Tajiri's mother's response to her daughter's inquiry about her traumatic experience in World War II was painful self-denial. In a tape-recorded conversation between the two, included in the video, the mother said:

> No, that's the truth, I don't remember. . . . When you hear people on television and everything, how they felt and everything, I don't remember any of that stuff. All I remember is . . . when I saw this woman. . . . This beautiful woman, young, you know, and uh, I thought to myself, why did this happen, you know? You can go crazy, you can go out of your mind, so you just put these things out of your mind, you know.[38]

Here, the boundary between memory and invention, history and myth, never seems clear. The filmmakers decide to merge facts and memory, or the actual and dreamed, because such a synthesis of techniques most aptly presents their sense of self, as well as their connections to their heritage.

Calling all her works "electronic reflections," Janice Tanaka feels that memory does not work in a linear fashion. "Memories are not always an understood compilation of linear ideas," she writes. "They seem instead to be fragments of stored, synthesized, edited sensory stimuli; bits of personalized perceptions."[39] This fluid and fragmentary memory has been skillfully turned into visual concepts by Tanaka in *Memories from the Department of Amnesia.* The video's richly textured opening sequence offers a good illustration. The video opens with a deep-focus shot of a dazed and frenzied bicyclist circling inside a bar. With a constant change of angles, the restless camera creates a series of quick cuts—a glance at the bar, a close-up of the turning wheel, and a long shot of a robed doctor advancing and retreating in a snowstorm. This dreamlike sequence becomes a metaphor that determines much of the video's thematic focus: the loss of her mother, Yuriko Yamate, and the elusiveness of the filmmaker's memories. As a multilayered visual text, Tanaka's use of dissolves, together with the repeated shifts between positive and negative images (transitions between color and black-and-white film stock), reinforce the subjective nature of personal memory and its impact on history. The experimental style of editing links scenes together in an ahistorical fashion.[40] Tanaka's narrative strategy informs the video's overriding message that our sense of history exists only as our memory of the past flows through our own existence. As a result, narrative causality in the video easily disappears in subjective reflections.

Trinh T. Minh-ha's feature-length film *Surname Viet Given Name Nam* also represents a radical break with the linear perspective. "Working in the realm of stories and popular memories," Trinh explains, "I was not interested in a linear construction of time, and I was not attempting to reconstruct any specific period of Vietnam history."[41] To displace the notion of fixed time, she employs various experimental strategies. For example, she intercuts restaged interviews of five Vietnamese women with black-and-white news footage and photographs that obviously do not belong to the same time period as the voice-over. A case in point she cited herself: 1950s footage of the north-south movement of Vietnamese refugees is juxtaposed with a young woman's voice in the form of a letter addressed to her sister, reminiscing about her contemporary refugee experience with her mother in Guam in 1975. Trinh explains that, in the scene described, "The focus is neither on the plight of the refugees in the 50s nor on that in the 70s; rather, what seems more important to me is the specific nature of the problems women of many times and many places have to undergo—as women."[42] In the ending sequence of the film, images of a group of refugees floating on a raft in the sea during the 1950s become the background for off-screen comments on the contemporary problems of "boat people." Using the narrative device of the jump-cut, the film has succeeded in breaking up the sequential time (with no beginning or ending) in the women's stories. One voice-over in *Surname Viet* comments, "There is always the tendency to identify historical breaks and to say 'this begins there,' 'this ends here,' while the scene keeps on recurring, as unchangeable as change itself."[43]

Juxtaposing images out of chronological order seems to be a common structural feature in almost all the films under discussion. Historical footage and contemporary events often occupy the same time and space. In *History and Memory*, Tajiri parallels her footage with found footage. In one scene, for example, when she revisits the Poston barracks in Arizona, she films the Japanese internment camp (or rather, traces of it), as it is today, and then intercuts it with government photos showing it under construction in 1942. The most eloquent example might be this scene: while showing clips from *Bad Day at Black Rock* (a 1954 Hollywood feature), the text from an August 28, 1990, *New York Times* article scrolls into the frame: "Assemblyman Gil Ferguson, Republican Orange County, California, seeks to have children taught that Japanese Americans were not interned in 'concentration camps' but rather were held in 'relocation centers' justified by military necessity."[44] Valerie Soe's twelve-minute *Picturing Oriental Girls* uses the technique of incongruous juxtaposition to an extreme. In almost every sequence, quick movie clips are overlapped with written texts from various sources, such as mail-order-bride catalogues, men's magazines, and *The World of Suzie Wong* (1960). The texts cleverly deconstruct, or subvert, the meaning of the collage of racist and sexist images by literally turning them upside down and against each other.

Counter-memory may not carry effective countercultural values for marginalized groups until it is related to the present. Put differently, collective memories are only meaningful insofar as they teach us about our current actions. In re-creating her family history, for example, Tajiri tries not only to rescue human memories, but also, and more significantly, to establish links between reminiscences about the past and then to compare them to present struggles. This existential theme is conveyed by the letter she reads from Uncle Shinkichi:

> You asked what I thought I gained or lost from the evacuation. Gained? Very little except a unique situation that a very tiny percentage of the American public had ever explained. What I lost was my faith in the American Constitution and it is for that reason that I left the U.S. 43 years ago, a year after I returned from the war.[45]

Here, Tajiri formulates a historical narrative that not only attempts to reshape our memory of the past but that also can inform the present political dialogue. In a sense, this struggle of memory against forgetting, as represented by the video, could become a rich source of community empowerment.

Besides the use of inventive camera techniques, these experimental artists have also used asynchronous sound to break the "law" of traditional film editing. A careful examination of the soundtrack of Valerie Soe's *New Year* reveals graphic and sound mismatches at several points. A major break occurs between picture and soundtrack when, for example, martial arts fighting is heard on the soundtrack, but no picture appears for two full minutes. In *Surname Viet*, out-of-sync editing is more intricate. Playing with the so-called time-image format,[46] Trinh T. Minh-ha deliberately creates gaps between what is read, what is heard, and what is seen on the screen. "Not only does the text not always enter at the same time as the speech," the filmmaker emphasizes in an interview, "its shorter duration on the screen also makes it quasi-impossible for the viewer to hear and read at the same time without missing parts of both."[47] This manipulation is further complicated, as Foster notes, by the "diegetic speech in both Vietnamese and English sometimes translated and subtitled, and sometimes left deliberately 'untranslated.' "[48] For Trinh, this kind of asynchronic editing becomes an inventive ideological and structural device to "displace the notion of fixed time and place."[49]

Indeed, avant-garde women filmmakers have attempted to represent time in gendered, experimental, and oppositional ways. In *Color Schemes*, Shu Lea Cheang adopted a circular or cyclical structure as an alternative to the self-enclosed linear narrative. Originally conceived as a multipart video installation, the videotape uses three 1954-era front-loading washing machines as a metaphor for the great American "melting pot" of ethnicity. In a reenactment of the Last Supper, twelve performers, of various ethnic backgrounds, gather and discuss American history and racism inside the washing machines. We view this poignant image with the full knowledge that the four cycles—soak, wash, rinse, and extract—become the narrative structures of the film. In each cycle a different historical theme is explored, from Chinese coolie labor to the genocide of Native Americans.

Yasui's cyclical narrative in *The Family Gathering* is embedded in the content of the film largely through the attitudes displayed by her father (Robert Shu Yasui), aunts, and uncles toward her grandfather's suicide: from denial and hesitancy, finally to acknowledgment. The way Yasui handles the process of her family's gradually coming to terms with their emotions is similarly revealing. As Cassandra Van Buren observes, "The way in which Yasui frequently comes back around to the specific conversation about Masuo's suicide is a striking example of the cyclical nature of the film. She first alludes to Masuo's wrongful internment in the introductory narration of the film, then leaves the subject untouched for nearly half of the duration of the documentary. It is about three-quarters of the way through the film that she weaves [in] her bit of narration mentioned earlier, in which she relates the climactic conversation with Robert and shows him explaining why many nisei kept this information from her generation."[50]

In comparison, Tajiri uses the technique of repetition to create a back-and-forth structure in *History and Memory*. The opening image of the video, for instance, is a dripping water faucet outdoors. Then there is a close-up of a pair of hands holding a canteen in the middle of the desert. On numerous occasions, the film circles back to this beautifully composed sequence, for at least two narrative purposes. First, it illustrates that personal memory is subjective and malleable; second, it symbolizes her family's experience of dealing with the trauma of internment. For example, Tajiri's mother's struggle with her traumatic experience functions as an important subtext of the video. As a victim of incarceration in relocation camps, her mother uses forgetting as a defense mechanism of self-preservation.

In short, working within the tradition of oral history, these Asian American women filmmakers have taken a nonlinear and open-ended approach in the stories they tell about their personal, family, and community histories. In contrast to Hollywood's temporal logics, these artists employ disjunctive structural techniques such as flashbacks, asynchronous sound and image, circular narrative, and blank spaces between shots. All these oppositional filmic techniques contribute to an Asian American subjectivity that challenges the notion of historical objectivity.

SCREEN SPACE AS SOCIAL SPACE

Euro-American culture has long valued time over space. While time carries the meaning of the story, space often figures as its passive setting. In recent years, however, there has been a growing recognition of the ideological construction of space, especially in theories of postmodernism. Edward Soja's book *Postmodern Geographies*, for example, calls for radical "spatial deconstruction by resituating the meaning of space in history and historical materialism."[51] "The 'East' is divided into 'Near,' 'Middle,' and 'Far,' " Ella Shohat and Robert Stam write, discussing the Eurocentric nature of spatial logic, "making Europe the arbiter of spatial evaluation, just as the establishment of Greenwich Mean Time produces England as the regulating center of temporal measurement."[52]

Indeed, the racial and cultural hierarchy in Hollywood is made up of relationships that are spatial as well as temporal. In his analysis of new Black films, Manthia Diawara points out that "spatial narration, in classical cinema, makes sense through a hierarchical disposition of objects on the screen. Thus, space is related to power and powerlessness, in so far as those who occupy the center of the screen are usually more powerful than those in the background or completely absent from the screen."[53] Indeed, the absence of minorities from the screen could be read as a symbol of their absence from the society constructed by Hollywood. This straightforward manipulation of spatially situated images provides an important dimension of spatial hierarchy. Some scholars see a direct relation between the geography of the world and the geography of the imagination.[54] Edward Said defines the "imaginative geography" as a typical example of Orientalism. "The Orient was almost a European invention, and had been since antiquity a place of romance, exotic beings, haunting memories and landscapes, remarkable experiences."[55] As a creator of grand narratives and ideology, Hollywood has long used physical, social, and psychological "distancing" as strategies in offering up its grotesque representations of Asians. Whether it is the yellow menace or the exotic image, this anti-Asian xenophobia has forever been frozen on the silver screen.[56] Asian locales in American films—from the mysterious Chinatown, U.S.A. to the Vietnamese jungle—are presented by Hollywood as, alternately, exotic tourist attractions and dangerous wilderness for colonialist adventurers. In a symbolic sense, immigrants from Asia and their descendants can *never* claim a place in America in the manner that their European counterparts have done. As Eugene Wong notes in *On Visual Media Racism*, "The commonly held belief that Asian Americans are an alien collective living within a white American sea has become a popular cliché of self-perpetuating dimensions."[57] This construction of space, symbolic as well as geographical, remains an important aspect in Hollywood's representation of Asians.

Abjuring the straightforward documentary style, avant-garde films and videos by Asian American women have together sought to break up this spatial logic as it operates in artistic and social space. *Color Schemes*, for one, is a parody of public space in America. The setting of the laundromat, plus the wash motif inside the frame of the washing machines, symbolizes limited social space for ethnic minorities. While the laundromat is "a racially mixed gallery," the wash motif is analogous to the power-mediated racial conflicts in American society. As director Shu Lea Cheang explains, "When you do a wash you separate whites and colors. The colors are always thrown in together with each other. . . . And that is the power structure that has us fighting each other. This is what the 'soak' cycle was to be about."[58] Likewise, in the pool table scene in the wash cycle, the pool balls are used "to represent assorted people of color, and how they are being banged around" and knocked into pockets where they remain out of sight, out of mind.[59]

The video's framing effect is equally suggestive. The entire frame of the screen is folded and unfolded, corresponding to each washing cycle in the machine. The washing machine door becomes the frame for Cheang's interviews, suggesting the spatial confinement experienced by many racial groups. Interracial conflicts, she argues, are rooted in the unbalanced spatiality of social life. "Minorities are the diverse colors constantly being thrown together by society," Cheang tells *CineVue*, "without knowing each other and feeling very uncomfortable."[60] The very concept of a homogeneous melting pot is dismantled in the film. On the surface, the washing process seems to imply assimilation, while the fading of color suggests the loss of individual identity. But Cheang's vivid characters defy the process, emerging as colorful and vibrant individuals. These representations, as semiotic imagery and ideologies, play a powerful role in reshaping the spatial dimensions of American society.

Janice Tanaka's highly geometric *Memories from the Department of Amnesia* provokes an equally significant but different spatial dialectic. In a surrealist manner, screen space becomes a symbol of her inner struggles to retrieve her mother's life history in America. Out-of-focus shots, whip pans, and split screens are some of the spacing mechanisms used. In the beginning sequence, for instance, during rapid zooms onto the pedaling bicyclist, the screen frame is radically tilted, blurred, and deformed into bizarre shapes. In a series of dissolves, the footage of the bicyclist cuts to a blank screen, soon to be occupied by a male physician in a surgical gown, which in turn cuts to a snowstorm scene, as mentioned earlier. Through superimposition, the two figures become part of the same space. From this point on, the spatial dimension of the video settles into a split screen. Frame by frame, as a series of small snapshot negatives of her mother develops into prints on the left, enlarged pictures (not in the same order) appear on the right with thirty-six (a typical number of frames in a roll of film for a personal camera) scrolling titles identifying the dates and events in Yuriko's life. While the past is represented graphically on the screen by the photographs, the filmmaker and her daughter are heard on the soundtrack reminiscing nostalgically about the woman. Thus, through experimental mise-en-scène and editing, Tanaka's own contemporary perspectives and her mother's stories of the past come to occupy the same space at one time. As Marina Heung observes, three incongruous images and sounds emerge in the sequence: the personal tragedies in the subtitles, the images of a smiling and radiant filmmaker and her daughter, and their lighthearted and loud voices. "This lighthearted and casual conversation runs counter to the mood and content of the subtitles," Heung writes, "as the two women laugh and giggle through their memories of Yuriko as a woman with a 'warped sense of humor,' a 'hot rod' who drove a Mustang, dated a lot of men, encouraged her family to eat arsenic-laced prune pits, and stored her wild outfits in a cedar trunk."[61] These spatial devices are extremely effective in supplying narrative authenticity to the family members' history. The screen space occupancy serves as a form of empowerment for them.

Strikingly similarly, Valerie Soe's *Picturing Oriental Girls* skillfully employs several spacing techniques, such as overlapping, cross-referencing, and ironic juxtaposition, to manipulate the screen space. For example, over the image of a geisha from *The Teahouse of the August Moon* (1956), a quotation starts to crawl across the screen: "Asian women are renowned for their beauty, femininity, traditional values, and loving dispositions." In this overlapping technique, the source of the quote defeats the purpose of the citation, as we see it is taken from the Sunshine International Catalogue.

In comparison, Trinh T. Minh-ha's approach to spatial form is more conceptual than structural. As a filmmaker and a theoretician, Trinh seeks a broader reexamination of the ideological constructs of hierarchies, oppositions, and boundaries used pervasively in Western media. As in her earlier films, *Reassemblage* (1982) and *Naked Spaces: Living Is Round* (1985), the artist attempts to create a hybrid place, or what she calls "interstitial space"—"the space in between, the interval to which established rules of boundaries never quite apply."[62] This hybrid place operates at several levels in her films. In formal terms, her film *Surname Viet* resists easy categories—whether documentary, narrative, or avant-garde. For instance, in the first part of the film, the viewer usually takes the staged or reenacted "fake" interviews (supposedly taking place in Vietnam) as real, only to confront a series of onsite interviews with the same women but in the explicit context of the United States. This mixture of genres presents a unsettling situation for the viewers. As Trinh recalls a statement made by a bewildered Vietnamese viewer, "Your film is different. I can't yet tell exactly how, but I know it's different from the documentary films I am used to seeing."[63]

To expose the "object-oriented camera," Trinh experiments with the notion of negative space both on-screen and off. For example, in many of the interview sequences in the early part of the film, the establishing shots are often of women's bodies, chests, hands, and legs. "Talking heads" literally become headless. When the faces of the women *do* appear, the restless camera never stays on them, but instead pans across the screen, creating a series of blank screens. What is more, the framing effects also heighten the importance of off-screen space. Very few full-frame images of the women are included. And half-face images are shown with the screen edge being cut, disconcertingly, directly on the women's noses. And old photographs and stills, large and small, are framed with disproportionately large black space. Sometimes, lighting is extremely low-key and reinforces this dark screen space. In addition to the manipulation of visual images, the film's soundtrack is interrupted with empty spaces (silences) or "sounding holes." The filmmaker relates all these strategies to the notion of the Void, derived from Zen Buddhism. "People often don't even know what you are talking about when you mention the vitality of the Void in the relationships between object and non-object, or between I and non-I," the filmmaker states.[64] This notion of the Void best explains Trinh's approach to spatial form.

One of the recurring motifs in the film is the critique of an essentialist identity, or what Trinh calls "identity enclosure."[65] The title itself—*Surname Viet Given Name Nam*—is a pun and a parody on the politics of naming a person, a nation, and a culture. Taken from an anecdote in which an unmarried Vietnamese woman claims her marital status as being married to her country, and from what this means to Vietnamese women exiles in the United States, this identity enclosure becomes one of the film's subtexts. "I keep on thinking despite our emigrating to the US," as Kim's voice-over goes, "if our surname is Viet, our given name ought to be Nam—Vietnam."[66] In acted interviews, Vietnamese women tell of war, exile, traditions, and daily lives from shifting perspectives as women, mothers, wives, Vietnamese, and Americans. With the wedding ceremony as another motif of the film, women transform their identities from "lady, and maid, to monkey." In these pluravocal formulations of identity politics, "the self loses its fixed boundaries," says Trinh, and hybridization occurs in its place.[67] In its critique of women's oppression, the film is "directed toward the condition of women—whether in socialist or capitalist context, whether back home in the nation-space or over here in the community-space."[68] A case in point: if the story of Kieu, a woman who sells her body to save her father's honor, serves as a critique of the patriarchal structure in Vietnamese society, how does it relate to the Miss Vietnam pageant held in the United States? Does it signify the multiple exploitation of women's bodies? And what is the difference between sexual oppression, on the one side, and the commodification of sexuality, on the other? *Surname Viet Given Name Nam* thus opens up several issues, ideological as well as cinematic, in the conventional ordering of the spatial form in commercial cinema.

These space-based techniques are used as a way of revealing and linking different forms of oppression that have been separated or suppressed in Hollywood. In other words, Asian American experimental filmmakers have opened up a new textual space in their films. Spatial narration has become a conduit to Asian women's' self-expression, a story-telling device that interrogates identity, memory, and Asian American ways of life. Taken together, their efforts, to borrow Foster's comments about Trinh's *Naked Spaces,* conflate "a number of theoretical attempts to reconstitute 'women's space'—for example, Laura Mulvey's 'lucid' space, Teresa de Lauretis' notion of off-screen space, Julia Kristeva's notion of the prelinguistic space of the chora, or Luce Irigaray's rereading of psychoanalytic 'lack' of a voicing of the female body."[69]

Historically, many of the techniques discussed in the chapter can be found in the avant-garde tradition from as long ago as the 1920s. As Stephen Kern has demonstrated in *The Culture of Time and Space* the disjunctive qualities can be found in several early-twentieth-century art movements such as the fracturing of time by the futurists, and the fracturing of space by the cubists.[70] Many of these strategies could also be seen in avant-garde films from the period, such as Man Ray's *Retour à la Raison* (1923) and Fernand Leger's *Ballet Mécanique* (1924). They may also be reminiscent of the New Wave filmmakers such as Jean-Luc Godard in the 1960s. However, unlike these early-twentieth-century visionary predecessors and the French New Wave directors, Asian American women artists have used their structural thrust not merely for special aesthetic effects, but instead to challenge the formulaic "verisimilitude" of Hollywood films.[71] Writer bell hooks's recent call to African American filmmakers to go "back to the avant-garde" serves as further affirmation of the significance of the experimental works by Asian American women:

> For too long black people and everyone else in this culture have been socialized to see the avant-garde solely as a marginal place where art that only a few understand resides. The time has come to rethink our assumptions. When we embrace the avant-garde as a necessary matrix of critical possibility, acknowledging that it is a context for cultural revolution, new and exciting representations of blackness will emerge.[72]

Indeed, Soe, Yasui, Tanaka, Cheang, Trinh, and Tajiri have used avant-garde techniques as a vehicle to approach both historical and social issues, literally turning this "marginal space" of the avant-garde into a vital space for an alternative historical discourse.

NOTES

1 Trinh T. Minh-ha, *Woman, Native, Other: Writing Postcoloniality and Feminism* (Bloomington: Indiana University Press, 1989), 1–2.

2 I use the term *hybrid cinema* in a broad sense, referring to films that make departures from the cinematic conventions or what Noel Burch calls "technological image norms." See Noel Burch, *Life to Those Shadows* (Berkeley: University of California Press, 1990), 257.

3 Directors Panel, 15th San Francisco International Asian American Film Festival, March 1997.

4 Asian American filmmaker and critic Renee Tajima acknowledges that the avant-garde has also been overlooked by Asian American critics, except for Daryl Chin; see Renee Tajima, "Moving the Image: Asian American Independent Filmmaking, 1970–1990," *Moving the Image: Independent Asian Pacific American Media Arts,* ed. Russell Leong (Los Angeles: UCLA Asian American Studies Center, 1991), 20.

5 P. Adams Sitney, for example, declares, "The structural film insists on its shape, and what content it has is minimal and subsidiary to the outline." *Visionary Film: The American Avant-Garde* (New York: Oxford University Press, 1974), 407–408.

6 bell hooks, "Back to the Avant-Garde: The Progressive Vision," *Reel to Real: Race, Sex and Class at the Movies* (New York: Routledge, 1996), 103.

7 Ibid., 106.

8 Ibid.

9 "The [Video] World According to Cheang and Chong," *CineVue* 3:1 (March 1988), 7.

10 For a critique of film theory and practice, see Robert Crusz, "Black Cinemas, Film Theory and Dependent Knowledge," *Screen* 26:3–4 (May–Aug. 1985), 152–56.

11 Trinh T. Minh-ha seems to be the only exception. Various reviews, articles, and interviews have been published on her films in journals and books. For example, there is a chapter on Trinh in Scott MacDonald's book *Avant-Garde Film: Motion Studies* (New York: Cambridge University Press, 1993).

12 Trinh T. Minh-ha, "Which Way to Political Cinema?" *Framer Framed* (New York: Routledge, 1992), 250.

13 Malcolm Le Grice, *Abstract Film and Beyond* (Cambridge: MIT Press, 1977), 7.

14 See Tim Bywater and Thomas Sobchack, *An Introduction to Film Criticism: Major Critical Approaches to Narrative Film* (New York: Longman, 1989), 145.

15 Robert A. Rosenstone, "History in Images/History in Words: Reflections on the Possibility of Really Putting History onto Film," *American Historical Review* 93:5 (Dec. 1988), 1174.

16 Fred Campter, "The End of Avant-Garde Film," *Millennium Film Journal* 16–18 (Fall/Winter 1986–1987), 99–124.

17 Ibid., 101.

18 Pierre Sorlin, *The Film in History: Restaging the Past* (Oxford, England: Basil Blackwell, 1980), 33.

19 See "Introduction," in *Resisting Images: Essays on Cinema and History*, ed. Robert Sklar and Charles Musser (Philadelphia: Temple University Press, 1990), 3–11.

20 John Grierson, *Grierson on Documentary*, ed. Forsyth Hardy (London: Faber and Faber, 1966), 145.

21 Stuart Hall on video, *Representation and the Media*, produced, directed, and edited by Sut Jhally of the University of Massachusetts, Amherst, who also introduces the presentation. The video is distributed by Media Education Foundation, 26 Center St., Northampton, Mass. 01060.

22 Stephen Kern, *The Culture of Time and Space* (Oxford, England: Basil Blackwell, 1980), 33.

23 Johannes Fabian, *Time and the Other: How Anthropology Makes Its Object* (New York: Columbia University Press, 1983), ix.

24 Mary Louise Pratt, "Scratches on the Face of the Country," *Critical Inquiry* 12 (1985–1986), 129.

25 See Edward Said, *Orientalism* (New York: Pantheon Books, 1978); and Pratt.

26 Russell Leong, "To Open the Future," *Moving the Image*, xv.

27 Teshome H. Gabriel, "Thoughts on Nomadic Aesthetics and the Black Independent Cinema: Traces of a Journey," *Blackframes: Critical Perspectives on Black Independent Cinema* (Cambridge, Mass.: MIT Press, 1988), 66.

28 Salman Rushdie, "Outside the Whale," *American Film* (Jan.–Feb., 1985), 16, 70–73.

29 *History and Memory* script, version 8/12/91, available from Video Data Bank, Chicago, 9.

30 Ibid.

31 Cassandra Van Buren, "*Family Gathering*: Release from Emotional Internment," *Jump Cut* 37 (1992), 56. Van Buren's insightful essay on the film offers some helpful points on its narrative structure, emotional texture, and soundtrack. Her ideas contribute substantially to my analysis of the film.

32 Michel Foucault, "Nietzsche, Genealogy, History," *Language, Counter-memory, Practice: Selected Essays and Interviews by Michel Foucault*, ed. Donald F. Bouchard (Ithaca, N.Y.: Cornell University Press, 1977), 139–64.

33 Carole Gerster, "The Asian American Renaissance in Independent Cinema and Valerie Soe's *New Year*," *A Gathering of Voices on the Asian American Experience*, ed. Annette White-Parks et al. (Fort Atkinson, Wis.: Highsmith, 1994), 195.

34 Van Buren, 62.

35 Foucault, 139–40.

36 George Lipsitz, *Time Passages* (Minneapolis: University of Minnesota Press, 1990), 213.

37 Teshome H. Gabriel, "Third Cinema as Guardian of Popular Memory: Towards a Third Aesthetics," *Questions of Third Cinema*, eds. Jim Pines and Paul Willemen (London: British Film Institute, 1989), 53–54.

38 *History and Memory* script, 10.

39 Janice Tanaka, "Electrons and Reflective Shadows," *Moving the Image*, 206.

40 For information about this editing technique in the visionary films, see P. Adams Sitney, *Visionary Film: The American Avant-Garde*.

41 Trinh, "Who Is Speaking," *Framer Framed*, 208–209.

42 Ibid., 209.

43 See film script in Trinh, *Framer Framed*, 56.

44 *History and Memory* script, 19.

45 Ibid., 20.

46 The text-image cinema refers to films in which the act of reading printed or written texts is a central viewing experience. For details, see Trinh T. Minh-ha, "A Minute Too Long," *When the Moon Waxes Red* (New York: Routledge, 1991), 114–15.

47 Trinh, "Who Is Speaking," 208.

48 Gwendolyn Audrey Foster, *Women Filmmakers of the African and Asian Diaspora: Decolonizing the Gaze, Locating Subjectivity* (Carbondale and Edwardsville: Southern Illinois University Press, 1997), 102.

49 Trinh, "Who Is Speaking," 209.

50 Van Buren, 62.

51 Edward Soja, *Postmodern Geographies* (New York: Verso, 1989), 73.

52 Ella Shohat and Robert Stam, *Unthinking Eurocentrism: Multiculturalism and the Media* (New York: Routledge, 1994), 2.

53 Manthia Diawara, *Black American Cinema* (New York: Routledge), 11.

54 Martin Blythe, "'What's in a Name?': Film Culture and the Self/Other Question," *Quarterly Review of Film and Video* 13:1–3, 205–15.

55 Said, 1.

56 Note, for example, as recently as in Joel Schumacher's *Falling Down* (1993), that the rude and incongruous Korean grocer still carries the enigmatic image of an ungrateful sojourner, in contrast to the white male's (Michael Douglas) image as a patriot and natural heir to this "white land."

57 Eugene F. Wong, *On Visual Media Racism: Asians in the American Motion Pictures* (New York: Arno Press, 1978), 265.

58 "Color Schemes: CineVue Interviews Video Artist Shu Lea Cheang," *CineVue* 4:1 (March 1989), 5.

59 Ibid.

60 Ibid.

61 See Marina Heung, "Representing Ourselves, Films and Videos by Asian American/Canadian Women," *Feminism, Multiculturalism, and the Media: Global Diversities,* ed. Angharad N. Valdivia (Thousand Oaks, Calif.: Sage, 1995), 101.

62 Trinh, "Why a Fish Pond," *Framer Framed*, 174.

63 Trinh, "From a Hybrid Place," *Framer Framed,* 146.

64 Ibid., 142.

65 Trinh, *Woman, Native, Other*, 95–97.

66 *Surname Viet Given Name Nam* script, *Framer Framed*, 86.

67 Trinh, "Film as Translation: A Net with No Fisherman," *Framer Framed*, 133.

68 Trinh, "Who Is Speaking," 196.

69 Foster, 100.

70 Kern.

71 It may not be a unique situation among Asian Americans to use experimental films and videos to make political statements. As Shu Lea Cheang says, "If you look at tapes now, you will find that a lot of experimental video makers are including a lot of social/political elements in their work. I think that's a very important element in the eighties. Conversely, you will find that tapes that deal with very serious subject matter use what we might call experimental techniques." "The [Video] World According to Cheang and Chong," 7.

72 hooks, 107.

Marginal Cinema and White Criticism

SEVERAL WEEKS BEFORE the 1996 Academy of Motion Picture Arts and Sciences Awards ceremony, emotions were running high and charges of racism were swirling around Hollywood. Critics pointed to the 166 Oscar nominees, of whom just one was Black: live-action short film writer-director Dianne Houston. Several filmmakers and politicians accused the Academy's members and Oscar voters of being "Ivory soap—99.4 percent white." Tim Reid, the Black writer-director of the critically acclaimed new film *Once Upon a Time . . . When We Were Colored* (1995), bitterly protested, "There's a white elite running this town. They think if they've got their tickets for the Lakers game they've done their part for race relations."[1] Falling short of calling for a major overhaul, the Rev. Jesse Jackson wrote in a letter to studio executives, "We seek not to embarrass the entertainment industry, but to educate the public that the standards of fairness should also be applied to the film and television industries." In response, Hollywood officials contended that those complaints were misguided.

The divisions over the controversy were not clearly drawn along racial lines. For one thing, Whoopi Goldberg and Quincy Jones, both Black, were the host and producer, respectively, of the ceremony. "You cannot single out this year as a banner year for racism. It's not," says Dianne Houston, nominated for making the short film *Tuesday Morning Ride*. For another, some of the year's most acclaimed white performers, from Nicole Kidman (*To Die For*) to John Travolta (*Get Shorty*), also failed to be nominated.

This controversy is strikingly meaningful not because of its racial theme, but rather because of legitimacy politics and marginalization. It at once demonstrates the dominance of the Academy Awards, and attests to the continuing marginality for Black filmmakers and performers despite their popular success and broad audience base. More important, it reinforces the obvious, but seldom acknowledged, perception in the entertainment industry that minority artists often

175

need a cultural chaperone, so to speak, to the "American" party. To put it differently, public recognition (read: prestige, money, and funding opportunities) comes only with an endorsement from the mainstream establishment.

The critical history of Asian American filmmaking, the focus of this chapter, shows similar practices of cultural marginalization and appropriation. Although Asian Americans have produced hundreds of films and videos over the past three decades, ultimately they have received little recognition by mainstream institutions of their cultural production, nor a substantive critique. Only after box-office breakthroughs by a group of younger filmmakers in the early 1990s did Asian American cinema begin to receive some of the critical attention that has been long overdue. However, the central argument of the chapter is that this late (and grudging) recognition signifies not a true assimilation of Asians into the American mainstream, but rather a mere repositioning of their marginality in the motion picture industry. Taking a close look at recent readings of Asian American films by both mainstream and community sources, this chapter attempts to provide a critique of the three coexisting but conflicting patterns, namely, historical marginalization, cultural misreadings, and market validation. I hope that this discussion will contribute to the ongoing dialogue on the so-called "minority discourse" in cultural studies.[2]

PRACTICES OF MARGINALIZATION

As early as the 1970s, Black film historian Thomas Cripps noted that Black films had long been marginalized. He saw two major reasons why Black cinema did not receive sophisticated critical attention. First, critical mass was never created because of either the lack of access to the media or simple neglect. Second, film criticism was too politically oriented. It was in turn influenced by the liberal progressivism in the 1930s, the World War II ideology of racial integration, and Marxist dialectics.[3] A similar assessment holds true for films made by Asian Americans in the last three decades. Except for a few highly acclaimed features like Wayne Wang's *The Joy Luck Club*, Asian American cinema, either as a movement or as a group of individual films, is still far removed from the general public. As Duane Kubo, one of the Visual Communications (VC) founders, commented, "The question is have there been enough Asian American films to be able to really critically analyze them. There have been quite a few Asian American films made, but they are so different and very few Asian American filmmakers are given a chance to fail and to continue and to make better films . . . most filmmakers, like any writer, need experience, seasoning, a chance to fail, and a chance to succeed."[4]

This lack of critical attention can be attributed to ideological and institutional racism. The traditions of independent filmmaking have always meant being outside of, and going against, the mainstream. As explained earlier in the book, the genesis of Asian American filmmaking was a direct result of the social and political movements of the 1960s. Inspired by civil rights struggles and ethnic studies programs, the concept of equity (both racial and cultural) has been one of the prime driving forces for the Asian American film movement. Started as an alternative movement, it has developed its own agenda and aesthetic in opposition to mainstream strategies and structures in the film and TV industries. From the outset these Asian American media groups have been deadly opposed to the media industry's motive of profits derived from mass appeal. Endorsement by the mainstream film establishment was likely the last thing on the minds of those artists.

In general, Asian American independents differentiated their artistry from Hollywood in two fundamental ways. First, they rejected the glossy technical sophistication that historically defines Hollywood's "classic realist" cinema. Renee Tajima wrote a few years ago that the products of independent cinema must be appreciated within their own "imperfections." Gregg Araki, the renowned underground guerrilla filmmaker, has best articulated an antiestablishment philosophy: "What The Movement . . . really needs are those formal/political thematic challengers of the Status Quo. . . . I'm talking about the next generation of Godards, Fassbinders, Derek Jarmans who push the envelope, who are not satisfied with the 'Good Story Well Told' Bullshit that Mainstreams of all stripes and colors unabashedly endorse."[5] Naturally, this antislick tradition has pulled the movement away from Hollywood. Second, instead of engaging in author-centered productions, Asian American filmmakers have been trying to abolish the division between art and life, between filmmakers and viewers. "I'm not interested in the artist being the most important person in the world," Loni Ding explained recently; "I think the artist is simply another worker in the world, another human being, who has certain skills and certain interests and absolutely a person has to use what they have and be who it is they are."[6] Asian American filmmakers' ideological differences with Hollywood—or rather, distancing from it—account partly for why mainstream film historians and critics have neglected their productions.

Even more important, in the context of the harsh reality of independent production, the Asian American film movement has been nurtured from its infancy by an advocacy network that includes community-based organizations and non-profit media arts centers, such as Visual Communications in Los Angeles, Asian CineVision in New York, and the National Asian American Telecommunications Association (NAATA) in San Francisco. Founded in 1971, 1976, and 1980 respectively, these pan-Asian arts centers organize annual film festivals, publish journals, provide news outlets, and serve as networks for disseminating films, ideas, and resources. Asian American film events as well as annual international film festivals in San Francisco, New York, Los Angeles, and Seattle have helped to define and maintain a cohesiveness for the film movement, whether imagined or real. Sponsored by Asian CineVision, the Asian American International Film Festival (AAIFF), now in its twentieth year, has been particularly effective in promoting Asian American works. Wayne Wang's *Chan Is Missing* was featured at the festival in 1982, and Ang Lee's thesis film from New York University was showcased at the festival in 1985. Based in New York, it also organizes tours each year to theaters across the country. This singular phenomenon of Asian American film events and festivals has not only provided venues for publicizing promising works but has also created a demand for particular kinds of films on the art house circuit, college campuses, and public television. What is more, without a specialized film journal such as *Black Film Review*, the most significant exchanges of ideas among filmmakers and critics take place on those occasions and in those venues. The fact that these special festivals exist for films made by Asian Americans also means that different standards have been developed for judging them.

However, this voluntary disassociation has been overshadowed by a marginalization process in the industry. Traditionally, the three kinds of American film histories—the aesthetic, the social, and the industrial—tell exclusively the stories of "the white immigrants, the Jewish moguls and WASP regulators."[7] "It is probably fair to say," Nick Browne astutely wrote, "that the critical perspective on American film has been centered on and privileged white experience, that it is an ethnocentric view inscribed within a Caucasian chalk circle."[8] Some film scholars, such as Black film historian Robert Crusz, have argued that the film medium itself is a European invention and has been judged largely by Eurocentric standards. In a revealing essay, "Black Cinemas, Film Theory and Dependent Knowledge," Crusz writes, "The technology of film-making has developed within the specific Euro-American context. As such it carries with it the particular history of that context. Linked to this particular technology are products, practices and theories which have developed within a world view confined to Europe, both east and west, and to North America."[9]

Brown's and Crusz's points on the Eurocentric nature of film criticism are very well taken. For example, the auteur theory—the conceptual foundation of a critical perspective—which was developed in the early 1960s and which emphasizes the determining role of a single individual (the director or "author") in the shaping of a film, could easily defeat the purpose of independent filmmaking as an alternative cinema. Robert Rosenstone's criticism on behalf of historians is pertinent to Asian American cinema: "Currently theories of cinema—structuralist, semiotic, feminist, or Marxist—all seem too self-contained and hermetic, too unin-terested in the flesh-and-blood content of the past, the lives and struggles of indi-viduals and groups, to be directly useful to the historian."[10] The ongoing debate over feminist film theory may be another telling example of this problem. Femi-nist film criticism became influential in the mid-1970s largely through two groundbreaking articles by Laura Mulvey and Claire Johnston, published in the British film journal *Screen*.[11] Employing psychoanalysis as their framework, espe-cially that of Jacques Lacan, they have raised provocative questions about the source and function of male visual pleasure, making the important shift from women's images to the signifying practices of the film medium itself. However, the theory's usefulness is undercut by two serious limitations: its ahistorical and antiempiricist bias and its reductionist logic. First, by focusing on subjectivity, the theory often downplays the social and historical contexts. What is more, the con-cept of male "look" or "gaze," so fundamental to feminist film theory, advocates a split in social totality, male and female. Unfortunately, film viewing and reception cannot be understood only in terms of our psychology or subject positioning, and of course women are not solely textual constructs. Since Western feminism empha-sizes sexual difference as the only social variable, matters of class, ethnicity, and race have disappeared from the equation. In fact, the theory reinforces white mid-dle-class values, for it keeps women from seeing other forms of oppressions. As bell hooks argues, "Feminist theory rooted in an ahistorical psychoanalytic framework that privileges sexual difference actively suppresses recognition of race, reenacting and mirroring the erasure of black womanhood that occurs in films."[12]

By the same token, many minority film artists have complained that they are deadlocked in a double bind. On the one hand, they are expected by their com-munities to reflect a cultural diversity based on their ethnic heritage, and on the other, their film school training is based on a Eurocentric mode, which is alien to their needs. Clyde Taylor, for example, pointed out in *Black Film Review* that "the seeds of authorism may have been sown among Black independents in film school. Formal cinema training is one of the defining characteristics of the current film movement. And most film schools train their students to be auteurs, demanding from them projects where they work as solo honchos."[13] With this auteur complex, Taylor asserted, Black filmmakers "want to write, produce, direct, edit and act in their films, offering as an excuse the limitations of their budgets, yet few are ener-getic and talented enough to do all these tasks and make good films."[14] For non-white filmmakers, rejecting auteur-based filmmaking does not mean giving up creative control, but instead means opening the filmmaking process. As Black woman scholar Barbara Christian said (in a different context), "People of color have always theorized—but in forms quite different from the Western form of abstract logic. And I am inclined to say that our theorizing (and I intentionally use the verb rather than the noun) is often in narrative forms, in the stories we create, in riddles and proverbs, in the play with language, since dynamic rather than fixed ideas seem more to our liking."[15]

In *Black Film/White Money*, Jesse Algeron Rhines highlights another important dimension of critical reception: the special role of distribution in today's film industry. Hollywood's "block-book" system (in which a film distributor, often a major studio, books a new film throughout the country in a block of hundreds, even thousands of theaters) prevents independent films from reaching most movie theaters and commercial outlets. Nearly all independent films have gone the route of limited distribution on the festival circuit and have had minimal exhibition. Even specialized ethnic-oriented theaters cannot help; nor can annual film festivals, despite their themes and hoopla. With limited budget and screening opportunities, an independent film's crossover potential coincides with its ability to secure a significant financial return from white American viewers. As Rhines argues in the case of Black cinema, "Black films must be presented to white distributors in particular ways that are consistent with white audience stereotyping of Blacks in order to predict crossover success."[16] Indeed, box-office appeal or indifference shows clearly the extent to which popular stereotypes shape audience expectations. Small films offering realistic treatments of everyday life in minority communities often fail to achieve broader distribution, owing to Anglo-America's patronization of products that reconfirm their assumptions. In comparison to the Black situation, there is an outright absence of venues for Asian American films. As Peter Wang advises, "You have to recognize that this market is dominated by the big studios, Hollywood. And Hollywood is telling the European cultural-oriented stories—it has been, it will be for a long time. Asian stories are something that deviates from the mainstream."[17] Tiana (Thi Thanh Nga) writes about her experience in distributing her critically acclaimed *From Hollywood to Hanoi*:

> This was the first American film shot in Viet Nam, for Viet Nam, to play in theaters. It has won major festival awards and pleased audiences enough that they have funded the prints and 35mm blow-up. I have taken the film on the college circuit from East Coast Harvard to West Coast Stanford. I've shown it in art centers as far north as Minneapolis and as far south as New Orleans. But no Hollywood studio has been willing to take it on for distribution. Distributing has been like waging war. You take a hill at a time. You go bunker to bunker. I had no choice, but I don't recommend it.[18]

Indeed, mainstream film industry continues to employ racist practices (through a rigid set of "rules" in distribution) to maintain artistic and political control and to marginalize artists of color. As Freude Bartlett comments on the difficulty in distribution of developing a mass audience for independent product, "The mass audience is kept asleep by overexposure to Hollywood studio product which is kept in the public eyes with the help of multimillion dollar promotion campaigns."[19]

In this regard, it is also important to note how the dynamics of Asian American cinematic experience differ from those of its Black counterparts. In the history of Black filmmaking, the element of spectatorship has served as one of the defining characteristics. The all-Black "race movies" in the 1930s and 1940s, for example, were produced specifically for Black Americans, never intended to be viewed by a white audience. Blaxploitation movies in the 1970s and 1980s, made by white directors, targeted the Black audience as well. Today, African Americans, who make up less than one-eighth of the population, comprise one-third of the paying audience for motion pictures. The NAACP estimates total industry revenues at $4.6 billion "with Black moviegoers making up over 25 percent of box office ticket sales."[20] In contrast, Asian Americans do not have that numerical leverage. Steven Okazaki believes that the existence or absence of a core audience decides how much creative control a filmmaker enjoys:

> The real hard thing is that the independent black films now are really given a certain amount of freedom because there is at least a core audience to support that vision. Just like Woody Allen can make his films as long as they are not too expensive, for a core audience, any way he wants. But if he wanted to reach a lot more people he'd have to make more concessions. . . . Black filmmakers [can do the same thing], if they can count on a core interest from Black ticket buyers. With Asian Americans, you're talking about several communities that are not necessarily relating to each other. . . . And I think that automatically changes it not necessarily for the worse, but it is affected.[21]

In addition, the audience for Asian American films is further diluted by the diverse nature of the communities. "It was not easy," Robert Nakamura recalls, "because the community at that time [1970s] was really fragmented, with many different viewpoints and conceptions of what the Asian American community was and how people should serve it. The radical left and the conservatives of the community had very different ideas about the role of media. We were criticized by both sides."[22]

Moreover, Renee Tajima is quoted as saying that one Asian American community does not readily recognize Asian Americans in *other* communities, and that the Asian American community only recognizes Asian American achievement after validation by white society.[23] Japanese American actor George Takei, best known as Mr. Sulu on the series *Star Trek*, agrees with Tajima:

Jazz is claimed as the singularly American musical form, but America
didn't produce jazz. It was the unique support and sustenance of the
African American community. Even in the most poverty stricken area
of the black ghetto, you'll find a record shop. The black community
nurtures their artists. But we don't see it happening with Asian Americans. . . . If our artists are going to flower and to deal with Asian
American material, they have to be sustained by an audience that best
understands what they're talking about.[24]

Director Kayo Hatta reflects on her experience as further proof: "When I
was making *Picture Bride*, I was really telling people that 'if the Asian community
doesn't come out to support the film, it's going to just show people like Miramax
that there really isn't much of an audience out there.' We have to keep developing
our audience as much as possible."[25] But she feels disappointed, saying: "One of the
frustrating things within the Asian American community sometimes can be that
they don't see something as worthwhile until it's validated by the mainstream. I
think that in many ways, if *Picture Bride* had not won the Audience Award at Sundance, it wouldn't have gotten as much recognition in the Asian American audience."[26] Hatta speculates on the reasons for the lack of community support:

[This is] partly because, say within a younger Asian American audience,
maybe people don't think these things have anything to do with them
and that it calls attention to their ethnicity. Maybe there's a more assim-
ilationist pressure or people just blending in. Maybe [it's] because they
are further away from all the ethnic roots that older Asian American
filmmakers are wrapped up in.[27]

The phenomenon of what I would term the "cultural gatekeepers" in contemporary Asian American discourse further marginalizes Asian American films.
Very much like the selective filtering in the Harlem Renaissance of the 1920s and
1930s, when white gatekeepers made decisions about what was worthy of publication and critical acclaim, some scholars and critics still arrogantly assume the
ultimate knowledge of Asian or Asian American life, while suppressing different
voices. The debate in the 1980s over Amy Tan, David Henry Hwang, and especially Maxine Hong Kingston has become the best-known case.[28] Frank Chin, for
example, in the name of preserving Asian American cultural integrity, has called
for "harsh and knowledgeable" Asian American critics to "police the difference
between the real and the fake."[29]

Whether working in literature or films, Asian Americans often find that
they have to pass a litmus test, administered by those community watchdogs. If
the result turns out to be unfavorable, they will be unfairly blamed for not living
up to the authenticity of the culture they try to represent. Again, take the major

cinematic work *The Joy Luck Club* as an illustration. The movie has become the target of crucifying scrutiny by some self-claimed cultural guardians. One Chinese film critic wrote, "That the filmmakers exercised such considerable license in interpreting the book was a great misfortune. . . . Their reinterpretation resulted in an alarmingly rich array of botched details." Here are some of the "botched details" he picked:

> As a young woman Auntie Ying Ying wears her long hair down, loosely about her shoulders, but in the 1930s and 1940s young unwed Chinese women invariably wore their hair in braids and married women in buns. (Loose hair would have drawn the suspicion of insanity.) As the Japanese close in on Guilin, Suyuan flees with the populace. The roads are clogged with people, but the river is inexplicably free of boats. . . . When Jing-mei finally goes to China to meet her half-sisters, she arrives in Shanghai by riverboat rather than by plane, as in the book. This would have required her to fly to Hong Kong, travel by plane or, more likely in the mid-1980s, by rail to an interior point such Qongqing (Chungking) or Wuhan in order to board a Changjiang (Yangtze River) ferry. Such a circuitous route would have been hard enough had she traveled in the company of a fluent Mandarin-speaker like her father, again as she did in the book, but what possible motive to tackle it alone when the goal was to reach her sisters without delay? . . . To top things off, Jing-mei makes her way through the crowd at the dock and, just when she reaches her sisters, sets her suitcase down on the ground. I can just imagine the scattered, stifled chuckling in theaters throughout the world. Anybody watching this scene who had lived or simply traveled substantially in China would know that in all probability when, after the hugs, Jing-mei bent down again to pick up her luggage nothing would be there.[30]

Some of the points made above may be well taken. However, the author, George Tseo, seems to take for granted "authenticity" as a test. Who gives him the ultimate authority to judge the accuracy of Chinese life in the 1930s and 1940s? What makes him so sure of his understanding of Chinese geography and Jing-mei's itinerary? How can we use our own rational judgment on other people's actions at very emotional moments of their lives? This kind of political reading of media texts can easily be taken out of context, and further it resembles so-called "redemptive readings," a concept developed by Charlotte Brunsdon. According to Brunsdon, media critics, taking this approach, constantly search out the incoherencies within a media text to salvage the work for a particular audience. "The redemptive reading," however, she writes, "frequently meets with a certain skepticism, a doubt that real readers read like that."[31] Furthermore, as Toni Morrison points out in the context of Black cultural criticism, there should be no "totalizing approaches to African-American scholarship which have no drive other than the exchange of domination—dominant Eurocentric scholarship replaced by dominant Afrocentric scholarship."[32] Morrison's comment is as pertinent to Asian Americans as to African Americans.

Since movie-making is such a capital-intensive and mass-audience-driven business, critical reception in the media is certainly shaped by whoever holds buying power. In a public forum such as the movie industry, filmmakers must ultimately seek validation in the marketplace, from viewers who lay down their dollars at the box-office window. However, in comparison with marketplace exploitation, the fundamental hurdles that Asian Americans must surmount to get into the industry remain the same forms of ideological and institutional racism discussed in Chapter 2. Until Asian Americans are fully accepted as equal members in American society, they will "remain on the margins except in cases where they can bring a decent return on the investment of the 'big boys.'"[33] Even this limited market validation of a few selected Asian American productions results in an outpouring of critical controversies, which will be examined in the next section.

VALIDATION AS APPROPRIATION

The last few years represent a landmark in Asian American filmmaking. "As if at the wave of a magic wand," in the words of *A. Magazine*, Asian American films have suddenly been transformed into highly marketable products. Making three times its production cost, *The Joy Luck Club*, directed by Wayne Wang, became the first commercial success for Asian American cinema. Produced on a budget of $750,000, Ang Lee's *The Wedding Banquet* grossed over thirty times its cost, making it the most profitable film of 1993, beating even *Jurassic Park* based on its cost-to-earnings ratio. With this critical success, we see expansion of major avenues for the Asian American drama. For example, Wang and Lee, among others, began to be recruited by Hollywood studios in making general movies (*Smoke* and *Blue in the Face* by Wang, *Sense and Sensibility* and *The Ice Storm* by Lee). It is, therefore, safe to suggest that Asian American cinema has left the margins to flirt with the mainstream.

This commercial breakthrough is celebrated widely by Asian American communities because it has proven that Asian American stories, which are different from Hollywood representations, can find a market and enjoy broad appeal. However, it also raises some fundamental issues about the paradoxical relationship between independent cinema and the film industry itself. In 1991, Black film critic Clyde Taylor framed these questions for Black filmmaking: "Should we look at the corps of Black independents as apprentices readying themselves for big studio 'breaks?' How has the goal of building a Black film culture beyond Hollywood control and supported by the Black community been affected?"[34] The questions raised by Taylor are debated also among Chicano/a filmmakers. Film historian Chon A. Noriega described the relations with Hollywood as a central cinematic dialectic, or dual emplacement, for Chicano/a cinema. He argues that, from the beginning, Chicano/a cinema operates within a dialectic between the political weapon of New Latin American Cinema and the economic formula of Hollywood. On the one hand, Chicano/a cinema has made some inroads into the American film and TV industries, although, ideologically, it also tries to sustain an intertextual dialogue with the Hollywood representation of Chicanos/as.[35]

Likewise, on their road to commercial success, some vexing questions have fueled controversies about the relationship of Asian Americans' independent status to the mainstream Hollywood establishment. What does commercial success mean for the artists? For the first time Asian American productions are validated by the commercial mainstream, and its endorsement has become means of legitimization. Does this indicate their maturation and a natural evolution toward a wider cinematic context? In other words, does it signify an end to the marginalization of Asian American themes? Or does it mean instead that mainstream cinema constantly feeds on independent cinema and appropriates its themes, stories, and even narrative styles? And, are Asian Americans losing artistic control? This concern over cultural appropriation by the mainstream was already registered at AAIFF a decade ago. Commenting on the shrinking number of annual submissions, Jeannie Park wrote, "Ironically, the major factor causing the current dearth seems to be that Asian American films are finally being noticed and picked up by commercial distributors, who often have exclusive agreements with theaters and would rather premiere the films in more prestigious forums where they control publicity and press access. These sorts of obligations have precluded Wayne Wang's *Dim Sum* as well as Steven Okazaki's *Living on Tokyo Time* and Peter Wang's hit *A Great Wall* from appearing at the festival."[36] Former AAIFF director Marlina Gonzalez took a positive spin on the situation, saying, "The filmmakers have become almost unreachable. I don't want to call it too much of a problem, though, because it's a big step forward for Asian American filmmaking. I'd like to see it as a positive result of the festival."[37] However, to borrow a concept from Black film scholar Mark Reid, one wonders whether this problem of losing access to the best Asian American films indicates the beginning of *two* Asian American film traditions operating at the same time: the "independent" and the "Asian-oriented."[38]

Perhaps Oliver Stone's *Heaven and Earth* (1993) provides a revealing example of this trend. The movie is based on two autobiographies of Le Ly Hayslip, a Vietnamese refugee woman. Proclaimed to be the first look at the Vietnam War from a Vietnamese perspective, the movie, in the hands of controversial director

Stone, very much defeats its proclaimed purpose of providing a counter-viewpoint. As a critic in the *San Francisco Examiner* put it poignantly, "How strange and disappointing, then, that though the words and stories we hear are Le Ly Hayslip's, the tone of voice, the emphatic style is so clearly Stone's. The point-of-view, it turns out, is one we already know quite well."[39] With his manipulative directorial style, and the personal agenda that imbues many of his films, Stone has become the dominant voice in the story. In looking at Black film reception, Ed Guerrero suggests that the Black screen image has been in "protective custody," meaning Black-oriented films controlled by Hollywood industry.[40] Perhaps it is not totally groundless to speculate that if Melvin Van Peebles's *Sweet Sweetback's Baadasssss Song* (1971) helped to launch Hollywood's blaxploitation era, would Oliver Stone's *Heaven and Earth* initiate an "Asianploitation" wave in Hollywood?

Viewed from another political angle, as some community people have charged, the general acclaim of an Asian American film in itself can be taken as evidence of both "selling out" and falling victim to the market imperative. It is not surprising that in a society obsessed with race, ethnic artists are bashed if they ever cross the lines. Asian American writers and directors are often simplistically dismissed for selling out to Hollywood. But it is a legitimate question to ask: does an ethnic filmmaker become more readily admitted into the mainstream when she or he becomes less of a filmmaker with a cause (that is, with content less disturbing to the mainstream) and less political in her or his own work? At root, does an independent film's going commercial constitute selling out?

The debate over Wayne Wang's Hollywood production *The Joy Luck Club*, the first Hollywood-financed Asian American–directed major movie, should be placed in this context. On the one hand, Asian American media watchdog groups criticized the adaptation of Amy Tan's book for perpetuating long-standing screen stereotypes of Asian males. Referring to the fact that two of the three contemporary young women are involved with sympathetically portrayed Caucasian men, Guy Aoki, president of the Media Action Network for Asian-Americans (MANAA), charges, "Asian-American males are not even attractive to their own women. . . . The message to women is, you've made it when you've got a white boyfriend. Unfortunately, that's still reflected in 'The Joy Luck Club.' "[41] What is more, Aoki has a problem with the change Tan and screenwriter Ronald Bass made for the obnoxious yuppie Chinese American character to whom the third daughter is married. In Tan's novel, the character is Caucasian rather than Chinese American. "Why did they change that?" Aoki asked. "And why no redeeming Asian?" Tan and Bass both defended the screenplay change for a Chinese American rather than have all three Caucasian husbands or boyfriends. "We said, 'Hey, we don't want to propose the notion that every Asian woman only marries a Caucasian guy,' " said Bass.[42] To Wayne Wang, the controversy is senseless: "Anyway, it's not about the men, it's about women. If the Asian men want to have a movie that's deeper and more complex about the men, well, let them write a great book about it, and I'll make a movie of it. But I do want to say that Chinese men—the Chinese Americans are less so—but Chinese men traditionally have been awful with women, with their wives, and this is a very clear, strong statement that I want to say about it."[43] Among filmmakers, Kayo Hatta has lodged the protest in more direct terms, stating:

> The more specific you are, the more universal you become and I really believe in that whole notion. If you treat a subject very specifically with the colors, the texture, the nuances, the details of an experience, whether it's your ethnicity, your sexual orientation, or whatever, it just points out in spite of those differences we're very similar. That's what makes it universal and that's what makes it interesting. I don't think that becoming universal means telling all stories from a white perspective or [telling stories] that are totally pasteurized.[44]

Poet, writer, and critic Garrett Hongo saw a similar "ideological battle within the field known as 'Asian American literature.'" To quote him, "They [Asian American literary critics] have alleged that recognition is itself a sign of a given writer's personal assimilation of an insidious bourgeois culture and a corruption of that which is the 'authentic' literary culture of Asian America. . . . They have engaged in the ideological practice of judging the cultural pertinence of a given literary work by employing a litmus test of ethnic authenticity."[45] Hongo angrily condemned this practice as "nothing more than fascism, intellectual bigotry, and ethnic fundamentalism of the worst kind."[46]

Even before the commercial breakthrough, some Asian American filmmakers and critics already sounded the alarm. John Esaki, for example, in 1990 called on fellow filmmakers to go "back to real Asian American filmmaking."[47] While citing Wayne Wang's first black-and-white feature *Chan Is Missing* as a recommended film, Esaki warned about the economic lure and the seduction of prestige in Hollywood for Asian American artists. Indeed, many Asian American filmmakers prefer to work independently for artistic control. Steven Okazaki, for example, declares in an interview, "I think your creative independence is kind of defined by who is paying for the film. . . . We've developed TV movies and it constantly becomes an issue. Putting in the white character and changing the focus toward the non-Asian audience."[48] Gregg Araki fiercely defends his independent status: "Any 'Independent' Film," he told his interviewer, "that reinforces and buys into the values of the Mainstream is an opportunity wasted."[49] Kayo Hatta agrees: "In independent films we are our own producers, we find our own money. That's how you can make films that truly reflect your perspective and your voice."[50] Hatta thinks Asian Americans have to compromise their principles in order to have big studios "take chances on telling an Asian American story." She believes that *The Joy Luck Club* was a real exception, "because the book was a bestseller and that was profitable. It was already proven. It's really a business."[51]

However, in a capital-intensive industry like filmmaking, it might be imperative for Asian American films to operate essentially as a business. "For me, I think I learned early on in film school how important money is. Just making like short films, ten-minute films you know, I had to work like two, three jobs just to pay it off myself. So definitely money is a huge part of the whole process. . . . I really don't think going commercial is selling out if you do it right," stated Justin Lin, co-director of *Shopping for Fangs*, at a film panel discussion.[52] Wayne Wang told bell hooks in their interview, "I believe that the truly independent films are completely financed outside of the studios. It is very hard to raise money to make true independent films. In my mind, I don't even know what independent films are any more, if they exist at all."[53]

To take Wang's point another step, does the ethnic background of the financial backers make a difference in terms of creative control? Spike Lee, for example, has often stated that it was the money contributed by wealthy Black entertainers that guaranteed his control of *Malcolm X*. But Wahneema Lubiano asks poignantly, "Would the financing from African American capitalists necessarily be more politically adventurous than that from Euro-American capitalists?"[54] The mixed reactions to Russell Wong's recent agreement to star in Miramax's updated Charlie Chan movies testify to the controversy from another angle. Obviously for Wong, the three-picture deal with Miramax promises to be the biggest break in his career, but the question remains: would the ethnicity of a Chinese American star help break the time-honored racist stereotype or revive it? Chinese American novelist Gish Jen is confident that Wong as Chan will break the stereotype: "It would be great to see an Asian American in that role rather than someone in yellow face." But Frank Chin cannot disagree more, claiming, "Charlie Chan will always be a symbol of white racism, no matter who plays him. If you put a black man in a hood, does that make the Ku Klux Klan a civil rights organization?" Jessica Hagedorn, who edited an Asian American anthology titled *Charlie Chan Is Dead,* has serious reservations, too: "I'm a little taken aback. It's like if you resurrected Sambo or Stepin Fetchit or Aunt Jemima. What if you said Angela Bassett will play Aunt Jemima?"[55]

This debate over strategies fits perfectly into the culturally resistant practices outlined by Black writer and critic Houston Baker. His concept of the "deformation of mastery" and "the mastery of form" represent the two ends of the strategic continuum in creating oppositional or culturally resistant productions.[56] Similarly, the recent critical success of Asian American films intensifies the existing debate among Asian American film practitioners about the pros and cons of the two strategies: seeking entry into the system to subvert the norm from within, versus remaining independent and challenging the system from without. Amy Tan's experience in making *The Joy Luck Club* might serve as an illustration for my point. As she recalled in her diary, published in the *Los Angeles Times*, while she was securing financing for the film, Oliver Stone agreed to be the executive co-producer with Janet Yang, who was by then vice president of his production company. In the spring of 1990, Stone helped them sign a contract to make *The Joy Luck Club* under his deal with Carolco. However, that same fall, Tan remembers, "after six months of negotiating, we found the contract did not really guarantee us the creative control we required, so we walked away from the Carolco deal."[57] In an entry two years later, dated March 1992, Tan and her team met with Disney Studios Chairman Jeffrey Katzenberg, Kathryn Galan, and Henry Hwang of Disney and its Hollywood Pictures division. Since Katzenberg had already read the script, it only took an informal discussion to sign what was described as a sweet deal. Tan wrote confidently a year later, "Katzenberg gave us exactly what we wanted: creative control. He expressed enormous respect for Wayne as a filmmaker. We would be able to make our movie just like an independent production, and we'd be supported by Hollywood Pictures, headed by Ricardo Mestres."[58] Tan has this to say for "the truth about Disney":

> Obviously, I'd be in a bad spot discussing working with the people at Disney if I had loathed it. Happily, that's not the case. Disney said we had creative control, and that's what we got. Sure, we got notes on the rough cut. But Ricardo Mestres and Jeffrey Katzenberg seemed to go out of their way to assure us that the notes were only suggestions. We had the final say. We did take some of their suggestions, of course, but there was never any pressure to do so. Could we tighten the pacing at this point? We looked at it—sure. Would the scene be better, if the mother lashed out in anger at the daughter as well? Let's try it and find out. From the beginning, they seemed very supportive and enthusiastic. We've also been included on marketing and distribution plans, as well as publicity and such details as the making of the trailer.[59]

In the final analysis, it would be debatable if this so-called sweet deal was exceptional or typical for Asian American independent filmmakers. As Amy Tan admits, "Yes, I'm aware of the fact that Hollywood might look at 'The Joy Luck Club' as some sort of proving ground."[60] Some critics predict most of these Asian American directors may only have limited or one-shot deals with the major studios. In their view, the recent popular acceptance of some Asian American films does not signify an assimilation of Asians into the American mainstream, but rather a mere repositioning of their marginality. It will be interesting to see in the coming years whether the oppositional aesthetics and thematics of their earlier independent films can be sustained for mass-market consumption. With Asian American cinema slowly moving from the margins to the mainstream, these questions are going to stay with us, understandably so. After all, they are legitimate questions that touch on important issues of representation, authenticity, and cultural domination and resistance.

CULTURAL MISREADINGS

With this increasing visibility come confusions and controversies within the affected communities and outside them. The number of such critiques of Asian American films is growing tremendously—undoubtedly a healthy sign of sophistication in Asian American film practices—although many of these critiques also yield and promote diverse cultural misreadings. Often, Asian American stories get patronized, and their attacks on Anglo-American sensibilities are neutralized or deflected in various ways. What is more, significant differences could easily be read between the so-called "white criticism" (that is, reviews from mainstream film journals) and "ethnic criticism" (commentaries from the communities). In writing this chapter, I have done a survey of film reviews published over the past five years. The survey reveals that because mainstream cinema critics misunderstand Asian American experiences, they misconstrue the significance of Asian American films, and often misinterpret them in a number of ways.

"Calling Their Ignorance Our Inscrutability"

Back in the early 1980s, Maxine Hong Kingston was feeling very much frustrated by the cultural misreadings of *The Woman Warrior* by two-thirds of her American reviewers. Despite their favorable commentaries, she complained that "they praise the wrong things." Insisting that "I am an American . . . an American writer," Kingston accused those critics of "measuring the book and me against the stereotype of the exotic, inscrutable, mysterious oriental." While books "written by Americans of European ancestry are reviewed as American novels," Kingston indignantly asked, "How dare they call their ignorance our inscrutability!"[61]

It is very clear in the critical literature how this notion about Asians and Asian Americans has been invoked in other nonliterary media. Films and videos made by Asians in this country are often considered specialized works, directed by foreigners who will never really belong to America. In the critical literature, Asian American films are taken for their anthropological or ethnographic values more than anything else. In a cursory survey of recent re-reviews of *The Joy Luck Club*, for example, the movie is universally described as authentically Chinese. Similarly, reviews of Ang Lee's *The Wedding Banquet* put the greatest emphasis on the Chinese marriage rituals in the film, which are described as colorful, attractive, and aesthetically pleasing. Even in a mainstream production like *Sense and Sensibility*, Ang Lee was credited not for his own individual vision or artistic choices, but instead for his ties to Asian culture. Film journals and other media commentaries emphasize the Asian values that Lee brought to the set. As an example, he performed a ritualistic blessing before starting the production. It was called the Big Luck Ceremony, involving symbolic uses of fruit, flowers, and incense, and calling for bows to the North, South, East, and West.[62]

Rituals, said to be an excellent tool in creating the desired mood for the movie, have become a shorthand guide to Chinese culture for the American audience. The rationale behind doing this, of course, is the selling point of "Oriental" exotica. Another ready example was how Kayo Hatta's *Picture Bride* was packaged in the video marketplace. The image of the hat on the original poster was replaced with the image of a couple in a waterfall, creating a very exploitive video cover. Hatta felt embarrassed, because in many ways "*Picture Bride* was a film that a lot of people were really excited about and really proud of the fact that it made into the mainstream and it felt awful to see it represented that way."[63] What is more, Hatta felt the cover defeated the purpose of the film. "It sort of almost undermined everything we were trying to do as a film. Trying to make a true and really complex and dignified representation of an Asian American woman. It [the waterfall] has nothing to do with the story. Plus, if you look really carefully, the naked couple in the waterfall are white. . . . It was very disturbing."[64] Hatta did eventually get Buena Vista, the distributor, to put out a different cover for later copies, but the waterfall package was never removed from store shelves.

It is apparent that Hollywood's image of Asians and Asian Americans is virtually one and the same. In 1993, *Time* magazine film critic Richard Corliss proclaimed the arrival of "Asian chic."[65] Although Corliss's mood was celebratory, he reinforces a critical misconception by lumping together films such as Chen Kaige's *Farewell My Concubine* (1993), Oliver Stone's *Heaven and Earth*, and Ang Lee's *The Wedding Banquet* with the videos for Madonna's "Rain" and Janet Jackson's "If." This mix seems innocent on the surface, but it reaches deeper into a more systematic problem. For one, in Asian American productions, Asian themes are automatically assumed to take primacy over American themes. Nor have most scholarly works on Asian representations attempted to differentiate between Asians and

Asian Americans. Charlie Chan, arguably the first Asian American character, is a "Chinese detective" who happens to speak English, but whose talk is still sprinkled with Chinese aphorisms. This confusion is not surprising in view of Hollywood's track record of portraying all Asians with one broad brush, replacing one Asian ethnic group with another (all "Orientals" look alike) and transposing one Asian culture for another (who cares about the difference). This misconception is not unique to America, but a more univeral problem. As Rea Tajiri comments about her European experience, "In terms of European buyers they are still not able to make a distinction between Asian and Asian American film. If I send them an American independent or if I didn't go there as an American independent, thinking about that, they kind of saw it as an Asian film. . . . We sort of have to break through that perception."[66]

To a certain extent, this lumping together of Asian and Asian American films is self-invented. At most film festivals organized by Asian Americans, both Asian and Asian American films are showcased together. This decision may be strategically advantageous, yet it carries some negative implications. Curtis Choy has some serious doubts as to the merits of AAIFF's international program. "Asian American International? What's that? It just means Asian movies get lumped in with the Asian American stuff."[67] Similarly, Spencer Nakasako has noted, "Anything Asian, anything that comes from Asia, is considered Asian America film: critics say it's a boon for Asian American filmmakers. You've got the Zhang Yimous and the Chen Kaiges and John Woo's *Hard Target* as Asian American Cinema. It just takes one Asian actor or director, and it gets classed as Asian American Cinema." He rightfully points out further, "You don't see films out of Africa called African American, you don't see Luis Bunuel called a Mexican American filmmaker."[68] Similarly, Maxine Hong Kingston commented several years ago, "I have never before read a critic who took a look at a Jewish American spouse and said, 'There's something wrong with that Saul Bellow and Norman Mailer. They aren't at all like the one I'm married to.' Critics do not ask whether Vonnegut is typical of German Americans; they do not ask whether J. P. Donleavy is typical of Irish Americans. You would never know by reading the reviews of Francine du Plessix Gray's *Lovers and Tyrants* that it is by and about an immigrant from France. Books written by Americans of European ancestry are reviewed as American novels."[69]

Many filmmakers believe it is critically important to differentiate Asian from Asian American films. "A logical place to start" defining Asian American cinema, one of them said, "would be to exclude movies made in Asia, especially movies which do not deal with life in America."[70] At a panel discussion organized by the 15th San Francisco International Asian American Film Festival in March 1997, Quentin Lee, co-director of *Shopping for Fangs* (1996), deemed it very crucial to distinguish Asian American productions from Asian films. He felt that Asian American films are sandwiched "right in between American independent and Asian films." Lee sees a better situation if Asian American films can be separated from Asian films, because "the Asian film circle is very small . . . quite elitist with a certain number of critics here dictating which films are good and bad." He believes that there is a niche for Asian American films to fit into the American independent scene, because "that has the most possibilities [and] people are much more open to you. [Also] people who would want to buy American independent films are much more open to what kind of films you have."[71] Peter Wang agrees with Lee: "Being Asian American, I grasp some opportunities, get my business on the road for quite a bit of mileage. I have to be very thankful for my cultural background. It is because I am an Asian American, Chinese American, that I can tell a simple story, probably somewhat differently. People will be interested."[72]

"Sociology Passes for Film Criticism"

Another disconcerting film-critical practice for Asian American works is the discounting of the films' artistic merits. Reviews of Asian American art works by mainstream media critics often reveal that the criteria they use to assess the works' merits have been something other than literary and aesthetic. Instead, the critics only expect the films to be instructive in Asian American life, rather than expressing artistic qualities and styles. In other words, the quality of the films is often defined in racial or ethnic terms alone, as if the art and the message of the works were mutually exclusive. The beauty, humor, and richness of the works are often overlooked in critical analysis. As Garrett Hongo describes the critical practices in the context of poetry, Asian American artists "weren't so much listened to as intellectuals, as employed as ritual objects of the culture." He observes cynically, "Our works weren't so much read, as our appearances and personalities were interpreted—and then along fairly simple lines of social image and racial pride, sociological themes of ethnicity, and political iconoclasm."[73]

Similarly, opposition has already been voiced among Asian American filmmakers that their works should not be seen only as history and sociology—but as art as well. As Renee Tajima laments, "To this day, whenever described as a group, Asian American independent filmmakers are made out to be saints or school teachers, rarely artists. Sociology passes for film criticism, and the work continues to be defined by thematic, not cinematic, significance."[74] Indeed, for better or for worse, the fact that most of their films comment on racism, sexism, oppression, and other social ills has caused critics and everyday viewers to respond more to the implicit or explicit social commentary than to the artistry of their films.

Bearing this in mind, Ang Lee's omission as director from the two Golden Globes and seven Oscar nominations for his romantic hit *Sense and Sensibility* was not surprising. Despite *Time* magazine film critic Richard Corliss' prediction that "Lee will probably become the first Asian to receive an Oscar nomination for Best Director,"[75] Lee was bypassed for best-director recognition. *Sense and Sensibility* won Best Picture, but as some commentator quipped, the movie apparently directed itself. Going over most film reviews of *Sense and Sensibility,* one sees that its success was entirely accredited to Emma Thompson (its featured actress and screenwriter). Very little, if any at all, attention was given to Lee's artistry. "Emma could have made the whole movie a big ego trip," said producer Lindsay Doran. "But she was very generous with her performance and her presence. She didn't try to take over the scenes from the other actors or from Ang. And she's incredibly generous with everyone."[76] It is incredible that the only thing Lee was credited for in making a "white" film was his understanding of the "tensions and conflicts with traditions that separate generations."[77] There is not the slightest doubt that when viewers see a Steven Spielberg movie, they would judge Spielberg's success or failure based on individual vision and artistry. In contrast, Ang Lee's credit is based on the fact that he has successfully integrated "Asian values" into a film that is British in nature. Thus, formal innovations are entirely overlooked, even where—as is often the case—they are an intrinsic part of the filmmaker's message. Generally, Asian American films are seen as providing, at best, easy sociological discussions at museums, in late-night educational programs, and on university campuses. This critical blindness has created a huge dichotomy between form and content.

Unfortunately, in the practice of cultural misreadings, community responses to the films reinforce the problem of the so-called culture/art divide. Often, a certain "burden of representation" is placed on Asian American films, and their entertainment quotient is very much overlooked by the communities. The primary focus of the criticism is placed on the films' value in the instruction they offer in Asian American life. Must Asian American filmmakers be totally and exclusively answerable to their own ethnic community, be spokespersons for that community, tell its stories and tell them accurately? Or can they claim the right to express an individual vision and personal concerns, and in doing so modify the myths and legends of a group for their own artistic purpose? More often than not, a filmmaker's "personal" concerns turn out to be the concerns of many, although the "many" may not necessarily be from the same ethnic community from which the artist comes. Asked whether Black filmmakers should have "social responsibility," as reported by Jesse Algeron Rhines, award-winning documentarian Stanley Nelson responded, "I don't think a filmmaker has any responsibility at all to the community. I don't think you can do that. It puts too much weight on you. Your responsibility is to yourself as an artist."[78] Wayne Wang concurs, proclaiming, "No story that is about individuals, about specific people, can represent all of Asian American culture, or Chinese American culture. It just represents those characters."[79]

This culture/art divide results at least partially from the role tokenism plays in criticism. Because of the dichotomy of the so-called "marked cultures" and "unmarked cultures," white directors and filmmakers, operating out of an unmarked cultural base, are often expected to explore universal themes, while their minority counterparts (whose masked cultures exist in relation to whiteness) are confined to do only specialized themes from their *own* cultures. As bell hooks writes recently:

> No one asks a white filmmaker in the United States or Britain who makes a film with only white characters if he or she is a white supremacist. The assumption is that the art they create reflects the world as they know it, or certainly as it interests them. However, when a black filmmaker, or for that matter any filmmaker of color, makes a work that focuses solely on subjects exclusively black, or white, they are asked by critics and their audiences to justify their choices and to assume political accountability for the quality of their representations.[80]

Indeed, because of the dearth of minority filmmakers in the industry, any news delivered by them will be interpreted as group representations. In other words, the majority filmmakers are taken as universal spokespersons for *all* people, while minority filmmakers are considered to be "tokens" of special interest groups. Warning against this specter of tokenism, Canadian video artist Midi Onodera pleads to the minority communities, "We must give our developing media artists a chance to experiment without elevating them to where they can be shot down."[81]

It is by now a well-acknowledged fact that when mainstream critics evaluate works of minority group members, the results are at best simplistic misreadings, and at worst cynical misappropriations. As cultural producers, critics, and consumers, Asian Americans need to become engaged in critical intervention in the realms of film criticism. There may be two approaches to accomplish this goal. First, Asian Americans need to build a broadly based interpretive community. Cultural studies scholar Janice Radway put forward the concept of an interpretive community, and she suggests including the audience in the traditional idea of academic scholars. Following this approach espoused by Radway, Asian American film viewers should be encouraged to transform themselves from a "social audience" to "spectators," to borrow a term from Annette Kuhn. Kuhn, a feminist film scholar, distinguishes between a "social audience" and "spectators" among media viewers. Social audience members, according to her, are the actual filmgoers and television watchers, while spectators are theoretical constructs used to analyze meaning

construction within the text/spectator relationship. A true Asian American interpretive community could only be developed out of a large base of Asian American
spectators.

With the interpretive community in place, an equally important task is to
develop a critical tool, a cinematic language in film criticism. A profitable way to
develop this language is perhaps through collaboration between different art
forms, especially Asian American literature. As one Black film scholar writes about
Black cinema, "Black film criticism, then, must start by considering structures that
inform other African American arts such as repetition, antiphony (call/response),
the use of folklore, polyrhythmic and polyvisual structure, to mention a few."[82]
Useful strategies such as Sau-Ling Cynthia Wong's two-pronged approach of contexts and intertexts in reading Asian American literature could be employed with
modifications and innovations in reading Asian American films. Asian American
cinematic critical mass could, therefore, be developed by Asian American spectators imbued with a distinctive and sophisticated voice.

NOTES

1   John Horn, "Movie-awards furor not just black and white," *The Denver Post* (March 22,
1996), 2A. See also Lewis Beale, "Blacks again ignored at Oscar time," *The Denver Post* (Feb. 22,
1998), 8K.

2   For a definition and discussions, see "Special Issue: The Nature and Context of Minority Discourse," *Cultural Critique* 6 (Spring 1987).

3   See the last chapter of Thomas Cripps, *Black Film As Genre* (Bloomington: Indiana University Press, 1979).

4   Interview with Katherine Leslie, April 1996.

5   As quoted by James M. Moran, "Gregg Araki, Guerrilla Film-maker for a Queer Generation," *Film Quarterly* 50:1 (Fall 1996), 20.

6   Interview with Katherine Leslie, April 1996.

7   Nick Browne, "Race: The Political Unconscious of American Film," *East-West Film Journal*
6:1 (Jan. 1, 1992), 6.

8   Ibid.

9   Robert Crusz, "Black Cinemas, Film Theory and Dependent Knowledge," *Screen* 26:3–4
(May–Aug. 1985), 154. The late Korean American artist and writer Theresa Cha's anthology *Apparatus, Cinematographic Apparatus: Selected Writings* (Tanam Press, 1980) also contains significant articles
addressing the Eurocentric nature of movie technology and language.

10   Robert A. Rosenstone, "History in Images/History in Words: Reflections on the Possibility
of Really Putting History onto Film," *American Historical Review* 93:5 (Dec. 1988), 1181.

11   See Laura Mulvey, "Visual Pleasure and Narrative Cinema," and Claire Johnston, "Feminist
Politics and Film History," *Screen* 16:3 (Autumn 1975), 6–18 and 115–124.

12   bell hooks, *Black Looks: Race and Representation* (Boston: South End Press, 1992), 123.

13   Clyde Taylor, "The Paradox of Black Independent Cinema," *Black Film Review* 4:4 (Fall
1988), 17.

14   As quoted by David Nicholson, "Which Way the Black Film Movement," *Cinemas of the
Black Diaspora*, ed. Michael T. Martin (Detroit: Wayne State University Press, 1995), 443.

15   Barbara Christian, "The Race for Theory," *Cultural Critique* 6 (Spring 1987), 52.

16   Jesse Algeron Rhines, *Black Film/White Money* (New Brunswick, N.J.: Rutgers University Press, 1996), 70.

17   Phone interview with Katherine Leslie, April 1996.

18   Tiana (Thi Thanh Nga), "The Long March—From Wong to Woo: Asians in Hollywood," *Cineaste* 21:4 (1995), 40.

19   Freude Bartlett, "Distributing Independent Films," *Jump Cut* 31 (1986), 29.

20   As quoted by Rhines, 6–7.

21   Phone interview with Katherine Leslie, April 1996.

22   As quoted by Stephen Gong, "A History in Progress: Asian American Media Arts Centers 1970–1990," *Moving the Image: Independent Asian Pacific American Media Arts,* ed. Russell Leong (Los Angeles: UCLA Asian American Studies Center, 1991), 3.

23   See Daryl Chin, "Writing an Unexpurgated History of Asian American Film," *CineVue* 3:2 (June 1988), 6.

24   *CineVue* interview with George Takei, " 'Mr. Sulu' Steers a New Course," *CineVue* 6:3 (Sept. 1991), 10.

25   Interview with Katherine Leslie, April 1996.

26   Ibid.

27   Ibid.

28   See Frank Chin, "Come All Ye Asian American Writers of the Real and the Fake," *The Big Aiiieeeee!* (New York: Meridian, 1991).

29   Robert Murray Davis, "Frank Chin: An Interview," *Amerasia Journal* 14:2 (1988), 85.

30   George K. Y. Tseo, "Joy Luck: The Perils of Transcultural 'Translation,'" *Literature/Film Quarterly* 24:4 (1996), 342.

31   Charlotte Brunsdon, "Text and Audience," *Remote Control: Television, Audiences, and Cultural Power,* ed. Ellen Seiter et al. (New York: Routledge, 1989), 122.

32   Toni Morrison, *Playing in the Dark: Whiteness in the Literary Imagination* (New York: Alfred A. Knopf, 1992), 8.

33   Quoting from Darrell Hamamoto's comments on the manuscript.

34   Clyde Taylor, "The Future of Black Film: The Debate Continues," *Black Film Review* 4:4 (Fall 1988), 7.

35   Chon A. Noriega, "Between a Weapon and a Formula: Chicano Cinema and Its Contexts," *Chicanos and Film: Essays on Chicano Representation and Resistance* (New York: Garland Publishing, 1992), 159–88.

36   Jeannie Park, "The First Decade: The Asian American International Film Festival," *Independent* (Nov. 1987), 26.

37   Ibid.

38   In the context of Black cinema, Reid's concept of blaxploitation refers to those Black-oriented films produced in Hollywood beginning in 1970 and continuing mostly until 1975. In addition to its historical context, the term is a way of labeling a film that largely fails to represent the aesthetic values of Black culture. Although the term is based on a misleading dichotomy between independent and nonindependent films, it acknowledges the role that production and distribution play in shaping a film's aesthetic characteristics.

39   Scott Rosenberg, "Vietnam journey cast in Stone," *San Francisco Examiner* (Dec. 24, 1993), C2, 4.

40   Ed Guerrero, *Framing Blackness: The African American Image in Film* (Philadelphia: Temple University Press, 1993), 69–71.

41   Yardena Arar, "Tan, Wang defend depiction of Asian men in 'Joy'," *The New York Daily News* (Sept. 8, 1993), C14, 105.

42   Ibid.

43   Ibid.

44   Phone interview with Katherine Leslie, April 1996.

45   Garrett Hongo, Introduction to *The Open Boat: Poems from Asia America* (New York: Anchor Books/Doubleday, 1993), xxxv.

46   Ibid., xxxv–xxxvi.

47   John Esaki, "Back to Real Asian American Filmmaking," *Moving the Image*, 34.

48   Interview with Katherine Leslie, April 1996.

49   As quoted by Moran, 20.

50   Phone interview with Katherine Leslie, April 1996.

51   Ibid.

52   Transcript from taped "Panel: Asian American Feature Films," 15th San Francisco International Asian American Film Festival, March 8, 1997.

53   bell hooks, "The critical mix: an interview with Wayne Wang," *Reel to Real: Race, Sex, and Class at the Movies* (New York: Routledge, 1996), 130.

54   Wahneema Lubiano, "But Compared to What?: Reading Realism, Representation, and Essentialism in *School Daze, Do the Right Thing*, and the Spike Lee Discourse," *Representing Blackness: Issues in Film and Video*, ed. Valerie Smith (New Brunswick, N.J.: Rutgers University Press, 1997), 102.

55   Somini Sengupta, "Charlie Chan Retooled for the 90's," *New York Times* (Jan. 5, 1997), col.1, Sec. 2, 20.

56   Ed Guerrero applied Baker's concepts to Black filmmaking and he brought them to my attention. See Guerrero, 181.

57   Amy Tan, "Joy, Luck and Hollywood," *Los Angeles Times* (Sept. 5, 1993), D4, 105.

58   Ibid.

59   Ibid.

60   Ibid.

61   Maxine Hong Kingston, "Cultural Mis-readings by American Reviewers," *Asian and Western Writers in Dialogue: New Cultural Identities*, ed. Guy Amirthanayagam (London: MacMillan, 1982), 55.

62   Susan Stark, "Movie in Review: Director brings artistic sense and sensibility to Austen film," *Detroit News* (Dec. 16, 1995).

63   Interview with Katherine Leslie, April 1996.

64   Ibid.

65   Richard Corliss, "The Asians Are Coming! The Asians Have Landed," *Time* (Sept. 13, 1993), 68.

66   Transcript from taped "Panel: Asian American Feature Films," March 8, 1997.

67   As quoted by Peter Feng, "In Search of Asian American Cinema," *Cineaste*, 21:1–2 (1995), 33.

68   Ibid.

69   Kingston, 63.

70   Feng, 33.

71   Transcript from taped "Panel: Asian American Feature Films," March 8, 1997.

72   Phone interview with Katherine Leslie, April 1996.

73   Hongo, xxxiv.

74   Renee Tajima, "Moving the Image: Asian American Independent Filmmaking 1970–1990," *Moving the Image*, 10.

75   Richard Corliss, "Ang Lee: Persuasian," *Time* magazine (Jan. 29, 1996).

76   Live online conference on *Women's Wire* on CompuServe.

77   Lin Neuman, "Cultural Revolution," *Far Eastern Economic Review* (Jan. 4, 1996), 97–98.

78   As quoted by Rhines, 132.

79   Arar.

80   hooks, *Reel to Real*, 69.

81   Midi Onodera, "A Displaced View: What Are We Reconsidering about the Yellow Peril?," *Yellow Peril: Reconsidered,* ed. Paul Wong (Vancouver: On Edge, 1990).

82   Gloria J. Gibson-Hudson, "African American Literary Criticism as a Model for the Analysis of Films by African American Women," *Wide Angle* 13:3–4 (July–Oct. 1991), 52.

Conclusion

ANYONE WHO HAS READ THIS BOOK should agree that as a force on both sides of the camera, Asian Americans have created a formidable oppositional discourse—and on their own terms. In search of a cinematic language, and operating against the conventions and practices of the mainstream industry, they have established a distinctive cinema that is unmistakably Asian American. As the late Steve Tatsukawa fittingly remarked years ago:

> Those Asian Americans who have chosen the film and television field to dedicate their energies and talents [to] are not only creating images; they are creating history. It is no longer the case that the only accurate and viable Asian American image is in our own mirrors. Asian Americans are finally, and firmly, moving beyond the looking glass.[1]

Given these remarkable accomplishments, it now seems to be an opportune time to ask: what is next? Some pioneers, such as Robert Nakamura, have vowed to continue with their Asian American–themed productions. "A lot of exciting films are being made these days by talented Asian American filmmakers," Nakamura wrote, "but there are still so many basic aspects about Asian American culture untapped by filmmakers. Developing these projects will keep all of us in Asian American media busy for at least another twenty years."[2] Opinions, however, diverge on future directions. Many filmmakers are already looking for new horizons, broader canvases, and perhaps even bigger budgets, too. Peter Chow, former executive director of Asian CineVision, feels strongly that "it should be possible to go beyond Asian-American subject matter into other territory."[3] The fundamental question remains: what are these other territories?

If Black independent cinema is any guide, Asian American filmmaking has indeed reached a stage of maturity, and with it maybe a midlife crisis. In the late 1980s, two decades after the emergence of new Black cinema, a serious, and sometimes acrimonious, debate was waged among Black filmmakers, scholars, and critics (such as the one among Clyde Taylor, David Nicholson, and Zeinabu Irene Davis in *Black Film Review*).[4] Important questions have been raised about the cohesiveness and future direction of Black filmmaking as a distinctive film culture. For example, accusations have been made that Black filmmakers have increasingly fallen victim to the auteur mode, which is part of Western aesthetics and thus is directly opposed to Black collaborative efforts. Some Black critics attribute this orientation toward auteurism to formal cinema training by the film schools, while others mention the economic lure and seductions of prestige of the Hollywood industry. In sum, African American critics and scholars have argued strongly that the time may have arrived to rethink the basis and rationales of Black filmmaking after its considerable commercial success.

Similar polemics have also been engaged in over Asian American cinema. Rather than joining this contentious debate, I would like to take a more constructive approach to assess the current status and future trends of Asian American cinema, by reviewing some new developments within the Asian American film movement and "sampling" a few important works from the Asian diasporic communities (especially in the English-speaking world).

A CINEMA IN TRANSITION: CROSS-OVER FILMS

American cinema in the 1990s is invariably referred to by mainstream media critics as the decade of "Pacific overtures" and "East Asian chic." An article in *The New York Daily News* comments:

> Major actors and directors from the Hong Kong, Taiwanese and mainland Chinese film industries are starting to work in Tinseltown [Hollywood]. This talent pool represents the most significant influx of foreign creativity since Mel Gibson, Judy Davis, Peter Weir, Gillian Armstrong and other Australians entered the industry in the early '80s.[5]

Indeed, since the early 1990s the American silver screen has been "invaded" by an "Asian wave." Films from "the three Chinas" (mainland dramas, Taiwanese domestic comedies, and Hong Kong action films) are marching into Hollywood together. According to Robert Sklar, "Special-effects disaster movies rule Hollywood and Brawny-hero action movies come next in importance."[6] Jackie Chan has become the biggest action star in Hollywood since Bruce Lee. Chan was interviewed on David Letterman and was presented a Lifetime Achievement Award on MTV. Without the usual steamy sex, dirty jokes, and hero-wins-it-all plot-line, Chan brings to the American cinema a creative vision in on-screen martial arts that he terms "happy-go-lucky."[7]

Not only has this new Asian wave brought some refreshing newfound aesthetics to Hollywood, but it has also created new opportunities and challenges for the indigenous Asian American cinema sandwiched in between. As it looks now, we probably will have to wait a few years to comprehend the specific influences of this new wave. In the meantime, however, we do witness some new developments that are beginning to reshape the present state, and the possible future, of the Asian American film movement. For one, Asian American filmmakers have increasingly outgrown the essentialist "ethnic" mode and have broadened their mass appeal. An increasing number of accomplished young veterans have moved beyond art house parameters and begun to make studio-backed mainstream productions. In the wake of the successful run of Ang Lee's *Sense and Sensibility*, it has become clearer than ever that Asian American filmmakers have been pursuing a variety of creative projects not prescribed by racially defined boundaries.

Narrative filmmakers Ang Lee, Wayne Wang, Mira Nair, and Gregg Araki, among others, have produced a growing body of what I would term *cross-over films*—films that are not directly related to Asian Americans in terms of subject matter or motifs. The story line of Jane Austen's novel should be familiar to us. Set in Devonshire and London, starring an all-English cast led by Emma Thompson, Kate Winslet, Hugh Grant, and Alan Rickman, Ang Lee's Oscar-winning *Sense and Sensibility* has very few Asian threads. The only Asian reference in the entire movie was a fanciful expression of a desire to travel to China. Lee's latest work, *The Ice Storm* (1997), a historical drama about a Connecticut family breaking apart on a Thanksgiving night in the 1960s, continues his exploration of familial themes across ethnic or racial lines. Similarly, none of the major characters hanging around the Brooklyn cigar shop in Wayne Wang's *Smoke* and its companion piece, *Blue in the Face* (co-directed by Paul Auster), are Asian or Asian American. Likewise, Mira Nair made her third feature, *The Perez Family* (1994), about the Cuban refugees reaching Miami in the Mariel boatlift and its aftermath. Starring Anjelica Huston and Alfred Molina, the film's theme, Nair says, "is on exile; it has its sexual moments (sex is as naturally accepted as the sun), and its raunchy, ribald humor and rich music capture Cuban culture, its way of life and the spirit of the Cubans who are not self-piteous; despite the many problems they face (separated from their families only by 90 miles and unable to meet for years) they choose to live, and their sheer vitality carries them through."[8] Obviously, Nair's own diasporic experience informs her film works. While shooting *Mississippi Masala* in Uganda, she met, fell in love with, and married Mahamood Mamdam, a professor of political science. Born in India, operating out of New York, she now has made her permanent home in Kampala, Uganda.

Not as well-known to mainstream moviegoers, Gregg Araki has represented perhaps the most daring and controversial voice in cross-over productions among Asian Americans. Proclaimed a pioneer of what has been dubbed the Queer New Wave, almost all of Araki's works are on gay and lesbian themes and characters: from *The Long Weekend (O'Despair)* (1989), the tragic story of a gay man haunted by a nostalgic longing for the past; to *The Living End* (1992), the sad tale of a film critic (Jon Gilmore) who falls into despair over his recent HIV-positive diagnosis; to *Totally F***ed Up* (1994), a diary-like compendium that records the everyday hopes and struggles of a close circle of gay and lesbian teens; and finally to *The Doom Generation* (1995), which chronicles the misadventures of three young Americans fleeing the neoconservative climate in a desperate effort to find love and the freedom of unfettered sexual experimentation. Araki's protagonists are, predominantly, gay white men. If an Asian character appears, he or she is just part of the social setting, or an "extra," to use film jargon. In his latest feature, *The Doom Generation*, for example, the violently murdered Korean owner at the local Quickie Mart is as stereotypical a character as the Korean grocer in Joel Schumacher's *Falling Down* (a role heavily criticized by the Korean American communities). Leaving aside for the moment the question whether his character is denigrating, Araki's treatment of the Korean is clearly not intended for ethnic image-making. Even for the multiethnic cast of players with Latino, Black, and Asian backgrounds in *Totally F***ed Up*, Araki has described the cast as "completely interchangeable. The ethnicity of the characters was like wardrobe, essentially."[9]

As an Asian American, Araki's queer sensibilities are informed by a gay agenda rather than one of ethnic activism. He has soundly rejected criticism of both his pursuit of gay themes and his seeming avoidance of racial issues. He has been quoted as saying, "I've found 'my' subcultures to be more repressive, more straitjacketing, more tunnel-visioned than the Majority culture they so relentlessly and demonstratively attack." Accordingly, he calls for more diversified voices in Asian American cinema: "There is room, in fact there is a dire need, for difference within our claustrophobic little elitist clubhouses. The pitfalls of generic stagnancy in gay, Asian American, and independent cinema(s) are not being avoided."[10]

In his introductory essay to *Cinemas of the Black Diaspora*, Michael T. Martin writes about the transnational nature of the Black diasporic cinemas: ". . . black filmmaking, in the diaspora, bridges the North and South, as well as the West and East. Practiced in the First and Third Worlds, it draws on both Western and non-Western sources of culture for its stylistic and aesthetic forms."[11] While it is debatable whether these cross-over films bear Asian American cultural or aesthetic values (and, if they do, how they exert that power), one thing is for sure: Asian American artists have used production techniques that they hold close to the vest. For example, Wayne Wang's characteristic management of screen space is amply demonstrated in both *Smoke* and *Blue in the Face*. Constant "spaces" of silence in *Smoke*, which is often assumed to be his signature narrative structure, leave the audience to deal with different kinds of emotions. In an interview with the *Denver Post* about *Smoke*, Wang explains, "People neglect the spaces between the notes. For instance, one of the scenes I really love is after that big fight between the father and son. There's this long silence. I love those moments of silence in movies where there's so much said and nothing is said. Just looks between people and things like that."[12] "In Hollywood movies," he continues, "they always think of narrative and emotional impact. I think that's a pity. Why do we always look at it in that one way, its emotional impact, its drama and its words? There are so many other aspects of film."[13]

Film critics have discovered many cinematic connections between Lee's *Sense and Sensibility* and the works of both Japanese and Chinese filmmakers. First, it shares a narrative link with Lee's Oscar-nominee *Eat Drink Man Woman*, which also features three sisters who live with a single parent (a widower) and ponder the marriage question. Better still, *Sense and Sensibility* is informed by both Asian and Western cultures in some other subtle ways. For example, the scene where Marianne and the youngest sister Margaret are walking up a hill in the rain reminds people of similar scenes in Akira Kurosawa's *Dreams* (1990) and *Rhapsody in August* (1991). What is more, moments of quiet intensity between characters in *Sense*, "where words are not exchanged, yet customs are still exchanged (the rituals of preparing meals, quietly courting and cleaning up), match some of the exquisite moments in Zhang Yimou's films [*Raise the Red Lantern* (1991), *The Story of Qui Ju* (1991), and *To Live* (1994)]."[14]

Perhaps the most debatable aspect of these Asian American cross-over films is the question of appropriation. Does the idea of cultural appropriation—a charge often lodged against mainstream media—apply to Asian Americans who choose to depict a culture other than their own? Indeed, the widespread proprietary feelings may turn *against* Asian Americans. *Smoke*, for example, generated some interesting political and cultural repercussions when it was first released. Some critics asked Wang how much he was paid by the tobacco industry for the movie title. Of course, the director was outraged by the suggestion. Wang did not hesitate to take "smoke" as the movie title, as he explains, because he believes smoking is good and bad at the same time. In Hong Kong, where he was born and raised, smoking binds people together despite the health hazards. Wang also likes the metaphoric meaning of smoke. As one actor said in the movie, "[S]moke is something that is constantly changing in shape, and never fixed."

Black scholar bell hooks was both "intrigued and enraged" by *Smoke*. "When I saw *Smoke*," hooks told Wang in an extended interview, "I was stunned by the way in which all the usual racial and sexual stereotypes are played out: the good guys are white, the bad guys black, loose women are working class or females of color. . . ."[15] hooks saw a difference between the screenplay, which "was skillfully deconstructive, challenging the process by which we make superficial judgment," and Wang's film as "a drama that not only does not allow us to really see the inner landscape of the characters, but undermines this radical message."[16] However, hooks had the following high praise for Wang's *Blue in the Face*: "What makes *Blue in the Face* as a movie of the moment right now, is that it does raise those questions of ethnicity and identity: who is who; what does it mean to be black; or what does it mean to have a national identity."[17]

Several years ago, in response to intense criticism of her works, Vietnamese American filmmaker Trinh T. Minh-ha wrote, "Maybe this is why my work has met with a certain resistance among Asian Americans. In the case of my two first films, shot in West Africa, *Reassemblage* and *Naked Space: Living Is Round*, Asian American curators found it difficult to program them, for their subject matter was not immediately classifiable."[18] More recently, many more Asian American filmmakers have moved away from the "ethnic" and activist line of works, experimenting with divergent forms of cinematic expression. This growing proliferation of cross-over films indicates a profound shift in political and artistic orientation, and further it may demand a redefinition of the culturally determined category of Asian American films.

This expansion of discursive parameters is also reflected in another direction. Since the late 1980s, Asian American filmmakers have produced a different kind of cross-over film: films set in and made for their ancestral homelands. Among the ever-growing homeland-themed films by Asian Americans are: Peter Wang's cross-cultural comedy *A Great Wall*, discussed in Chapter 4; Nancy Tong's documentary *In the Name of the Emperor* (1996), dealing with the 1937 Nanjing Massacre and the 200,000 "comfort women" who were forced into prostitution by the Japanese government in World War II; Ramona S. Diaz's *Spirits Rising* (1995), a compelling story of Corazon Aquino's People Power revolution over the Marcos regime, embedded in the historical role of women in the Philippines; Xiao-Yen Wang's *The Monkey Kid* (1995), a touching story about a nine-year-old's struggle for survival during China's Cultural Revolution; and Tiana Thi Thanh Nga's *From Hollywood to Hanoi*, a documentary of the filmmaker's journey back to post-war Vietnam. These homeland-based films are often meant to inform the American audience by providing a much-needed corrective. As Tiana (Thi Thanh Nga) explains: "What did [Forrest] Gump say about his experiences in 'Nam? 'We were lookin' for some guy named Charlie.' The audiences thought that was hilarious. I cringed. Was this to be our legacy? Three million Indochinese dead. The nation of Viet Nam ravished, fit now only to be the butt of a Hollywood joke?"[19] To help address the misrepresentation of her ancestral homeland, currently she is working on another film set in Vietnam, *Rice Dreams*.

Not all Asian American filmmakers, however, are welcomed home as good-will ambassadors. Mira Nair's *Children of Desired Sex* (1985), a documentary about sex-determination tests and their impacts on female infanticide in India; her award-winning first feature *Salaam Bombay!*, a fictional narrative about homeless children, prostitutes, and drug addicts in the slums of Bombay through a child beggar's perspective; and *India Cabaret*, an ethnographic film on the lives of Indian strippers—each of these films was challenged by both Indian viewers at home and their compatriots abroad. Indian immigrants in New York City, for example, succeeded in persuading WNET (the New York public television station) to cancel plans to screen *India Cabaret* as initially scheduled.[20] Nair was accused of presenting a "male gaze," and displaying Indian women as sex objects. Not swayed by the critcism, the director countered that her critics, mostly upper middle-class and middle-class women, had come to see the film with preconceptions. She states, "What is unsettling perhaps about *Indian Cabaret* is that the women in it do not ask for our help, refuse to be viewed as victims, and do not need our pity. They struggle and survive with great humor, strength, and resilience."[21]

In comparison, Nair's latest movie, *Kama Sutra: A Tale of Love*, caused an uproar in India. The sexually explicit film takes its title from the Kama Sutra, the ancient Indian manual of "erotic science." Set in sixteenth-century India, it is an erotic court tale of a courtesan named Maya (Indira Varma). Nair has come under heavy criticism for "exploiting" her own culture. India's censor board was outraged and banned the film, and Nair is taking her censorship case to India's Supreme Court. It is interesting to note that, inside India, the movie has been debated largely in terms of morality. However, it has become an issue of ethnic betrayal for some of the Indian expatriates abroad. As one Indian American viewer commented, "I am not putting the responsibility on her to present 'the' South Asian woman, but I certainly didn't expect to be betrayed by my own. . . . I had expected a celebration of South Asian women's sexuality but it was simply a 'showgirl,' Indian style."[22] Not budging amid the controversy, Nair fiercely defends her movie, insisting *Kama Sutra* is about "sexual politics, not sexual positions—politics between men and women and between women and women," about "the many faces of love," as seen from a feminine, even a feminist, perspective.[23] Obviously her radical message did not get through to all members of her audience. "She talked of radical ideas in historical literature," another Indian viewer said, "but women using their bodies for power is hardly radical, and the principles of how to please a man are explored regularly in women's magazines today."[24]

This growing trend of hybrid films, containing as they do a much wider range of content, styles, and perspectives, calls into question any essentialist or authenticity claims to Asian American productions. At the same time, it may also represent a growing desire among Asian American filmmakers to move beyond the genre conventions of an Asian American cinema that has been shaped within an explicitly racialized context. Thus, a more inclusive formulation of Asian American films is called for in the field. In addition to cross-over productions discussed here, this new framework should also consider cinematic works from other Asian diasporic communities.

FILMS FROM THE ASIAN DIASPORA

Over recent years scholars have begun to pay close attention to the critical space created by the cultural politics of diaspora as well as to the limits imposed by them. Homeland and travel, the two defining elements in diasporas, paradoxically highlight both its liberating power and its limitations for ethnic minorities in the West. On the one hand, the idea of diaspora advocates de-territorialized identities and creates hybrid sensitivities through the themes of travel and migration. "Since diasporas are fundamentally and inevitably transnational in their scope," Ien Ang puts it nicely, "always linking the local and the global, the hear [sic] and the there, past and present, they have the potential to unsettle static, essentialist and totalitarian conceptions of 'national culture' or 'national identity' which are firmly rooted in geography and history."[25] In other words, the idea of diaspora enables the imagined communities to fight racism based on the politics of "nation-states." Writing about immigrant literature by Asian women, Inderpal Grewal stresses the importance of studying Asian American cultural productions in transnational contexts. "Asian cultural formations are not unconnected with Asian Americans," she writes, "and these complex linkages across generations of immigrants need to be understood through what can be called a transnational perspective, one that encompasses the politics of multiple locations within a framework of transnational capital and its cultural effects."[26]

On the other hand, the notion of diaspora can also become a marginalizing force of transnational capitalism.[27] For the diasporic peoples, the promise and potential of a diaspora culture is often contingent on their recognition of the particular historical and specific conditions within and between specific diasporas. As transnational sociocultural groups, various diasporas, from the Jewish and the African, to the Indian and the Chinese, develop under very different historical conditions and circumstances. However, all diasporas are imagined communities that are sustained by the myth of an ancestral "homeland," whether real or symbolic. This mythic attachment to the homeland often creates contradictions in subject positioning for the diasporic people in the West. By identifying single-mindedly with a real or imagined "homeland," which is elsewhere, ethnic minorities could fall victim to a new form of self-marginalization. Instead, minority cultures "should privilege neither host country nor (real or imaginary) homeland," and should creatively define themselves in diasporic terms through "hybrid cultural forms borne out of a productive, creative syncretism."[28]

Cognizant of these contradictions, I still believe diaspora is a powerful framework to move discussion of Asian American films beyond the U.S. context by looking at the dispersed Asian-descended communities in other parts of the world. At this point, I must admit that there is very little literature available. Occasionally, at festivals and through art houses, we do hear about and see on the screen some narratively provocative and cinematically sophisticated works produced by Asians from Canada, Britain, Australia, and France. Learning more about these various Asian diasporic filmmakers, and exchanging ideas with them, may represent another uncharted territory for Asian immigrants in this country.

Asian Canadian visual artists are probably the most productive and best known (at least among those working in the United States). Since Vancouver has lately become the focus for immigrants from Hong Kong, it is hardly surprising that Canada is witnessing a booming Asian Canadian cinema. "Yellow Peril: Reconsidered," a 1990–1991 traveling show of film and video by Asian Canadian artists, showcased an impressive array (twenty-five in all) of Asian Canadian productions, in all styles from straightforward documentaries to experimental short films and performance pieces.[29] *Chinese Cafes in Rural Saskatchewan* (1985) by Anthony Chan, *Ati Ati Han* (1986) by Marlin Oliveros, *The Journey* (1986) by Ruby Truly, *The Displaced View* (1988) by Midi Onodera, *Rage* (1988) by Jay Hirabayashi, *The Morning Zoo* (1989) by Daisy Lee, *The Compact* (1990) by Brenda Joy Lem, and *Masala* (1991) by Srinivas Krishna are some of the titles listed in the catalogue.[30] Mina Shum, Richard Fung, Helen Lee, Srinavas Krishna, and Michelle Wong are a few of the better known Asian Canadian filmmakers. Recently, Indian Canadian filmmaker Deepa Mehta received media attention in both Canada and the United States. Her first feature, *Sam and Me*, caught the eyes of George Lucas, who asked her to direct a one-hour episode for his *Young Indiana Jones* series.

"Because of Canada's geographic and cultural proximity to the United States," Valerie Soe wrote in *The Independent*, "it's tempting to try to compare the Asian Canadian experience with that of Asians living in the US. There is, of course, a danger in drawing too many parallels between US and Canadian Asian communities—not the least is the inclination to discount Canada's distinct and particular historical milieu," she continued, "However, shared issues and concerns exist when any oppressed minority group struggles for sovereignty within a hegemonic social structure."[31] Although Asian Canadian films are distinguished from

Asian Americans' efforts by national, cultural, and ideological orientations, they do share similar thematic concerns, and they have developed comparable representational strategies and aesthetic sensitivities. Perhaps Helen Lee best embodies the cross-pollination of ideas between the two. As Peter Feng notes, "Lee lists both Canada and the US as countries of origin for *My Niagara*; the film was shot primarily in Toronto, but postproduction took place in New York as well, when Lee worked for Women Make Movies and attended New York University."[32] This cross-referencing between the two cultures is also reflected in her other works. Lee's twelve-minute *Sally's Beauty Spot* (1990) anatomizes the Asian female body as represented in Hollywood movies. As its title suggests, Sally (played by Lee's real-life sister) is obsessed with a mole on her chest, which is emblematic of her physical difference and, for that matter, of racial and sexual identities. Over repetitive shots of Sally looking in the mirror, cross-cut with clips from *The World of Suzie Wong*, we see Sally brushing her hair, or scrubbing at her mole, and trying to hide it by covering it up with heavy make-up. Even a surgical method of removal was suggested by a female voice-over at one point in the film. Lee's radical message is clearly articulated in the contrasting close-ups in the beginning and ending of the film. In the first part of the film, there are repeated close-up shots of Sally kissing a Caucasian man. Near the end, Sally begins to kiss a Black man where the Caucasian used to stand in the frame.

Richard Fung is another notable Asian Canadian diasporic filmmaker. Fung was born in Trinidad, is based in Toronto, and films, writes, and publishes regularly in the United States. As a video artist, he is an active proponent of gay representation in general. For example, his 1984 feature-length video *Orientations* profiles more than a dozen gay men and women of different Asian backgrounds, who speak frankly about coming out, homophobia, racism, cultural identity, and the ways in which being both gay and Asian have shaped their lives. His visual and written works on the marginal genre of interracial pornography have received particular attention.[33] *Chinese Characters* (1986), an experimental documentary, deconstructs the discourse of gay male pornography by portraying an eroticized Asian male image that has routinely been excluded. His film critique challenges the limited and racist construction of the gay male body in pornography. Unlike Gregg Araki, whose films deal invariably with gay representation, Fung *does* work on Asian Canadian themes. Two of his videos, *The Way to My Father's Village* (1987) and *My Mother's Place* (1991), are the videomaker's attempts to reconstruct his family history. While the former video is more conventional in style, the latter, shot in Trinidad and Canada, weaves a diasporic family migration story through a series of interviews with Rita Fung, the videomaker's mother. As Fung explains in a voice-over near the end of the video, "[My mother] connects me to a past I would have no other way of knowing. And in this sea of whiteness, of friends, enemies and strangers, I look at her and know who I am."

Like Lee and Fung, Srinivas Krishna crossed Canada's southern border and made two short dramatic films in New York before returning to his hometown, Toronto, to make his debut feature, *Masala*. The director plays an ex-junkie (also named Krishna) who is still trying to recover from the death of his family in a plane crash on their way from Toronto to a vacation in India. After years away from home, Krishna returns to his family in Toronto to seek financial and emotional stability. Instead, he soon finds himself involved in a series of intrigues and violence. Uncle Lallu is plotting with Sikh terrorists to monopolize the world sari trade. Lallu's cousin Tikkoo, a postal worker, is locked in a battle with the Canadian post office over control of a priceless stamp. The Indian children are hopelessly fighting the old-country tradition of arranged marriages. The violence-prone Krishna quickly jumps into the fray by insulting his uncles and seducing Tikkoo's daughter Rita. Eventually, his visit home is cut short by an impending danger to his life. According to the director, diaspora is the key motif for *Masala*, which comes from "a long history of what happened when you go abroad. You step outside of caste and religion. You become an individual, and there is great resistance to this in India. And yet all of the nation's recent history has been about returning diasporas."[34] Because of its biting satire of community politics and graphic sexual scenes, the movie has infuriated many elders from the British and Canadian Indian communities. However, among hip young children of Indian and Pakistani backgrounds, the young and handsome Krishna has become "something of a sex symbol." "I think they like the irreverence of the film," the filmmaker says. "There is a great deal that is surreal about life in the diaspora, and I think these kids connect with that. This is also a representation of them, which they can't find in Hollywood or the Hindi movie houses."[35]

Mina Shum is probably the best-known Chinese Canadian director to the American public, largely because of her widely distributed feature *Double Happiness* (1995). The movie shares its domestic/familial focus with Asian American dramas. Some critics have even hailed it as the "heterosexual *Wedding Banquet*." As the title suggests, the film's narrative revolves around Jade Li (Sandra Oh), a twenty-two-year-old aspiring actress who struggles to balance the traditional expectations of her Chinese family with her own wishes.[36] The opening scene captures the essence of the plot. Jade is talking to the camera: "I said [to my family] I would never make a big deal out of being Chinese," she begins. "They're very Chinese, if you know what I mean. But for the moment, just forget they're Chinese. Just think of them as any old white family. Though you could probably just turn on a TV set and see that. I grew up wondering why we could never be the Brady Bunch. *The*

Brady Bunch never needed subtitles." As Jade's estrangement from her parents (Stephen Chang and Alannah Ong) grows, the parents try to marry her off to Andrew, a handsome Chinese lawyer. By intention or accident, she picks a white university student named Mark (Callum Rennie), sleeping with him the same night they meet outside a trendy nightclub. *Double Happiness* cannot be dismissed as another regular entry into the overworked genre of growing-up stories, because it speaks to the complexity of being Asian in a race-conscious Canadian society. This theme of racialism is captured in a hilarious scene: Jade is auditioning for a part as a waitress in a TV drama. In front of a tribunal of filmmakers, she playfully reads her two lines, "Anything to drink with that?" and "Would you like gravy with your fries?" The director suggests she try it again with an accent. "What kind of accent do you want me to do, a Parisian accent?" Jade asks, with a smile and a sassy French inflection. Visibly irritated, the director looks back at her in an embarrassed silence. Sensing her potential job hanging in the balance, Jade apologizes and gives him what he wants. "Yes," she says, lowering her gaze and looking suddenly docile, "a very good Chinese accent I can do for you."

Having written and directed six short films, Mina Shum placed great hopes on what critical acclaim would bring her as a filmmaker.[37] "The most fortunate thing about *Double Happiness* is the critical acclaim it has received," she said, "which has moved me beyond the token figurehead, the 'Oh, she's the Chinese Canadian filmmaker from Canada.' [Instead, it's] the 'she is the award-winning filmmaker from Canada.' "[38] In a more personal sense, the success would also help convince her parents of her career choice. "[My parents] were really wary of me going into the arts," she recalled in an interview, "I come from an immigrant background and my family wanted me to get a steady job. But to go out and become a profound artist? It didn't make sense to them. It's not a safe career. The word 'freelance' doesn't even exist in my parents' vocabulary."[39] Shum got more than she expected. The film was named best first feature at the Berlin Film Festival and won the audience award at the Turin Festival in Italy in 1995. Sandra Oh, who plays Jade, won a Genie, Canada's equivalent of the Oscar. In describing her feelings about the film's success, Shum stated, "The whole film was very much a part of me in terms of the sensibilities and the camera angles and colors. You can walk into my house, and you know that the person who lives there would love *Double Happiness*. It's not the fact that she is the director, but because all the colors are the same and there is that sensibility that is similar."[40] With this success under her belt, plus her fifth short film, *Me, Mom and Mona*, which won an award at the Toronto Film Festival in 1993, and her second feature, *Drive, She Said*, in the works, Shum is already being hailed as "Canada's most successful Chinese-Canadian filmmaker."[41]

Michelle Wong, a young documentarian from St. Paul, Alberta, has also received critical attention, including several awards at the 16th Asian American International Film Festival in New York, for *Return Home* (1996). The biographical film is essentially a frank discussion about her family history with her grandparents (who passed away a few months after the film was released). Wong found that being raised in a Western culture did not allow her to understand why her grandparents acted the way they did. Like her American counterparts, Wong admits that for most of her life she suffered a double personality. "I grew up uncomfortable with being Chinese. I had internalized a lot of Western stereotypes and negative images of what a Chinese person was. In the Chinese community, I was not Chinese enough."[42] It disturbed her that she was not accepted by her own community. In an effort to reconcile with herself, she made a very political move by providing a private screening for more than three hundred members of the local Chinese community, in a theater that could only seat about one hundred. Two screenings were held, with different dialects used for subtitles. Michelle Wong reflected on the experience: "One thing I am particularly happy-proud-of is the decision to have a Chinese subtitled version, so that Chinese from Taiwan, Hong Kong and the Mainland, who may speak other dialects, were able to share the experience."[43]

Not surprisingly, the Asian independent voice in the United Kingdom is represented predominantly by South Asians. Partly because of the former colonial relationship, South Asian involvement in the British film industry goes as far back as 1924, when Heman Surayi, with an all-Asian cast, made *Light of Asia* (1924). Independent films made by Asian Indians, and, to a lesser degree, by Pakistanis, have exploded during the last two decades. Since the 1980s, a large group of documentaries, of different styles and uneven quality, appeared. Patel and Laxmi Jamdagni's *Stepping out of Frame* (1987) deals with media stereotypes of Asian women. Yogesh Walia's *Mirror, Mirror* (1980) reveals the divided loyalties by a young Asian woman toward her parents and her white boyfriend. The issue of "arranged marriages," from a woman's perspective, is explored in Faris Karmani's *The Wall* (1981). *The Garland* (1981), by H. O. Nazareth and Horace Ove, looks at the experience of a biracial child.[44] The field is not as prolific in narrative cinema. *A Private Enterprise* (1975) is the first Asian-directed independent feature to come out of the United Kingdom. Set in the grim urban wasteland of Birmingham, the movie tells the story of Shiv, a new young immigrant, and his struggle to survive. *Majdhar* (1984) by Retake is a strikingly similar story of Fauzia, a young Pakistani woman abandoned by her husband soon after their arrival in London.

Among South Indian documentarians in Britain, Pratibha Parmar is one of the very few who have received critical attention in the United States.[45] Parmar was born in Kenya and settled in London in the mid-1960s. She began "making videos and films from a background in political activism and cultural practice, not from film school or art school."[46] Her works are often noted for their activist and confrontational orientation against British racism, sexism, and homophobia. As an Asian lesbian, many of her works are dedicated to the struggle against homophobia. For example, she directed *Reframing AIDS* (1987), *Memory Pictures* (1989), *Flesh and Paper* (1990), *Khush* (1991), and *Double the Trouble, Twice the Fun* (1992) for "Out on Tuesday," a series dedicated to gay, lesbian, and bisexual issues. Among these, *Khush* represents a unique diasporic sensitivity. Named for the Hindi and Urdu word "khush," which means happy, and, by extension, "gay," the documentary explores a globalized South Asian queer identity through interviews with community members of Asian lesbian, gay, and bisexual activist groups from Europe and North America, including Shakti of London, Trikon of California, and Khush of Canada. Read closely, Parmar's films are truly diasporic, crossing the boundaries of different kinds of essential identity politics. Radical deconstruction of identity politics becomes the hallmark of her works. Her film *A Place of Rage* (1991), featuring June Jordan, Angela Davis, Alice Walker, and Trinh T. Minh-ha, underscores the political ties among women of color. As Gwendolyn Foster explains, "Parmar was able to move across borders of prescribed identity politics only after she began to question the reinforcement of proscribed 'territories' determined by essentialist fixed identity tags."[47]

Not confined to identities, Parmar's diasporic aesthetics inform the subject and topics of her production. Anti-Asian violence, a topic frequently covered in films by Asian American filmmakers, is treated in *Sari Red* (1988). Produced in memory of Kalbinder Kaur Hayre, an Asian woman who was murdered in a racially motivated attack by three white men in 1985, Parmar's twelve-minute video offers a powerful examination of racial violence in contemporary British society. The sari and the blood, as in the title phrase, are key metaphors in the film. The oral history of the racist murder of Kalbinder Kaur Hayre is narrated with a sari folding and unfolding around a South Asian woman's body. The full implication of the sacred Sari for the migrant South Asian community cannot be fully appreciated until the viewers come to understand its cultural meanings as both the temple cloth of the Mother Goddess and the cloth of all diasporic Asian women. The color red is equally significant, as its catalog description reminds us, referring to "the color of blood spilt and the red of the sari." As the other central symbol, the video opens with and cuts back and forth to the spectacle of blood. Foster observes perceptively,

> In *Sari Red*, Parmar evokes a violent racist attack through the visual repetition of an image of blood as it is splattered on a brick wall. Blood and its color, red, act as shifting signifiers that at once connote memory of

what "must not be forgotten," racist sexist violence. At the same time, red and blood denote positive images of the survival of Indian cultural traditions, traditions that celebrate red as the color of India, of the Great of India, of "the very essence of energy, of joy, of life itself."[48]

Like Choy and Tajima's *Who Killed Vincent Chin?*, the film *Sari Red* does not tell a straightforward story of a brutal hate crime, but instead poses soul-searching questions about race, nation, class, and popular memory.

Inspired by Alice Walker's novel *Possessing the Secret of Joy*, Parmar's highly inventive documentary *Warrior Marks* (1993) deals with the controversial subject of female genital mutilation. On-camera interviews were filmed with both women victims of the ritual and women who actually perform the ritual of female genital mutilation. The interviews, with women from Senegal, Gambia, Burkina Faso, and England, are intercut with Alice Walker's views on the subject and a dancing performance by "Richelle," an African American woman. In Alice Walker and Pratibhar Parmar's book on the making of *Warrior Marks*, Parmar discusses the critical reception of the film with regard to questions on cultural imperialism, essentialism, and the taboo against Western intervention against female genital mutilation. As Walker, who is also the producer, writes about the significance of *Warrior Marks*,

> It is a powerful and magnificent film, thanks to Pratibha's brilliance as director, constructed from our grief and anger and pain. But also from our belief in each other, our love of life, our gratitude that we are women of color able to offer our sisters a worthy gift after so many centuries of tawdriness, and our awareness of those other "companion spirits" we know are out there.[49]

Indeed, Parmar's works embody the vision of a transnational feminist film practice, or, in her own words, "diasporan sensibilities."[50] As the filmmaker reflects, "Women of color have been organizing and creating communities which have inspired a new sense of collective identity, and it is only through our own efforts that we have ensured against our erasure as artists and cultural producers."[51] However, this very claim of collective international identity, like any notion of transnational feminism, is politically suspect among feminist scholars. It is often accused of overlooking the important question of power relations between women living in the First World and women in the Third World. "There is a fine line," as one critic suggests, "which is never agreed upon, between claims of 'cross-cultural feminist interests' and cultural imperialism and the imposition of cultural gender norms."[52]

Also born in Kenya and raised in Southall (a Punjabi enclave in West London), the Punjabi filmmaker Gurinder Chadha is probably the best-known South Asian filmmaker in Britain. With a growing international reputation, Chadha is often compared to two other women filmmakers from the Indian diaspora, Mira

Nair in the United States and Deepa Mehta in Canada. In her works Chadha explores the motif of what it means to be Asian and British in her adopted country. Her first documentary *I'm British, but . . .* (1990) celebrates British Bhangra and Bangla music, a musical language created and enjoyed by the South Asian community. But it is the poignant portraits of a group of immigrants from the Indian subcontinent that is most striking. We meet a Scottish Pakistani sheep farmer, a Bangladeshi woman in Belfast, and an Indian girl in Glasgow with a Welsh twang in her voice. Their mindboggling accents highlight the complexity of being an Asian in contemporary British society. As the director puts it, "Brown faces talking in those accents subverts the stereotype image. Most white people were shocked!"[53]

Gurinder Chadha's highly acclaimed debut feature, *Bhaji on the Beach* (1994), is a collection of stories about violently oppressed women caught between Asian ties and British cultures. The film begins when a group of nine Asian women, spanning three generations, go on a day trip to the resort town of Blackpool. Organized by a feminist-activist leader, Simi (Shaheen Khan), the women seek a brief respite from their woes back in London. Like the Indian-English bread snack called "bhaji," the various characters split up in Blackpool, taking the story down myriad paths that reveal clashing values both within individuals and between generations, over such matters as behavior, decorum, love, sex, and family obligation. Their experiences on the trip are as varied as the colors of their saris. The older immigrants, Bina (Surendra Kochar) and Pushpa (Zohra Segal), confront an act of ugly racism under the carnival veneer of Blackpool's attractions. The middle-aged Asha (Latita Ahmed) encounters a wide range of discomforts over the ill fit of British traditions. The medical school–bound Hashida (Sarita Khajuria) anguishes over the discovery that she is pregnant by her secret, Black lover Oliver (Mo Sesay). Ginder (Kim Vithana), seeking a divorce from her husband, the brutal Ranjit (Jimmi Harkishin), takes heat from the older women about breaking up her family while remaining unaware that she is being stalked by Ranjit and two male relatives. The youngest travelers, teenage girls Ladhu (Nisha Nayer) and Madhu (Renu Kochar), have perhaps the hardest time trying to reconcile antiquated family obligations with their increasingly unrepressible sexual impulses. "*Bhaji* . . . is essentially a film about women and choice," the director explains. "The choices we make, the choices we do not make. What stops us from making the choices we want to make. It throws up as many conflicts and contradictions as it resolves."[54] However, in the end, everyone in the group turns out to be a survivor in one way or another.

It is interesting to note that Chadha is very critical of Asian Indian filmmakers who came to the West relatively late in their lives, accusing their films of being "terribly damaging and soul destroying because they look at the questions of identity and culture from a problematic point of view."[55] She tells her inter-viewer, "I am different from a person raised in India who came to the West com-paratively late. Like Mira Nair. Her perspective in *Mississippi Masala* was totally different from my perspective on Black and Asian relationships. Similarly, you can-not assess *Bhaji* . . . the way you would *Salaam Bombay!*" She emphasizes that "There is more to my life than racism. For me, there is an empowerment, a tremen-dous excitement about being able to partake in so many different things."[56] Chadha's "diasporic consciousness" makes her reject the traditional concept of a binary identity. "I am struggling against the binary position," she states. " I want to talk about new ideas that are not fixed." The new ideas she is articulating are based on the premise of redefining British national identity. "We cannot be fully British," she declares, "until the idea of being British acknowledges re-definition from the other cultures. Until then, we live in Britain but belong to the diaspora."[57]

In another corner of the British empire, in Australia, where the traditional motto "Australia for the White Man" still rules in some political circles (as evi-denced by the anti-Asian demagogue Pauline Hanson, the head of One Nation Party and a first-term member of Parliament), Asian independent arts are still in their budding stage.[58] Teck Tan, a Chinese Australian; Solrun Hoaas, a Japanese Australian; and Pauline Chan, a Chinese Vietnamese Australian—these three are part of a small group of Asian filmmakers operating independently in Australia. Tan has written and directed several short films, dramas, and documentaries about different aspects of Chinese immigrant life in Australia. Her best-known work is *My Tiger's Eyes* (1993). The narrative revolves around a young Chinese boy caught between two different cultures, represented by his own Chinese family and the O'Hallorans, his family's traditional Irish Australian neighbors. While his family resists assimilation, by trying to re-create a little China within Australia, the Irish Australian couple are overtly anti-immigrants. The boy fails to belong to either world. His struggle is symbolized by a line in the film, "Dim Sum versus the meat pie." Most of Tan's works are inspired by her personal experiences. "I think it is eas-ier to write about your own culture," Tan is quoted as saying, "especially when you are starting out in the industry. While I do enjoy making films about my own cul-ture, they are not the only films I intend to make."[59] Solrun Hoaas's historical drama *Aya* (1990) describes the touching experiences of a Japanese war bride—the title character, Aya (Eri Ishida)—and her marriage with Frank (Nicholas Eadie) in post-war Australia. "Our media are obsessed with the war," the director explains, "neglecting the occupation and the treatment of the Japanese war brides, who were the first Japanese allowed to enter Australia after the war."[60] Although the movie won a special jury prize for art and innovation at the 1990 Toronto Film Fes-tival, it was very much overlooked by audiences in Australia.

In comparison, Pauline Chan is better known and more widely screened. After several award-winning shorts and documentaries (including the controversial *Hang Up, The Space between the Floor and the Door*, which was exhibited at the Cannes Film Festival), Pauline Chan finished her first feature *Traps* in 1993, making it the first feature film ever directed by an Asian Australian. Set in her homeland, Vietnam, in the 1950s, Chan tells the story of a British photographer, Louise, and her Australian journalist husband, Michael Duffield (Saskia Reeves and Robert Reynolds), who arrive in French-occupied Indochina at the request of the French government. The couple stays at a rubber plantation managed by a Frenchman, Daniel Renouard (Sami Frey), and his precocious daughter, Viola (Jacqueline McKenzie). Like an "ensemble film," the four characters are joined by Tuan (Kiet Lam), Daniel's Vietnamese houseboy, who turns out to be a secret member of the Vietminh, Vietnamese guerrillas seeking to get rid of the French in the 1950s. Although Louise, the English wife, seems to be the focus of the drama (and it is largely her journey), the most complex character is Viola, who interacts with the local culture at a deeper level than anybody else in the movie. She speaks the language, dabbles in superstition with Tuan's old mother, and is implicitly in love with Tuan.

Although the movie is loosely based on the novel *Dreamhouse* by Kate Grenville, the director sees her own experience in the story. Chan identifies with Louise. "There's actually a lot of myself in Louise," Chan said in an interview with *Cinemaya*, "in the mirror effect as an Asian woman going to the west and feeling alienated and challenged by the culture and therefore having to find my own voice and my own identity."[61] Like her Asian American counterparts, Chan (as the best-known Asian Australian director) refuses to be tagged with any ethnic label and "be pushed into a little box." To quote her:

> In the broadest sense, when people say "ethnic," the things they associate with it are alien people, alien cultures and charity, because these people need help. In a film sense, it involves serious matters that may not be suitable for mainstream audiences. The minute you mention that you are making an ethnic film or one about ethnic issues, I notice that producers' eyes glaze over. "It's not commercial. You better go and find government funding," they say. What I would like to do is make the boundaries less narrow. Ethnic is part of us. We are not aliens. To do this you need to reveal a bit more about yourself, and perhaps be able to laugh at yourself and to show pain and joy and make the characters real. Everyone can relate to those emotions if they are allowed access to them.[62]

The Vietnam-born and Paris-based Tran Anh Hung is the only Asian filmmaker from the Francophone world whose works we know relatively well in the

United States, largely through his Oscar-nominated family drama *The Scent of Green Papaya* (1993). In the film, set in Saigon in 1951, the central character is a ten-year-old shy peasant girl named Mui (Lu Man San). She spends ten years as a maid in a wealthy merchant family in Saigon and grows up into womanhood. After the merchant abandons the family a decade later, the adult Mui (Tran Nu Yen-Khe) is sent to live with Khuyen (Vuong Hoa Hoi), a French-educated bachelor musician, and the two fall in love. With a story made up of intimate moments rather than major events, the movie enlightens the audience, whose exposure to Vietnam has been derived primarily from war films and propaganda. We are shown the other side of Vietnam, a peaceful land of rich culture, and not a bloody and scarred battlefield. Hung's "unwarring" story, with no helicopters, no napalm, and only hints of war in the film's soundtrack, provides the perfect antidote to Oliver Stone's similarly plotted melodramatic *Heaven and Earth*. As Hung comments, "Vietnam in the movies has meant images of war. For years now, violence has masked the humanity of my people."[63] In addition, watching the film we also learn much about the class structure of Vietnamese society, gender differences, and the suppression of women. For example, the mistress of the house (Trung Thi Loc) supports the family by running a small fabric shop, while the father (Tran Ngoc) sits on his bed, doing nothing but playing his guitar all day long. When the husband disappears with all the family's savings, it is the wife who is blamed for not satisfying her man. Nevertheless, women in the movie are portrayed as being courageous and possessed of great staying power. In more subtle terms, the movie also suggests the effects of French colonialism through the character of Khuyen, who studied in Paris and plays only Debussy, Chopin, and other European composers.

Cinematically, the movie is commended for its great lyrical beauty and sensitivities. Especially impressive is the evocative mise-en-scène. The heat and humidity of Vietnam pour through every frame. "'The Scent of Green Papaya,'" writes a critic, "is a marvel of what the French call mise-en-scène, of atmosphere in depth, but more elemental than that. Tran taps into unexplainable depths. He fuses our attention to the mysterious beauty that things, people and patterns of living have by fullness of presence, when deeply seen."[64] The "meditative" temperament of Mui, the protagonist, as suggested both by the Buddhist references (for example, the Bodhisattva figure in the pianist-lover's home) and by the pace, the colors, and the light of the film, shows Tran Anh Hung as an artist at his best. The heroine strikes the audience as a person who is capable of what some Buddhists call "nonjudgmental awareness" or "meditative attention." The windows in the mise-en-scène carry special importance for this "meditative attention." Literally, Mui lives inside and relates to the outer world largely via windows, and figuratively, the windows open into her inner world.

Following the critical success of *The Scent*, Tran Anh Hung returned to Vietnam where he completed his second feature, *Cyclo* (1995). His latest movie takes its title from the occupation of the central character, an eighteen-year-old driver of a three-wheeled pedal taxicab. Set again in Saigon, now renamed Ho Chi Minh City, *Cyclo* tells the story of a bicycle rickshaw driver, Kien, who lives with his grandfather and two sisters. The movie opens with the "Cyclo," as he is nicknamed, drenched in sweat, pedaling his passengers down Saigon's bustling streets. In a voice-over, his dead father, also a cyclo driver killed in a road accident a year ago, expresses regret at leaving nothing for his son or his family. As the story progresses, in a wrenching scene, his rickshaw is stolen and he is beaten up by the thieves. The protagonist vows to repay the Boss Lady, the owner of the rickshaw who actually orchestrated the theft herself as a means of forcing Cyclo into crime. Cyclo is initiated into a gang, whose leader is the enigmatic Poet. Lost and frightened at first, Cyclo is quickly drawn by the lure of money and falls deeper and deeper into a life of crime, from vandalizing a rice warehouse, to an arson attack and delivering drugs. Meanwhile, the Poet is recruiting Cyclo's elder sister Lien as a prostitute. The film reaches its moral climax when Cyclo is ordered to commit a murder.

Like his first film, Hung intends *Cyclo* to inform us about his homeland from different angles. First, it eloquently captures the weariness and the daily rhythms of the working class in modern urban Vietnam. On a deeper level, it also paints a vivid portrait of Vietnam, a nation and a people facing a changing economy and negotiating the process of integrating into a global economic order, while still recovering from the ravages of wars. But the heart of the movie is the universal theme of the tragic but binding father–son relationship. Although Cyclo's father died a year before the story begins, he constantly counsels his son. By contrast, the Poet has been disowned by his father, but he becomes a surrogate father to Cyclo and his older sister. Like Oliver Stone, Tran Anh Hung is reported to be working on the third feature, *Rice Wine and Dried Shrimp*, of his Vietnamese trilogy.

The films and the filmmakers selected here for discussion do not, of course, represent the full breadth of Asian diasporic cinemas. In fact, filmmaking in the Asian diaspora is not, and cannot be, a unified and monolithic undertaking. The works, however, do demonstrate a dialectical relationship between Asian American cinema and other cinematic movements in the Asian diaspora. On the one hand, because of their common historical experience of migration, displacement, and colonialism, they share similar thematic interests about identity, history, and social change, and they too have developed comparable, often oppositional, filmmaking practices. On the other hand, because of historical contingency and regional cinematic traditions (for example, European vs. North American), they are also distinguished by their national, cultural, gender, class, and ideological differences. A comparative framework is called for in locating and interpreting the Asian American cinematic experience in this transnational and intercultural context.

In their book *Unthinking Eurocentrism: Multiculturalism and the Media*, Ella Shohat and Robert Stam have argued for a "relational strategy," or "dialogical" (Mikhail Bakhtin's term) approach, to media representation—"one that operates at once within, between, and beyond the nation-state framework."[65] According to Shohat and Stam, ethnic representation in this context will benefit from what Bakhtin calls "mutual illumination." "A cross-cultural 'mutually illuminating' dialogical approach," they write, "stresses not only the analogies within specific national film traditions—for instance, the analogies between the representation of African-Americans and Native Americans within Hollywood cinema—but also the analogies and disanalogies between the representations of both groups in Hollywood cinema and their representation in the other multiethnic film cultures of the Americas."[66] By the same token, a "mutually illuminating" dialogical approach will demonstrate the thematic and aesthetic similarities (as well as the differences) among Asian diasporic films; for example, Indian Canadian films (*Sam and Me* and *Masala*), Indian British films (*I'm British, but . . .* and *Bhaji on the Beach*) and Indian American films (*Knowing Her Place* and *Mississippi Masala*). A separate critical project, similar to Michael T. Martin's *Cinemas of the Black Diaspora*, should be undertaken in the study of Asian diasporic films to "perform a conceptual 'remapping' of the field within a global space."[67] This conceptual "remapping," both within Asian American cinema and within the growing ranks of films from other Asian diasporic communities, holds the promise of a dynamic Asian diasporic culture in the future.

NOTES

1 Steven J. Tatsukawa, "Beyond the Looking Glass," *Anthology of Asian American Film and Video* (New York: Third World Newsreel, 1984), 45.

2 Robert Nakamura, "Visual Communications: The Early Years," *In Focus* 6:1, 9. Nakamura has just completed an hour-long documentary titled *Looking Like the Enemy*, a film about various Asian American soldiers who fought in the U.S. military in the three wars in which the enemy were Asians. He has also put out a video recently, entitled *Something Strong Within*, composed of footage shot by inmates in U.S. internment camps.

3 As quoted by Luis Francia, "Made in America," *Film Comment* 19 (Sept./Oct. 1983), 58.

4 Four pieces by the three are anthologized also in "The State and Future of the Black Film Movement: An Exchange," *Cinemas of the Black Diaspora,* ed. Michael T. Martin (Detroit: Wayne State University Press, 1995), 431–460.

5 Lewis Beale, "Hollywood is reaching out to Chinese filmmakers and actors," *New York Daily News* (Feb. 15, 1996).

6 Robert Sklar, "Taking Hollywood by Storm: Behind the Triumph of Independent Films," *Chronicle of Higher Education* (March 14, 1997), B7.

7 Constance Sommer, "Asian Film Star Jackie Chan Returns to U.S. and Finds Wild Fan Following," *SOURCE News and Reports* [http://www.sddt.com/files/libraryw...2_96DN96_02_12/DN96_02_12. cj.html].

8   Manjula Negi, "Mira Nair," *Cinemaya* 25–26 (1994–1995), 27.

9   As quoted by James Moran, "Gregg Araki, Guerrilla Film-maker for a Queer Generation," *Film Quarterly* 50:1 (fall 1996), 25.

10   Ibid.

11   Michael T. Martin, "Framing the 'Black' in Black Diasporic Cinemas," *Cinemas of the Black Diaspora*, 1.

12   Howie Movshovitz, "Indirection plays a role in films of Wayne Wang," *Denver Post* (July 16, 1995), F-01.

13   Ibid.

14   Richard Chang, "Sense and Sensibility: An Asian-English Affair," [http://www.lib.berkeley.edu/MRC/Asianfilm.html].

15   bell hooks, "The cultural mix: an interview with Wayne Wang," *Reel to Real: Race, Sex, and Class at the Movies* (New York: Routledge, 1996), 126.

16   Ibid.

17   Ibid., 134.

18   Trinh T. Minh-ha, "At the Edge," *Cinemaya* 25–26 (1994–1995), 29.

19   Tiana (Thi Thanh Nga), "The Long March—From Wong to Woo: Asians in Hollywood," *Cineaste* 21:4 (1995), 40.

20   See Mira Nair, "Indian Cabaret: Reflections and Reactions," *Discourse* 8 (fall/winter 86/87), 69.

21   Ibid., 67.

22   Farah Nousheen, "South Asian Women's Cinema," *The Sawnet Movie Page*, 7 [http://www.umiacs.umd.edu/users/sawweb/sawnet/cinema.html].

23   As quoted by Douglas S. Barasch, "The Politics of Sex: With her lavish, explicit new film, *Kama Sutra*, Indian director Mira Nair finds herself in a most unusual position," *Elle Magazine* 138 (Feb. 1997), 50.

24   Susan Chacko, "The Sawnet Movie Page" [http://www.umiacs.umd.edu/users/sawweb/cinema.html#Reviews].

25   Ien Ang, "To Be or Not to Be Chinese: Diaspora, Culture and Postmodern Ethnicity," *Southeast Asian Journal of Social Science* 21:1 (93), 13.

26   Inderpal Grewal, "The Postcolonial, Ethnic Studies, and the Diaspora: The Contexts of Ethnic Immigrant/Migrant Cultural Studies in the US," *Socialist Review* 24:4 (1994), 58.

27   On this point, I want to acknowledge Darrell Hamamoto for his comments on the manuscript: "The term [diaspora] is imprecise at best, perfect for the use of elite 'postcolonial' (read 'immigrant') intellectuals who invoke it to earn 'third world' minoritarian status while maintaining their class privilege that travels across national boundaries. . . . It [diaspora] implies a random, unstructured scattering of peoples whereas contemporary global migration is the result of transnational corporate capitalism and its ruinous effects." Although I do not fully agree with Hamamoto's argument, I have quoted him here to invite further discussion. While Hamamoto raises legitimate concerns, I do not fully agree with his class-deterministic argument. Not all immigrant intellectuals who advocate a "diasporic" identity are middle-class. For example, Pratibha Parmar, a "diasporic" filmmaker to be discussed in this section, hardly carries any class privilege when her family moves to Britain as refugees. She writes, "I first arrived in Britain with my family on a rainy March day in 1967. We were refugees from East Africa coming to the 'mother country' of Great Britain with hopes of a better future. Unlike many other Indians living in Kenya, my family barely had money for decent housing or adequate food. Our passage to England was paid for by rich, middle class Indians who used us to transport some of their wealth out of Africa into European banks." See "True Colours: The Asian Diaspora in Motion," by Pratibha Parmar, *NAATA/CrossCurrent Media* [http://www.lib.berkeley.edu/MRC/NAATA.TrueColours.html].

28   Ang, "To Be or Not to Be Chinese," 13.

29   Curated by Paul Wong, a programmer for Vancouver's artist-run video exhibition and distribution organization Video In/Video Out, this was the third section of a series of exhibitions. Two previous exhibitions concentrated on films, videotapes, and photography by Asians in Canada and the United States: "Asian New World," presented at Video In in 1987, and "Yellow Peril: New World Asians," shown in London in 1988.

30   See Lloyd Wong, "Remodeling Asian Media," *Afterimage* (May 1991), 14–15.

31 Valerie Soe, "Visions of An Asian New World," *Independent* (July 1991), 22.

32 Peter Feng, "In Search of Asian American Cinema," *Cineaste* 21:1–2 (1995), 34.

33 Richard Fung, "Looking for my penis: the eroticized Asian in gay video porn," *How Do I Look?: Queer Film and Video*, ed. Bad Object-Choices (Seattle: Bay Press, 1991), 145–60.

34 As quoted by Noah Cowan, "Srinivas Krishna: Writer/Director," *Independent* (April 1993), 15.

35 Ibid.

36 "Double happiness" is the Chinese symbol for marriage, which is literally two happinesses joined in union. But the movie title is a pun about Jade, the leading character, in a futile search for two types of happiness: one that her family wants, and one that she wants.

37 Her previous short films include *Picture Perfect*, which received the nomination for Best Drama under thirty minutes at the 1989 Yorkton Film Festival; *Shortchanged, Love In*, and *Me, Mom and Mona* (a documentary about the women in her family), which won a Special Jury Citation for Best Canadian Short at the Toronto Festival of Festivals in 1993; and *Hunger*.

38 Monique Harvey, "Achieving Double Happiness: An Interview with Mina Shum" [http://fas.sfu.ca/1h/cs/research/p.../the-peak/95-2/issue12/dblhap.html].

39 Ibid.

40 Ibid.

41 Sheila Benson, "Chinese but Not Chinese, And Revealing the Difference," *Denver Post* (July 23, 1995).

42 Chinacity Entertainment, Montreal, "Alberta Filmmaker Michelle Wong Returns Home," *Entertainment*, 4 [http://www.alvin.org/acr/retrun.html].

43 Ibid.

44 See also Jasvinder Phull's *The Arranged Marriage* (1986), Perminder Dhillon-Kashyap's *Shattering Illusions* (1987), and Munawar Nizam's *Changing Images* (1988).

45 Gwendolyn Audrey Foster has a chapter on Pratibha Parmar in her book *Women Filmmakers of the African and Asian Diaspora: Decolonizing the Gaze, Locating Subjectivity* (Carbondale and Edwardsville: Southern Illinois University Press, 1997), 73–94.

46 Pratibha Parmar, "That Moment of Emergence," *How Do I Look?*, 4.

47 Foster, *Women Filmmakers of the African and Asian Diaspora*, 74.

48 Ibid., 77.

49 Alice Walker and Pratibha Parmar, *Warrior Marks: Female Genital Mutilation and the Sexual Binding of Women* (New York: Harcourt Brace Jovanovich, 1993), 4.

50 Parmar, "That Moment of Emergence," 3.

51 Ibid.

52 This is a quote from comments on my manuscript made by Jennifer Collier at AltaMira Press.

53 Mohini Kent, "Gurinder Chadha: A Woman's Eye," *Cinemaya* 25–26 (1994–1995), 25.

54 Ibid.

55 Ibid.

56 Ibid.

57 Ibid.

58 For a historical overview of Chinese stereotypes in Australian language and culture, see Lachlan Straban, " 'The Luck of a Chinaman': Images of the Chinese in Popular Australian Sayings," *East Asian History* 3 (June 1992), 53–76.

59 As quoted by Pat Gillespie, "The New Breed of Ethnic Filmmakers," *Cinema Papers* 90 (Oct. 1992), 25.

60 Quoted by Sylvie Shaw, "The Asian Screen Test," Cinema Papers 87 (Mar. 1992), 38.

61 Chris Berry, "Pauline Chan," *Cinemaya* 25–26 (1994–1995), 66.

62 Gillespie, 24.

63 Russell Smith, "The Scent of Green Papaya," *Dallas Morning News* (March 4, 1994), A11, 38.

64 David Elliot, "Native filmmaker's fresh story has the scent of a masterpiece," *San Diego Union* (Feb. 10, 1994), 27-A9.

65 Ella Shohat and Robert Stam, *Unthinking Eurocentrism: Multiculturalism and the Media* (New York: Routledge, 1994), 9.

66 Ibid., 242.

67 Ibid., 243.

Selected Bibliography

Althusser, Louis. *Lenin and Philosophy, and Other Essays*. New York: Monthly Review Press, 1971.

Andersen, Erika Surat. "Review: *Mississippi Masala*." *Film Quarterly* 46:4 (Summer 1994).

Ang, Ien. "To Be or Not to Be Chinese: Diaspora, Culture and Postmodern Ethnicity." *Southeast Asian Journal of Social Science* 21:1 (93).

Anton, Saul. "A Search for Roots and Identity: An Interview with Tiana Thi Thahn Nga." *Cineaste* 20:3 (Summer 1993).

Arar, Yardena. "Tan, Wang defend depiction of Asian men in 'Joy.' " *New York Daily News* (Sept. 8, 1993).

Asian CineVision. "Tributes, Retrospectives, and New Films to Celebrate AAIFF's First Decade." *CineVue* 2:3 (May 1987).

Asian Society Galleries. *Asia/America: Identities in Contemporary Asian American Art*. New York: The New Press, 1994.

Bad Object-Choices, ed. *How Do I Look?: Queer Film and Video*. Seattle: Bay Press, 1991.

Bakhtin, Mikhail. *The Dialogic Imagination*. Austin: University of Texas Press, 1981.

Bartlett, Freude. "Distributing Independent Films." *Jump Cut* 31 (1986).

Beale, Lewis. "Hollywood Is Reaching Out to Chinese Filmmakers and Actors." *New York Daily News* (Feb. 15, 1996).

Benson, Sheila. "Chinese But Not Chinese, and Revealing the Difference." *Denver Post* (July 23, 1995).

Berger, John. *The Look of Things*. New York: Viking Press, 1974.

Bernardi, Adria. "Heat in the Delta: Reactions to the Triangle." *Southern Exposure* (July/Aug., 1984).

Bernstein, Matthew, and Gaylyn Studlar, eds. *Visions of the East: Orientalism in Film*. New Brunswick, N.J.: Rutgers University Press, 1997.

Berry, Chris. "Pauline Chan." *Cinemaya* 25–26 (1994–1995).

Bhabha, Homi. *The Location of Culture*. New York: Routledge, 1994.

Blythe, Martin. " 'What's in a Name?': Film Culture and the Self/Other Question." *Quarterly Review of Film and Video* 13:1–3.

Browne, Nick. "Race: The Political Unconscious of American Film," *East-West Film Journal* 6.

———. "The Undoing of the Other Woman: Madame Butterfly in the Discourse of American Orientalism." *The Birth of Whiteness: Race and the Emergence of U.S. Cinema*. Ed. Daniel Bernard. New Brunswick, N.J.: Rutgers University Press, 1996.

Brownlow, Kevin. *Behind the Mask of Innocence*. New York: Alfred A. Knopf, 1990.

Campter, Fred. "The End of Avant-Garde Film." *Millennium Film Journal* 16–18 (Fall/Winter 1986–1987).

Carmen, John. "Margaret Cho Breaks Ground in Sitcom Role." *San Francisco Chronicle* (May 10, 1994).

Carson, Diane. "Cultural Screens: Teaching Asian and Asian-American Images." *Shared Differences: Multicultural Media and Practical Pedagogy*. Ed. Diane Carson and Lester Friedman. Urbana: University of Illinois Press, 1995.

Cham, Mbye B., ed. *Blackframes: Critical Perspectives on Black Independent Cinema*. Cambridge, Mass.: MIT Press, 1988.

Chan, Sucheng. *Asian Americans: An Interpretive History*. Boston: Twayne Publishers, 1991.

Chang, Lia. "Filmmaker as Activist: Arthur Dong makes award-winning films that also seek to change the world." *AsianWeek* (May 10, 1996).

Chen, Chiung Hwang. "Feminization of Asian (American) Men in the U.S. Mass Media: An Analysis of 'The Ballad of Little Jo.'" *Journal of Communication Inquiry* 20:2 (1996).

Chin, Daryl. "After Ten Years: Some Notes on the Asian American Film Festival," *Program Notes* (New York: Asian CineVision, 1988).

———. "Asian American Filmmakers Harvest Oscar Nominations," *CineVue* 4:1 (March 1989).

———. "Film Forums: The Asian American Case." *CineVue* 1:3 (1986).

———. "Girlfriend in a Coma: Notes on the Films of Gregg Araki." *How Do I Look?: Queer Film and Video*. Ed. Bad Object-Choices. Seattle: Bay Press, 1991.

Chin, Daryl. "Writing an Unexpurgated History of Asian American Film." *CineVue* 3:2 (June 1988).

Chin, Frank. "Confessions of a Chinatown Cowboy." *Bulletin of Concerned Asian Scholars* 4:3 (Fall 1972).

Chinacity Entertainment, Montreal. "Alberta Filmmaker Returns Home." *Entertainment* 4 [http://www.alvin.org/acr/return.html].

Choy, Christine. "Images of Asian-Americans in Films and Television." *Ethnic Images in American Film and Television*. Ed. Randall Miller. Philadelphia: Balch Institute, 1978.

Christian, Barbara. "The Race for Theory." *Cultural Critique* 6 (Spring 1987).

CineVue. "Color Schemes: *CineVue* Interviews Video Artist Shu Lea Cheang." *CineVue* 4:1 (March 1989).

CineVue. Interview with George Takei. "'Mr. Sulu' Steers a New Course." *CineVue* 6:3 (Sept. 1991).

CineVue. "The [Video] World According to Cheang and Chong." *CineVue* 3:1 (March 1988).

Comer, Brooke. "*Eat Drink Man Woman*: A Feast for the Eyes." *American Cinematographer* (Jan. 1995).

Corliss, Richard. "Asian Invasion." *Time* (Aug. 14, 1995).

Cortés, Carlos E. "What Is Maria? What Is Juan? Dilemmas of Analyzing the Chicano Image in U.S. Feature Films." *Chicano and Film: Essays on Chicano Representation and Resistance*. Ed. Chon A. Noriega. New York: Garland Publishing, 1992.

Cowan, Noah. "Srinivas Krishna: Writer/Director." *The Independent* (April 1993).

Cowen, Paul S. "A Social-Cognitive Approach to Ethnicity in Films." *Unspeakable Images: Ethnicity and the American Cinema*. Ed. Lester Friedman. Urbana and Chicago: University of Illinois Press, 1991.

Cripps, Thomas. *Black Film As Genre*. Bloomington: Indiana University Press, 1979.

Crusz, Robert. "Black Cinemas, Film Theory and Dependent Knowledge." *Screen* 26 (May–Aug. 1985).

Daniels, Roger. *Asian America: Chinese and Japanese in the United States Since 1850*. Seattle: University of Washington Press, 1988.

Davis, Robert Murray. "Frank Chin: An Interview." *Amerasian Journal* 14:2 (1988).

Denzin, Norman. "Chan Is Missing: The Asian Eye Examines Cultural Studies." *Symbolic Interaction* 17:1 (1994).

Ding, Loni. "Strategies of an Asian American Filmmaker." *Moving the Image: Independent Asian Pacific American Media Arts*. Ed. Russell Leong. Los Angeles: UCLA Asian American Studies Center, 1991.

Dittus, Erick. "Mississippi Triangle: An Interview with Christine Choy, Worth Long and Allan Siegel." *Cineaste* 14:2 (1985).

Dower, John. *War Without Mercy: Race and Power in the Pacific War*. New York: Pantheon Press, 1986.

DuBois, W. E. B. "Krigwa Players Little Negro Theater." *Crisis* 32 (July 1926).

Esaki, John. "Back to Real Asian American Filmmaking." *Moving the Image: Independent Asian Pacific American Media Arts*. Ed. Russell Leong. Los Angeles: UCLA Asian American Studies Center, 1991.

Espiritu, Yen Le. *Asian American Panethnicity: Bridging Institutions of Identities*. Philadelphia: Temple University Press, 1992.

Fabian, Johannes. *Time and the Other: How Anthropology Makes Its Object*. New York: Columbia University Press, 1983.

Feng, Peter. "In Search of Asian American Cinema." *Cineaste* 21:1–2 (1995).

———. "Redefining Asian American Masculinity: Steven Okasaki's 'American Sons.' " *Cineaste* 22:3 (1996).

Fiske, John. *Understanding Popular Culture*. London: Routledge Press, 1989.

Foster, Gwendolyn Audrey. *Women Filmmakers of the African and Asian Diaspora: Decolonizing the Gaze, Locating Subjectivity*. Carbondale and Edwardsville: Southern Illinois University Press, 1997.

Foucault, Michel. "Nietzsche, Genealogy, History." *Language, Counter-memory, Practice: Selected Essays and Interviews by Michel Foucault*. Ed. Donald Bouchard. Ithaca, N.Y.: Cornell University Press, 1977.

Francia, Luis. "Asian and Asian American Cinema: Separated by a Common Language?" *Moving the Image: Independent Asian Pacific American Media Arts*. Ed. Russell Leong. Los Angeles: UCLA Asian American Studies Center, 1991.

———. "Made in America." *Film Comment* 19 (Sept./Oct. 1983).

Fregoso, Rosa Linda. *The Bronze Screen: Chicana and Chicano Film Culture*. Minneapolis: University of Minnesota Press, 1993.

Fung, Richard. "Centering the Margins." *Moving the Image: Independent Asian Pacific American Media Arts*. Ed. Russell Leong. Los Angeles: UCLA Asian American Studies Center, 1991.

———. "Looking for my penis: The eroticized Asian in gay video porn." *How Do I Look?: Queer Film and Video*. Ed. Bad Object-Choices. Seattle: Bay Press, 1991.

———. "Shortcomings: Questions about Pornography as Pedagogy." *How Do I Look?: Queer Film and Video*. Ed. Bad Object-Choices. Seattle: Bay Press, 1991.

Gabriel, Teshome. "Third Cinema as Guardian of Popular Memory: Towards a Third Aesthetics." *Questions of Third Cinema*. Ed. Jim Pines and Paul Willemen. London: British Film Institute, 1989.

———. "Thoughts on Nomadic Aesthetics and the Black Independent Cinema: Traces of a Journey." *Blackframes: Critical Perspectives on Black Independent Cinema*. Ed. Mbye B. Cham. Cambridge, Mass.: MIT Press, 1988.

Gee, Bill J. *Asian American Media Reference Guide*. 2d ed. New York: Asian CineVision, 1990.

Gerster, Carole. "The Asian American Renaissance in Independent Cinema and Valerie Soe's *New Year.*" *A Gathering of Voices on the Asian American Experience.* Ed. Annette White-Parks et al. Fort Atkinson, Wis.: Highsmith Press, 1994.

Gibson-Hudson, Gloria J. "African American Literary Criticism as a Model for the Analysis of Films by African American Women." *Wide Angle* 13:3/4 (July–Oct. 1991).

Gillespie, Pat. "The New Breed of Ethnic Filmmakers." *Cinema Papers* 90 (Oct. 1992).

Gilroy, Paul. *"There Ain't No Black in the Union Jack": The Cultural Politics of Race and Nation.* Chicago: University of Chicago Press, 1991.

Gong, Stephen. "A History of Progress: Asian American Media Arts 1970–1990." *Moving the Image: Independent Asian Pacific American Media Arts.* Ed. Russell Leong. Los Angeles: UCLA Asian American Studies Center, 1991.

Gramsci, Antonio. *Prison Notebooks.* New York: International Publishers, 1970.

Grewal, Inderpal. "The Postcolonial, Ethnic Studies, and the Diaspora," *Socialist Review* 24:4 (1994).

Guerrero, Ed. *Framing Blackness: The African American Image in Film.* Philadelphia: Temple University Press, 1993.

Guttman, Monika. "One-Woman Cho." *USA Weekend* (Sept. 16–18, 1994).

Hagedorn, Jessica. "Asian Women in Film: No Joy, No Luck," *Ms.* (Jan./Feb. 1994).

Hall, Stuart. "Cultural Identity and Cinematic Representation." *Framework* 36 (1989).

———. "Encoding/Decoding." *Culture, Media, Language.* Ed. Stuart Hall et al. London: University of Birmingham, 1980.

Hamamoto, Darell Y. *Monitored Peril: Asian Americans and the Politics of TV Representation.* Minneapolis: University of Minnesota Press, 1994.

Harvey, Monique. "Achieving Double Happiness: An Interview with Mina Shum." [http://fas.sfu.ca/1h/cs/research/p.../the-peak/95-2/issues12/dblhap.html].

Heung, Marina. "Representing Ourselves: Films and Videos by Asian American/Canadian Women." *Feminism, Multiculturalism, and the Media: Global Diversities.* Ed. Angharad N. Valdivia. Thousand Oaks, Calif.: Sage Publications, 1995.

Hirano, Ron. "Media Guerrillas." *Counterpoint: Perspectives on Asian America.* Ed. Emma Gee. Los Angeles: UCLA Asian American Studies Center, 1979.

hooks, bell. *Black Looks: Race and Representation.* Boston: South End Press, 1992.

———. *Reel to Real: Race, Sex and Class at the Movies.* New York: Routledge Press, 1996.

Hongo, Garrett. "Introduction." *The Open Boat: Poems from Asia America.* New York: Anchor Books/Doubleday, 1993.

Hoppenstand, Gary. "Yellow Devil Doctors and Opium Dens: A Survey of the Yellow Peril Stereotypes in Mass Media Entertainment." *Popular Culture Reader.* Ed. Christopher D. Geist and Jack Nachbar. Bowling Green, Ohio: Bowling Green University Popular Press, 1983.

Horikawa, Herbert. "Psychological Implications of Asian Stereotypes in the Media." *Ethnic Images in American Film and Television.* Ed. Randall M. Miller. Philadelphia: Balch Institute, 1978.

Horn, John. "Movie-awards furor not just black and white." *Denver Post* (March 22, 1996).

Horrigan, Bill. "Bruce and Norman Yonemoto: Assimilated." *Art and Text* 55 (Oct. 1996).

Hurston, Zora Neale. *Their Eyes Were Watching God.* Champaign: University of Illinois Press, 1979.

Ishizuka, Karen, and Robert A. Nakamura. "Conversations: An Experiment in Community-based Filmmaking." *Moving the Image: Independent Asian Pacific American Media Arts.* Ed. Russell Leong. Los Angeles: UCLA Asian American Studies Center, 1991.

Issacs, Harold R. *Scratches on Our Minds: American Images of China and India.* New York: John Day Company, 1958.

Jacobson, Brooke. "A Great Wall." *Film Quarterly* (Winter 1986–1987).

Jones, Dorothy B. *Portrayal of China and India on the American Screen, 1896–1955.* Cambridge, Mass.: MIT Press, 1955.

Kaw, Eugenia. "Medicalization of Racial Features: Asian American Women and Cosmetic Surgery." *Medical Anthropology Quarterly* 7:1 (March 1993).

Keller, Gary D. *Chicano Cinema: Research, Reviews, and Resources.* Binghamton, N.Y.: Bilingual Review/Press, 1985.

Kent, Mohini. "Gurinder Chadha: A Woman's Eye." *Cinemaya* 25–26 (1994–1995).

Kern, Stephen. *The Culture of Time and Space.* Oxford, England: Basil Blackwell, 1980.

Khush. "Fighting Back: An Interview with Pratibha Parmar." *A Lotus of Another Color: An Anthology of the South Asian Gay and Lesbian Experience.* Ed. Rakesh Ratti. Boston: Alyson Publications, 1993.

Kim, Elaine. *Asian American Literature: An Introduction to the Writings and Their Social Context.* Philadelphia: Temple University Press, 1982.

———. "Defining Asian American Realities Through Literature." *Cultural Critique* 6 (Spring 1987).

Kimura, Lillian. "Aloha, Issei! *CineVue* Interviews *Picture Bride* Director Kayo Hatta." *CineVue* 10:1 (May 1995).

Kingston, Maxine Hong. "Cultural Mis-Readings by American Reviewers." *Asian and Western Writers in Dialogue: Cultural Identities.* Ed. Guy Amirthanayagam. London: MacMillan, 1982.

———. *Tripmaster Monkey.* New York: Vintage Books, 1990.

Kirihara, Donald. "The Accepted Idea Displaced: Stereotype and Sessue Hayakawa." *The Birth of Whiteness, Race and the Emergence of U.S. Cinema.* New Brunswick, N.J.: Rutgers University Press, 1996.

Kishi, Yoshio. "Pioneers and Groundbreakers." *Moving the Image: Independent Asian Pacific American Media Arts.* Ed. Russell Leong. Los Angeles: UCLA Asian American Studies Center, 1991.

Kristeva, Julia. "Women's Time." *The Kristeva Reader.* Ed. Toril Moi. New York: Columbia University Press, 1986.

Kwan, Shirley. "Asian American Women Behind the Camera." *Anthology of Asian American Film and Video.* New York: Third World Newsreel, 1984.

Lane, Jim. "Notes on theory and the autobiographical documentary film in America." *Wide Angle* 15:3 (1993).

Lang, Robert. *American Film Melodrama: Griffith, Vidor, Minnelli.* Princeton, N.J.: Princeton University Press, 1989.

Lears, T. J. Jackson. "The Concept of Cultural Hegemony: Problems and Possibilities." *American Historical Review* 90:3 (March 1985).

Lee, Helen. "A Peculiar Sensation: A Personal Genealogy of Korean American Women's Cinema." *Cineaste* 23:1 (Winter 1997).

Lee, Joann Faung Jean. "Margaret the 'All-American Bust' of TV." *AsianWeek* 2 (Dec. 1994).

Le Grice, Malcom. *Abstract Film and Beyond.* Cambridge, Mass.: MIT Press, 1977.

Leong, Russell, ed. *Moving the Image: Independent Asian Pacific American Media Arts.* Los Angeles: UCLA Asian American Studies Center, 1991.

Lim, Gerard. "The Different Hues of 'The Color of Fear.'" *AsianWeek* (Jan. 2, 1994).

Lipsitz, George. *Time Passages*. Minneapolis: University of Minnesota Press, 1990.

Lowe, Lisa. "Heterogeneity, Hybridity, Multiplicity: Marking Asian American Differences." *Diaspora* 1:1 (Spring 1991).

Mapp, Edward. *Blacks in American Films: Today and Yesterday*. Metuchen, N.J.: Scarecrow Press, 1972.

Marchetti, Gina. "Ethnicity, the Cinema and Cultural Status." *Unspeakable Images: Ethnicity and the American Cinema*. Ed. Lester Friedman. Urbana and Chicago: University of Illinois Press, 1991.

————. *Romance and the Yellow Peril: Race, Sex, and Discursive Hollywood Strategies in Hollywood Fiction*. Berkeley: University of California Press, 1993.

Mark, Diane Mei Lin. *Chan Is Missing*. Honolulu: Bamboo Ridge Press, 1984.

Martin, Michael T. "Framing the 'Black' in Black Diasporic Cinemas." *Cinemas of the Black Diaspora*. Ed. Michael T. Martin. Detroit: Wayne State University Press, 1995.

McCunn, Ruthanne Lum. "Adrienne Telemaque." *Chinese American Portraits: Personal Histories 1828–1988*. San Francisco: Chronicle Books, 1988.

Mendez, Carlos. "Melodramatic Margaret Minces the Media Mavens." *AsianWeek* (Dec. 23, 1994).

Miller, Stuart Creighton. *The Unwelcome Immigrant; The American Image of the Chinese, 1785–1882*. Berkeley: University of California Press, 1969.

Moran, James. "Gregg Araki, Guerrilla Film-maker for a Queer Generation." *Film Quarterly* 50:1 (Fall 1996).

Morrison, Toni. *Playing in the Dark: Whiteness in the Literary Imagination*. New York: Alfred A. Knopf, 1992.

Moy, James. *Marginal Sights: Staging the Chinese in America*. Iowa City: University of Iowa Press, 1993.

Murray, James P. *To Find an Image: Black Films from Uncle Tom to Super Fly*. Indianapolis: Bobbs-Merrill, 1973.

Nair, Mira. "Indian Cabaret: Reflections and Reactions." *Discourse* 8 (Fall/Winter 86/87).

Nakamura, Robert. "Visual Communications: The Early Years." *In Focus* 6:1 (Winter 1990).

Nash, Michael. "Bruce and Norman Yonemoto." *Journal of Contemporary Art* 3:2 (Fall 1990).

Negi, Manjula. "Mira Nair." *Cinemaya* 25–26 (1994–1995).

Nguyen, Lan. "Rising Sun Presents Damaging Portrayal of Japanese, Asians." *Rafu Shimpo* (July 1, 1993).

Nicholson, David. "Which Way the Black Film Movement." *Cinemas of the Black Diaspora*. Ed. Michael T. Martin. Detroit: Wayne State University Press, 1995.

Noble, Peter. *The Negro in Films*. London: S. Robinson, 1948.

Noriega, Chon A., ed. *Chicanos and Film: Essays on Chicano Representation and Resistance*. New York: Garland Publishing, 1992.

Nousheen, Farah. "South Asian Women's Cinema." *Sawnet Movie Page* [http://www.umiacs.umd.edu/users/sawweb/sawnet/cinema.html].

Oehling, Richard. "The Yellow Menace: Asian Images in American Film." *The Kaleidoscopic Lens: How Hollywood Views Ethnic Groups*. Ed. Randall Miller. Englewood, N.J.: Jerome S. Ozer, 1980.

Onodera, Midi. "A Displaced View: What Are We Reconsidering about the Yellow Peril." *Yellow Peril: Reconsidered*. Ed. Paul Wong. Vancouver: On Edge, 1990.

Orenstein, Peggy. "Salaam America! An Interview with Director Mira Nair." *Mother Jones* (Jan./Feb. 1992).

Pao, Angela. "The Eyes of the Storm: Gender, Genre and Cross-Casting in Miss Saigon." *Text and Performance Quarterly* 12 (1992).

Park, Jeannie. "The First Decade: The Asian American International Film Festival." *The Independent* (Nov. 1987).

Parmar, Pratibha. "Other Kinds of Dreams." *Feminist Review* 31 (Spring 1989).

————."That Moment of Emergence." *How Do I Look?: Queer Film and Video*. Ed. Bad Object-Choices. Seattle: Bay Press, 1991.

Pines, Jim and Paul Willemen. *Questions of Third Cinema*. London: British Film Institute, 1989.

Pratt, Mary Louise. "Scratches on the Face of the Country." *Critical Inquiry* 12 (1985–1986).

Price, Darby Li Po. " 'All American Girl' and the American Dream." *Critical Mass: A Journal of Asian American Cultural Criticism* 2:1 (Winter 1994).

Ravitch, Diana. "Diversity and Democracy: Multicultural Education in America." *American Educator* (Spring 1990).

Rhines, Jesse Algeron. *Black Film/White Money*. New Brunswick, N.J.: Rutgers University Press, 1996.

Rosenberg, Scott. "Vietnam journey cast in Stone." *San Francisco Examiner* (Dec. 24, 1993).

Rosenstone, Robert A. "History in Images/History in Words: Reflections on the Possibility of Really Putting History onto Film." *American Historical Review* 93:5 (Dec. 1988).

Rushdie, Salman. "Outside the Whale." *American Film* (Jan./Feb. 1985).

"Sa-I-Gu's Dai Sil Kim-Gibson and Elaine Kim." *International Documentary* 12:8 (Sept. 1993).

Said, Edward. *Culture and Imperialism*. New York: Alred A. Knopf, 1993.

————. *Orientalism*. New York: Pantheon Books, 1978.

Schiller, Herbert. *The Mind Managers*. Boston: Beacon Press, 1973.

Shohat, Ella and Robert Stam. *Unthinking Eurocentrism: Multiculturalism and the Media*. New York: Routledge Press, 1994.

Singer, Michael. *Oliver Stone's Heaven and Earth: The Making of An Epic Motion Picture*. Boston: Charles E. Tuttle, 1993.

Singerman, Howard. "Bruce and Norman Yonemoto, 'Green Card': An American Romance, Long Beach Museum of Art." *Artforum* 21:2 (Oct. 1982).

Sklar, Robert. "Taking Hollywood by Storm: Behind the Triumph of Independent Films." *Chronicle of Higher Education*. (March 14, 1997).

Sklar, Robert, and Charles Musser, eds. *Resisting Images: Essays on Cinema and History*. Philadelphia: Temple University Press, 1990.

Smith, Russel. "The Scent of Green Papaya." *Dallas Morning News* (March 4, 1994).

Smith, Valerie. *Representing Blackness: Issues in Film and Video*. New Brunswick, N.J.: Rutgers University Press, 1997.

Snead, James. *White Screens/Black Images: Hollywood from the Dark Side*. New York: Routlege, 1994.

Soe, Valerie. "Inspired Purpose and Exhibition Practices: A Review of the Show the Right Thing Conference." *The Independent* (March 1990).

————. "On Experimental Video." *Moving the Image: Independent Asian Pacific American Media Arts*. Ed. Russell Leong. Los Angeles: UCLA Asian American Studies Center, 1991.

————. "Visions of an Asian New World." *The Independent* (July 1991).

Soja, Edward. *Postmodern Geographies*. New York: Verso, 1989.

Sollors, Werner. *Beyond Ethnicity: Consent and Descent in American Culture*. New York: Oxford University Press, 1986.

Sommer, Constance. "Asian Film Star Jackie Chan Returns to U.S. and Finds Wild Fan Following." *SOURCE News and Reports* [http://www.sddt.com/files/libraryw...2_96DN96_02_12DN96_02_12.cjhtml].

Sorlin, Pierre. *The Film in History: Restaging the Past.* Oxford, England: Basil Blackwell, 1980.

Spiegel, Tamio. "Horror! Sci-Fi! Action! Asian American Genre Filmmakers." *CineVue* 8:2 (July 1993).

Spigner, Clarence. "Race, Gender, and the Status-Quo: Asian and African American Relations in a Hollywood Film." *Explorations in Ethnic Studies* 17:1 (January 1, 1994).

———. "Teaching Multiculturalism from the Movies: Health and Social Well-being." *Shared Differences: Multicultural Media and Practical Pedagogy.* Ed. Diane Carson and Lester Friedman. Urbana and Chicago: University of Illinois Press, 1995.

Spivak, Gayatri. *In Other Worlds: Essays in Cultural Politics.* New York: Methuen, 1987.

Stam, Robert. "Bakhtin, Polyphony, and Ethnic/Racial Representation," *Unspeakable Images: Ethnicity and the American Cinema.* Ed. Lester Friedman. Urbana and Chicago: University of Illinois Press, 1991.

Stam, Robert, and Louise Spence. "Colonialism, Racism, and Representation: An Introduction." *Movies and Methods: An Anthology.* Ed. Bill Nichols. Berkeley: University of California Press, 1976.

Straban, Lachlan. " 'The Luck of a Chinaman': Images of the Chinese in Popular Australian Sayings." *East Asian History* 3 (June 1992).

Stromgen, Dick. "The Chinese Syndrome: The Evolving Image of Chinese and Chinese-Americans in Hollywood Films." *Beyond the Stars: Stock Characters in American Popular Film.* Ed. Paul Loukides and Linda K. Fuller. Bowling Green, Ohio: Bowling Green State University Popular Press, 1990.

Stuart, Andrea. "Mira Nair: A new hybrid cinema." *Women and Film: A Sight and Sound Reader.* Ed. Pam Cook and Philip Dodd. Philadelphia: Temple University Press, 1993.

Tajima, Marsha. "Carte Jaune Fantasies." *CineVue* 6:3 (Sept. 1991).

Tajima, Renee. "Asian Women's Images in Film: The Past Sixty Years," *In Color: Sixty Years of Minority Women in Film: 1921–1981.* New York: Third World Newsreel, 1993.

———. "Ethno-Communications: The Film School Program That Changed the Color of Independent Filmmaking." *Anthology of Asian American Film and Video.* New York: Third World Newsreel, 1984.

———. "Intersection in the Delta." *Southern Exposure* (July/Aug. 1984).

———. "Lotus Blossoms Don't Bleed: Images of Asian Women." *Making Waves: Anthology of Writings By and About Asian American Women.* Ed. Asian Women United of California. Boston: Beacon Press, 1989.

———. "Moving the Image: Asian American Independent Filmmaking 1970–1990." *Moving the Image: Independent Asian Pacific American Media Arts.* Ed. Russell Leong. Los Angeles: UCLA Asian American Studies Center, 1991.

———. "To Be Asian American." *Cinemaya* 25–26 (1994–1995).

Tan, Amy. "Joy, Luck and Hollywood." *Los Angeles Times* (Sept. 5, 1993) 105:D-7.

Tanaka, Janice. "Electrons and Reflective Shadows." *Moving the Image: Independent Asian Pacific American Media Arts.* Ed. Russell Leong. Los Angeles: UCLA Asian American Studies Center, 1991.

Tatsukawa, Steven J. "Beyond the Looking Glass." *Anthology of Asian American Film and Video.* New York: Third World Newsreel, 1984.

Taylor, Clyde. "The Future of Black Film: The Debate Continues." *Black Film Review* 4:4 (Fall 1988).

————. "The Paradox of Black Independent Cinema." *Black Film Review* 4:4 (Fall 1988).

Tchen, John Kuo Wei. "Believing Is Seeing: Transforming Orientalism and the Occidental Gaze." *Asia/America: Identities in Contemporary Asian American Art.* New York: New Press, 1994.

Tiana (Thi Thanh Nga). "The Long March—From Wong to Woo: Asians in Hollywood." *Cineaste* 21:4 (1995).

Trinh, T. Minh-ha. "A Minute Too Long." *When the Moon Waxes Red.* New York: Routledge, 1991.

————. "At the Edge." *Cinemaya* 25–26 (1994–1995).

————. "Difference: A Special Third World Woman Issue." *Feminist Review* 25 (March 1987).

————. "Film as Translation: A Net with No Fisherman." *Framer Framed.* New York: Routledge, 1992.

————. "From a Hybrid Place." *Framer Framed.* New York: Routledge, 1992.

————. "Which Way to Political Cinema?" *Framer Framed.* New York: Routledge, 1992.

————. "Who Is Speaking?" *Framer Framed.* New York: Routledge, 1992.

————. "Why a Fish Pond?" *Framer Framed.* New York: Routledge, 1992.

————. *Woman, Native, Other: Writing Postcoloniality and Feminism.* Bloomington: Indiana University Press, 1989.

Tseo, George K. Y. "Joy Luck: The Perils of Transcultural 'Translation.'" *Literature/Film Quarterly* 24:4 (1996).

Van Buren, Cassandra. "Family Gathering: Release from Emotional Internment." *Jump Cut* 37 (1992).

Viviano, Frank. "From Charlie Chan to Hyphenated Cinema." *Far Eastern Economic Review* (July 30, 1987).

Waldman, Diane. "There's More to a Positive Image Than Meets the Eye." *Jump Cut: Hollywood, Politics and Counter Cinema.* Ed. Peter Steven. New York: Praeger, 1985.

Walker, Alice, and Pratibha Parmar. *Warrior Marks: Female Genital Mutilation and the Sexual Binding of Women.* New York: Harcourt Brace Jovanovitch, 1993.

Walsh, Andrea S. *Women's Film and Female Experience: 1940–1950.* New York: Praeger, 1984.

Weis, Elizabeth. "Family Portraits." *American Film* 1:2 (Nov. 1975).

Wilkinson, Endymion. *Japan Versus the West: Image and Reality.* London: Penguin Books, 1990.

Wong, Eugene F. *On Visual Media Racism: Asians in the American Motion Pictures.* New York: Arno Press, 1978.

Wong, Lloyd. "Remodeling Asian Media." *Afterimage* (May 1991).

Wong, Paul, ed. *Yellow Peril: Reconsidered.* Vancouver: On Edge, 1990.

Wong, Sau-ling. *Reading Asian American Literature: From Necessity to Extravagance.* Princeton, N.J.: Princeton University Press, 1993.

Selected Filmography

THIS STUDY IS BASED ON A LARGE GROUP of selected films and videos I have viewed and collected in the past six years.[1] I have adopted some specific guidelines for the selection of the films listed here: the film must be a product with significant Asian American or Asian immigrant involvement in the creative process as screenwriter, producer or director; the film may be historical or related to current events, but it should address significant Asian American or Asian diasporic–related themes; the film should be original and significant. Like books, films vary in quality and viewpoints. Some are critically acclaimed while others are very uneven in quality.

In case a film or video has multiple distributors, only one is listed. When no distribution or rental source is given, please contact the filmmaker directly. For more information on hard-to-locate films or videos, I would suggest contacting Bill J. Gee of Asian CineVision and his *Asian American Media Reference Guide* (3rd edition forthcoming).

Films

a.k.a. Don Bonus, Sokly Ny and Spencer Nakasako, 1995, NAATA.

All Orientals Look the Same, Valerie Soe, 1986, NAATA.

American Sons, Steven Okazaki, 1995, NAATA.

Anatomy of a Springroll, Paul Kwan and Arnold Iger, 1993, Filmakers Library.

Ancestors: Coolies, Sailors, Settlers in the Americas, Loni Ding, 1996, Center for Educational Telecommunications.

Animal Appetites, Michael Cho, 1991, NAATA.

Another Day in America, Michael Chan, 1989, Third World Newsreel.

Art to Art: Expressions of Asian American Women, Valerie Soe, 1993, NAATA.

Ati Ati Han, Marlin Oliveros, 1986, Video Out Distribution.

Aya, Solrun Hoass, 1990.

Banana Split, Kip Fulbeck, 1990, NAATA.

---

1. In selecting films as primary sources, I have not included films by and about Pacific Americans, who, as I have argued, deserve a separate treatment. For information on Pacific Islander films, contact Pacific Islanders in Communication (PIC), 1221 Kapiolani Blvd. #6A-4, Honolulu, Hawaii 96814.

Between Two Worlds: The Hmong Shaman in America, Taggart Siegel and Dwight Conquergood, 1985, Filmakers Library.

Bhaji on the Beach, Gurinder Chadha, 1994, Columbia Tristar Home Video.

Blue Collar and Buddha, Taggart Siegel, 1988, NAATA.

Breathing Lessons: The Life and Work of Mark O'Brien, Jessica Yu, 1997, Inscrutable Films/Pacific News Service.

Bui Doi: Life Like Dust, Ahrin Mishan and Nick Rothenberg, 1994, NAATA.

Carved In Silence, Felicia Lowe, 1988, NAATA.

Chan is Missing, Wayne Wang, 1982, New Yorker Video.

Children of Desired Sex, Mira Nair, 1985, Facets Multimedia.

Children of the Railroad Workers, Richard Gong, 1981, Amerasia Bookstore.

China: Land of My Father, Felicia Lowe, 1979, Coronet/MTI Film & Video.

Chinese Cafes in Rural Saskatchewan, Anthony Chan, 1985, Video Out Distribution.

Chinese Characters, Richard Fung, 1986, Video Data Bank.

Claiming a Voice: The Visual Communications Story, Arthur Dong, 1991, Visual Communications.

The Color of Fear, Lee Mun Wah, 1995, Stir Fry Productions.

The Color of Honor: The Japanese-American Soldier in World War II, Loni Ding, 1988, NAATA.

Color Schemes, Shu Lea Cheang, 1989, Women Make Movies.

Combination Platter, Tony Chan, 1993, Arrow Video.

Coming Out Under Fire: The History of Gay Men and Women in World War II, Arthur Dong, 1994, Zeitgeist Films.

The Compact, Brenda Joy Lem, 1990, Video Out Distribution.

Conversations: Before the War/After the War, Robert A. Nakamura, 1986, NAATA.

Cyclo, Tran Anh Hung, 1995, New Yorker Video.

Days of Waiting, Steven Okazaki, 1988, NAATA.

Dim Sum: A Little Bit of Heart, Wayne Wang, 1985, Facets Multimedia, Inc.

The Displaced View, Midi Onodera, 1988, Women Make Movies.

The Doom Generation, Gregg Araki, 1995, Trimark Home Video.

Double Happiness, Mina Shum, 1994, New Line Home Video.

Double the Trouble, Twice the Fun, Pratibha Parmar, 1992, Women Make Movies.

The Dragon Painter, Sessue Hayakawa, 1919, George Eastman House.

Eat a Bowl of Tea, Wayne Wang, 1989, Columbia Tristar Home Video.

Eat Drink Man Woman, Ang Lee, 1994, Hallmark Home Entertainment.

Eight-Pound Livelihood, Yuet-Fung Ho, 1984, New York Chinatown History Project.

En Ryo Identity, Paul Mayeda Berges, 1991, NAATA.

The Fall of the I-Hotel, Curtis Choy, 1993 Revised (1983), NAATA.

Family Gathering, Lise Yasui, 1988, NAATA.

Fated to be Queer, Pablo Bautista, 1992, NAATA.

Flesh and Paper, Pratibha Parmar, 1990, Women Make Movies.

Forbidden City, U.S.A., Arthur Dong, 1989, NAATA.

Freckled Rice, Stephen C. Ning, 1983, NAATA.

Fresh Kill, Shu Lea Cheang, 1994, The Airwaves Project/ITVS/Channel Four/Woo Art International. Strand Releasing.

From Hollywood to Hanoi, Tiana (Thi Thanh Nga), 1992, Indochina Film Arts Foundation.

From Spikes to Spindles, Christine Choy, 1976, Third World Newsreel.

Game of Death, Kip Fulbeck, 1994, NAATA.

The Garland, Horace Ove, 1981, Anancy Films.

Great Branches, New Roots: The Hmong Family, Rita Laboux, 1983, Facets Multimedia.

A Great Wall, Peter Wang, 1986, Facets Multimedia.

Green Card: An American Romance, Bruce Yonemoto, 1982, Video Data Bank.

Hang Up, the Space Between the Floor and the Door, Pauline Chan, 1996, Australian Film Commission.

History and Memory: For Akiko and Takashige, Rea Tajiri, 1991, Women Make Movies.

Hito Hata: Raise the Banner, Duane Kobo and Robert Nakamura, 1980, NAATA.

Honor Bound: A Personal Journey, Wendy Hanamura, 1996, Filmakers Library.

I Told You So, Alan Kondo, 1974, NAATA.

I'm British, But . . ., Gurinder Chadha, 1990, NAATA.

In the Name of the Emperor, Nancy Tong and Christine Choy, 1994, Filmakers Library.

India Cabaret, Mira Nair, 1986, Filmakers Library.

Island of Secret Memories, Loni Ding, 1987, Center for Educational Telecommunications.

Jazz is My Native Language: A Portrait of Toshiko Akiyoshi, Renee Cho, 1983, NAATA.

The Journey, Ruby Truly, 1986, Video Out Distribution.

The Joy Luck Club, Wayne Wang, 1993, Buena Vista Home Video.

Kama Sutra: A Tale of Love, Mira Nair, 1996, Trimark Home Video.

Khush, Pratibha Parmar, 1991, Women Make Movies.

Khush Refugees, Nidhi Singh, 1991, NAATA.

Knowing Her Place, Indu Krishnan, 1990, Women Make Movies.

Licensed to Kill, Arthur Dong, 1997, Deep-Focus Productions.

The Living End, Gregg Araki, 1992, Academy Entertainment.

Living on Tokyo Time, Steven Okazki, 1986, New Line Home Video.

Long Weekend (O'Despair), Gregg Araki, 1991, Academy Entertainment.

Looking Like the Enemy, Karen Shizuka and Robert Nakamura, 1996, Japanese American National Museum.

The Love Thang Trilogy, Mari Keiko Gonzales, 1994, NAATA.

Made in China: A Search for Roots, Lise Hsia, 1986, Filmakers Library.

Majdhar, 1984, Retake Film and Video Collective.

Masala, Srinivas Krishna, 1991, Facets Multimedia.

Maya Lin: A Strong Clear Vision, Freida Lee Mock, 1994, NAATA.

Maxine Hong Kingston Talking Story, Joan Saffa, 1990, NAATA.

Me, Mom and Mona, Mina Shum, 1993, NAATA.

Meeting at Tule Lake, Scott T. Tsuchitani, 1994, NAATA.

Memories from the Department of Amnesia, Janice Tanaka, 1991, NAATA.

Memory Pictures, Pratibha Parmar, 1989, Frameline Distribution.

Mirror, Mirror, Yogesh Walia, 1980.

Mississippi Masala, Mira Nair, 1991, Facets Multimedia.

Mississippi Triangle, Christine Choy, Worth Long, and Allan Siegel, 1984, Third World Newsreel.

Mitsuye and Nellie: Asian American Poets, Allie Light and Irving Saraf, 1981, Women Make Movies.

Monterey's Boat People, Spencer Nakasako and Vincent Digirolamo, 1982, NAATA.

The Morning Zoo, Daisy Lee, 1989, Video Out Distribution.

My American Friends, Cheng-Sim Lim, 1989.

My Mother Thought She Was Audrey Hepburn, Sharon Jue, 1992, Filmakers Library.

My Mother's Place, Richard Fung, 1990, Video Data Bank.

My Niagara, Helen Lee, 1992, Women Make Movies.

My Tiger's Eyes, Teck Tan, 1993, Australian Film Commission.

The New Puritans: The Sikhs of Yuba City, Ritu Sarin and Tenzing Sonam, 1985, NAATA.

New Year: Parts I and II, Valerie Soe, 1987, Woman Make Movies.

Nisei Soldier: Standard Bearer for an Exiled People, Loni Ding, 1984, Center for Educational Telecommunications.

None of the Above, Erica Surat Andersen, 1994, Filmakers Library.

Not a Simple Story, Christine Choy, 1994, NAATA.

Orientations, Richard Fung, 1982, Video Data Bank.

Out in Silence: *AIDS in the Pacific American Community*, Christine Choy, 1994, NAATA.

Perceptions: A Question of Justice, Sandra Yep, 1984, KCRA-TV Channel 3.

A Personal Matter: Gordon Hirabayashi vs. the United States, John de Graaf, 1992, NAATA.

Picture Bride, Kayo Hatta, 1994, Buena Vista Home Video.

Picturing Oriental Girls: A {Re}Educational Videotape, Valerie Soe, 1992, NAATA.

A Place of Rage, Pratibha Parmar, 1991, Women Make Movies.

Play It Again, Nam!, Nam June Paik, 1993, Films for the Humanities & Sciences.

A Private Enterprise, Salmaan Peer, 1975, British Film Institute Production Board.

Pushing Hands, Ang Lee, 1992, Triboro Entertainment Group.

Rage, Jay Hirayabashi, 1988, Video Out Distribution.

Reframing AIDS, Pratibha Parmar, 1987.

Return Home, Michelle Wong, 1993, National Film Board of Canada, Montreal's CineRobotheque.

Sa-I-Gu: From Korean Women's Perspectives, Christine Choy, 1993, NAATA.

Salaam Bombay!, Mira Nair, 1988, Facets Multimedia.

Sally's Beauty Spot, Helen Lee, 1990, Women Make Movies.

Sam and Me, Deepa Mehta, 1996, Video Out Distribution.

Sari Red, Pratibha Parmar, 1988, Women Make Movies.

The Scent of Green Papya, Tran Anh Hung, 1993, Columbia Tristar Home Video.

Sewing Woman, Arthur Dong, 1982, NAATA.

Shoot for the Contents, Trinh T. Minh-ha, 1991, Women Make Movies.

Shopping for Fangs, Justin Lin and Quentin Lee, 1996.

The Shot Heard 'Round the World, Christine Choy, 1997, NAATA.

Slaying the Dragon, Deborah Gee, 1988, NAATA.

So Far from India, Mira Nair, 1983, Filmakers Library.

Some Divine Wind, Roddy Bogawa, 1991, Third World Newsreel.

Some Questions for 28 Kisses, Kip Fulbeck, 1994, NAATA.

Spirits Rising, Ramona S. Diaz, 1995, NAATA.

Stepping Out of Frame, Patel and Laxmi Jamdagni, 1987.

Stolen Ground, Lee Mun Wah, 1993, Stir Fry Productions.

The Story of Vinh, Keiko Tsuno, 1990, NAATA.

Strawberry Fields, Rea Tajiri, 1997, Open City Films.

Surname Viet Given Name Nam, Trinh T. Minh-ha, 1989, Women Make Movies.

Survivors: Forty Years After Hiroshima, Steven Okazaki, 1982, NAATA.

A Tale of Love, Trinh T. Minh-ha, 1995, Women Make Movies.

Thousand Pieces of Gold, Nancy Kelly and Kenji Yamamoto, 1991, Ingram International Films.

Through Struggle and Strength, Helen Liu, 1988.

Toc Storee, Ming-Yuen S. Ma, 1995, NAATA.

Totally F***ed Up, Gregg Araki, 1994, Facets Multimedia.

Traps, Pauline Chan, 1994, Australian Film Commission.

Two Lies, Pam Tom, 1989, Women Make Movies.

Unfinished Business: The Japanese American Internment Cases, Steven Okazaki, 1986, NAATA.

The Wall, Faris Karmani, 1981.

Warrior Marks, Pratibha Parmar, 1993, Women Make Movies.

The Wash, Michael Uno, 1988, Academy Entertainment.

The Way to My Father's Village, Richard Fung, 1987, Video Data Bank.

The Wedding Banquet, Ang Lee, 1993, FoxVideo.

Who Killed Vincent Chin?, Christine Choy and Renee Tajima, 1987, Filmakers Library.

Who's Going to Pay for These Donuts Anyway?, Janice Tanaka, 1992, Women Make Movies.

Wong Sinsaang, Eddie Wong, 1971, Visual Communications.

Yellow Tale Blues: Two American Families, Christine Choy and Renee Tajima, 1990, Filmakers Library.

Yuki Shimoda: Asian American Actor, John Esaki, 1985, NAATA.

Yuri Kochiyama: Passion for Justice, Rea Tajiri, 1993, NAATA.

Distributors

Academy Entertainment
9250 Wilshire Blvd., Ste. 400
Beverly Hills, CA 90212
Ph: (310) 275-2170
Fax: (310) 275-2195

Amerasia Bookstore
129 Japanese Village Plaza
Los Angeles, CA 90012
Ph: (213) 680-2888

Anancy Films
3 Kelly St.
London NW1 8PG, England
Ph: (171) 482-3332

Arrow Video, Inc.
135 W. 50th St., Ste. 1925
New York, NY 10020
Ph: (212) 258-2200
Fax: (212) 245-1252

Asian CineVision
32 E. Broadway
New York, NY 10012
Ph: (212) 925-8685

Australian Film Commission
150 William St.
Woolloomooloo NSW 2011, Australia
Ph: (2) 321-6444
Fax: (2) 357-3737
E-mail: info@AFC.gov.au

British Film Institute
Production Board (BFI)
21 Stephen St.
London W1P 1PL, England

Buena Vista Home Video
350 S. Buena Vista St.
Burbank, CA 91521-7145
Ph: (818) 562-3568
Fax: (818) 569-5900

Center for Educational Telecommunications
1460 Washington St.
San Francisco, CA 94109
Ph/Fax: (415) 673-6428

Columbia Tristar Home Video
Sony Pictures Plaza
10202 W. Washington Blvd.
Culver City, CA 90232
Ph: (310) 280-5418
Fax: (310) 280-2485

Coronet/MTI Film & Video
4350 Equity Dr.
P.O. Box 2649
Columbus, OH 43216
Ph: (614) 876-0371
Fax: (614) 771-5481

DeepFocus Productions
22-D Hollywood Ave.
Hohokus, NJ 07423
Ph: (800) 343-5540

Arthur Dong
4506 Palmero Dr.
Los Angeles, CA 90065
Ph: (213) 254-7072
E-mail: AdongLA@aol.com

Facets Multimedia, Inc.
1517 W. Fullerton Ave.
Chicago, IL 60614
Ph: (312) 281-9075
Fax: (312) 929-5437

Filmakers Library, Inc.
124 E. 40th St.
New York, NY 10016
Ph: (212) 808-4980
Fax: (212) 808-4983

Films for the Humanities & Sciences
Box 2053
Princeton, NJ 08543
Ph: (800) 257-5126
Fax: (609) 275-3767

FoxVideo
2121 Ave. of the Stars, 25th Fl.
Los Angeles, CA 90067
Ph: (310) 369-3900
Fax: (310) 369-5811

Frameline Distribution
346 9th St.
San Francisco, CA 94103
Ph: (415) 703-8650
Fax: (415) 861-1404
E-mail: info@Frameline.org
George Eastman House
900 East Ave.
Rochester, NY 14607-2298
Ph: (716) 271-3361
Fax: (716) 271-3970

Hallmark Home Entertainment
6100 Wilshire Blvd., Ste. 14000
Los Angeles, CA 90048
Ph: (213) 549-3790
Fax: (213) 549-3760

Hemdale Home Video
7966 Beverly Blvd.
Los Angeles, CA 90048
Ph: (213) 966-3700
Fax: (213) 653-5452

Indochina Film Arts Foundation
665 Chestnut St., 2nd Fl.
San Francisco, CA 94133
Fax: (415) 441-1783
E-mail: tianatiana@aol.com

Ingram International Films
790 Hickman Rd.
Des Moines, IA 50322
Ph: (515) 254-7000
Fax: (515) 254-7021

Inscrutable Films/Pacific News Service
The Lemonade Factory
1678 Shattuck Ave., Ste. 267
Berkeley, CA 94709
Ph: (510) 548-2530
E-mail: pacificnews@pacificnews.org

Japanese American National Museum
369 E. 1st St.
Los Angeles, CA 90012
Ph: (213) 625-0414
Fax: (213) 625-1770

KCRA-TV
Channel 3
3 Television Circle
Sacramento, CA 95814
Ph: (916) 446-3333
Fax: (916) 325-3731

National Asian American Telecommunications Association (NAATA)
346 9th St., 2nd Fl.
San Francisco, CA 94103
Ph: (415) 552-9550
Fax: (415) 863-7428
e-mail: naata@sirius.com

National Film Board of Canada (NFB)
1251 Ave. of the Americas, 16th Fl.
New York, NY 10020
Ph: (800) 542-2164
Fax: (212) 596-1779

New Line Home Video
116 N. Robertson Blvd.
Los Angeles, CA 90048
Ph: (310) 967-6670
Fax: (310) 854-0602

New Yorker Video
16 W. 61st St., 11th Fl.
New York, NY 10023
Ph: (212) 247-6110
Fax: (212) 307-7855

Open City Films
198 6th Ave.
New York, NY 10013
Ph: (212) 343-1850
Fax: (212) 343-1849
E-mail: ocfilms@aol.com

Orion Home Video
1888 Century Park E.
Los Angeles, CA 90067
Ph: (310) 282-0550
Fax: (212) 282-9902

Retake Film and Video Collective
25 Bayham St.
London NW1, England

Stir-Fry Productions
1222 Preservation Parkway
Oakland, CA 94612
Ph: (800) 370-STIR

Third World Newsreel
335 W. 38th St., 5th Fl.
New York, NY 10018
Ph: (212) 947-9277
Fax: (212) 594-6417

Triboro Entertainment Group
12 W. 27th St., 15th Fl.
New York, NY 10001
Ph: (212) 686-6116
Fax: (212) 686-6178

Trimark Home Video
2644 30th St.
Santa Monica, CA 90405
Ph: (310) 314-2000
Fax: (310) 392-0252

Video Data Bank
School of the Art Institute of Chicago
37 S. Wabash Ave.
Chicago, IL 60603
Ph: (312) 345-3550
Fax: (312) 541-8073

Video Out Distribution
1965 Main St.
Vancouver, BC, V5T 3C1, Canada
Ph: (604) 872-8449
Fax: (604) 778-3194

Visual Communications
263 S. Los Angeles St., Ste. 307
Los Angeles, CA 90012
Ph: (213) 680-4462
Fax: (213) 687-4848

Women Make Movies
462 Broadway, Ste. 500 R
New York, NY 10012
Ph: (212) 925-0606
Fax: (212) 925-2052
E-mail: orders@wmm.com

Zeitgeist Films, Ltd.
247 Centre St., 2nd Fl.
New York, NY 10013
Ph: (212) 274-1989
Fax: (212) 274-1644

Index